Check out of
Perkins - p. 43.

p 165

. . . .

GERMAN SEED IN TEXAS SOIL

Immigrant Farmers in Nineteenth-Century Texas

. . . .

. . . .

GERMAN SEED IN TEXAS SOIL

Immigrant Farmers in Nineteenth-Century Texas

. . . .

by Terry G. Jordan

UNIVERSITY OF TEXAS PRESS

AUSTIN   LONDON

International Standard Book Number
0-292-73629-0 (cloth)
0-292-72707-0 (paper)
Library of Congress Catalog Card Number 66-15703
Copyright © 1966 by Terry G. Jordan
Printed in the United States of America
First paperback edition, 1975

.... *Dedication* ....

To my wife Marlis, for her patience in the lean, financially unproductive years of my graduate work, her persistence in the seemingly endless task of typing and retyping the manuscript, her suggestions regarding its form and content, her help with many matters pertaining to the German language, and her diligence in working part-time to supplement the family income, all of which she did while still performing the functions of wife, housekeeper, and mother.

. . . . *Acknowledgments* . . . .

The present study represents essentially a revision of my doctoral dissertation, written for the Department of Geography of the University of Wisconsin at Madison. I am, therefore, deeply indebted to my advisor, Dr. Andrew H. Clark, who supervised the writing of the dissertation and contributed materially to its improvement through his advice and criticism. His enthusiasm and inquisitiveness were a source of continual inspiration to me during the three years I worked under his guidance. Other members of the faculty of the Department of Geography at the University of Wisconsin are also due my thanks, including Dr. Karl W. Butzer, who was particularly helpful in matters pertaining to the European background of the German settlers, and Dr. Clarence W. Olmstead, who had a great influence in the formulation of my concept of agricultural geography in general. Dr. Carl O. Sauer, a visiting member of the University of Wisconsin faculty in the spring of 1965, most graciously consented to read the manuscript and offered some valuable suggestions for its improvement. I owe a similar debt of thanks to Dr. Allan G. Bogue of the Department of History at the University of Wisconsin.

The research for this study was financed in part by a College Teaching Career Fellowship Award granted by the Southern Fellowships Fund of Chapel Hill, North Carolina. The views expressed herein are not, however, necessarily those of the Fund. Additional financial assistance was provided by the University of Wisconsin, in the form of a research assistantship, a travel grant, and funds to cover some of the expenses involved in the use of an electronic computer.

I wish to thank Mr. Kirby C. Smith, a lifelong friend, for his help in computer programming and Mrs. Anita A. Jurevics, my sister-in-law, for her assistance in card-punching. Both performed their services largely as a kindness to me, since funds were not available to pay them adequately.

To my parents, Dr. and Mrs. Gilbert J. Jordan, my gratitude is equally great for their encouragement and help all through my graduate studies. I came to know and appreciate the academic life through my father, a professor of German for some thirty-six years at Southern Methodist University in Dallas, and it was also he who awakened in me an appreciation of my German heritage.

The staff of the Texas State Archives, Austin, was extremely cooperative, helpful, and friendly during my months of research there, for which I am most grateful. Dr. Llerena Friend of the Barker History Library of the University of Texas is also due my thanks, as are the staffs of the Dallas Public Library and the Wisconsin State Historical Association.

Southern Methodist University, with which I had no academic affiliation during the period of my research, nevertheless rendered me a number of valuable services. Mr. R. G. McAfee of the S.M.U. Computing Laboratory allowed me the use of the facilities there free of charge, amounting to over one hour of computer time, and he supplied, also at no cost, over 4,000 I.B.M. punch cards. Dr. Edwin J. Foscue of the Department of Geography at S.M.U. provided space for me to work in the Cartography Laboratory and lent me numerous map-making tools. I was also allowed free and complete use of the library at the university, for which I am indebted to Miss Agnes E. Glaab.

T.G.J.

Arizona State University, Tempe

. . . . Contents . . . .

· · · · *Illustrations* · · · ·

(following page 82)

. . . . *Tables* . . . .

．．．． *Figures* ．．．．

. . . .

GERMAN SEED IN TEXAS SOIL

Immigrant Farmers in Nineteenth-Century Texas

. . . .

.... *Chapter One* ....

Introduction

Texas is a land where many cultures have met and mingled, for peoples of varied national origins have contributed to the development of the state. From Latin America came Spaniards and Mexicans, who colonized for a century prior to the arrival of any other groups; from the United States came hundreds of thousands of southerners, who first effectively occupied the soil; and, finally, from nineteenth-century Europe came smaller but significant numbers of Old World immigrants, who added diversity to the population. The rural areas of Texas reflect the varied ethnic character of the state as a whole, and communities of Germans, Czechs, Scandinavians, and Poles, are island-like in a sea of Anglo-Americans. These different immigrant groups brought the strands of Old World agricultural heritages to be woven into the rural fabric of Texas.

THE PURPOSE OF THE PRESENT STUDY

The present study focuses attention on the Germans, the largest of the groups of European immigrant farmers that settled in nineteenth-century Texas. It seeks to discover on the basis of their experience whether rural Texas became a mosaic bearing the marks of the various ethnic groups which inhabited it, or whether the agricultural individuality of the immigrants was erased through the process of assimilation. The significance of the European farming heritage of the Germans in shaping the agriculture of the areas in which they settled is evaluated.[1] The

[1] Studies on this same general topic are not too numerous, but some of the better ones which have been made are Walter M. Kollmorgen, "A Reconnaissance of Some Cultural-Agricultural Islands in the South," *Economic Geography*, 17 (1941), 409–430, and 19 (1943), 109–117; two more detailed works by Kollmorgen entitled *The German Settlement of Cullman County, Alabama: An*

study involves a rather detailed description and analysis of the changing farming practices of the Germans during their first half-century or
so in Texas, the crucial decades in the development of an immigrant
group's agricultural way of life. During this forty- or fifty-year period,
all major adaptations and changes were accomplished, and those aspects of the Old World farming heritage that were to survive in the
new homeland met their great testing-time. The study is a close look at
the workings of agricultural assimilation on a large immigrant group
that was loosely bound together by the tie of a common language.

Central to the study is the device of comparison, by means of which
the agricultural practices of the immigrant group may be seen in proper
perspective against the background of the practices of other cultural
groups in the same, or closely similar, areas. It would be meaningless to
study the Germans alone, for so to limit the investigation would re-
move the basis for judging whether or not the Germans were different
from other Texas farmers. Accordingly, an evaluation was made of the
practices of southern farmers to parallel that for the Germans. The result is an agricultural comparison of these groups as they lived side
by side in certain portions of Texas during much of the last century.

If comparison is the device of the present study, its major method is
the generous use of the manuscript census schedules of agriculture and
population for 1850 through 1880.[2] On the manuscript schedules of
agriculture, diverse information is found for each farm enumerated,
including the name of the farmer; while the population schedules list,

Agricultural Island in the Cotton Belt, and _The German-Swiss in Franklin
County, Tennessee: A Study of the Significance of Cultural Considerations in
Farming Enterprises;_ two articles by Leslie Hewes, "Cultural Fault Line in the
Cherokee Country," _Economic Geography_ 19 (1943), 136–142 and "Tontitown:
Ozark Vineyard Center," _ibid.,_ 29 (1953), 125–143; Russell W. Lynch, _Czech
Farmers in Oklahoma;_ William H. Gehrke, "The Ante-Bellum Agriculture of
the Germans in North Carolina," _Agricultural History,_ 9 (1935), 143–160;
Arthur B. Cozzens, "Conservation in German Settlements in the Missouri
Ozarks," _Geographical Review,_ 33 (1943), 286–298; H. F. Raup, "The Italian-
Swiss Dairymen of San Luis Obispo County, California," _Yearbook of the
Association of Pacific Coast Geographers,_ 1 (1935), 3–8; Loyal Durand, Jr.,
"Dairy Barns of Southeastern Wisconsin," _Economic Geography,_ 19 (1943),
37–44; and Glenn T. Trewartha, "The Green County, Wisconsin, Foreign Cheese
Industry," _Economic Geography,_ 2 (1926), 292–308. Of limited value are: Ed-
mund de S. Brunner, _Immigrant Farmers and Their Children;_ and Joseph T.
Och, _Der deutschamerikanische Farmer...._

[2] The manuscript agricultural schedules are kept in the Texas State Archives,
Austin, and microfilms of the population schedules are available there also.
Unfortunately, all schedules for 1890 were destroyed, and no microfilms exist.

among other things, the birthplace of each inhabitant. Through the combined use of these schedules, a great wealth of information in the form of averages and percentages for farmers of different origins was compiled, providing a statistical framework for the study. So embarrassing were these riches, that the use of the censuses was confined to a number of carefully chosen counties, and for the years 1870 and 1880 random samples were taken within these selected counties. A more complete discussion of the procedures employed in the use of the manuscript census is contained at the beginning of Chapters IV and V.

In order to put flesh on the dry bones of the census statistics and expand the study beyond the limits of the sample counties, thorough use was made of other contemporary sources, such as travelers' accounts, immigrant guide books, letters, reminiscences, diaries, newspapers, minute books of the meetings of agricultural societies, and almanacs. Through field work, the present-day landscape was scanned for relics of the past which might aid in a better understanding of the nineteenth-century farming systems, and descendants of the original settlers were informally questioned about the agricultural practices of their fathers and grandfathers.

POPULAR BELIEF AND THE GERMAN-AMERICAN FARMER

There long has been a popular belief in the United States that farmers of German origin were superior to the native inhabitants as tillers of the soil. As early as 1789 one writer describing the Pennsylvania Germans enumerated sixteen ways "in which they differ from most of the other farmers" of the state,[3] and similar remarks can be found in eighteenth- and nineteenth-century literature dealing with other areas where Germans settled. In Texas the popular notion of German agricultural distinctiveness began to gain acceptance quite early. In 1843 an English-language newspaper in Galveston contained an article on the German farmers who had settled a portion of the Republic, lauding them as "patient, industrious, and untiring," with skill, energy, and "a most scrupulous regard to punctuality in their contracts," as a result of which they gave "indications of fine prosperity." The Anglo-American farmers of Texas were chided for being inferior to the Germans in these respects.[4] In the following year the British consul in Texas, William Kennedy, wrote in a dispatch that German farmers in the Republic

---

[3] Benjamin Rush, *An Account of the Manners of the German Inhabitants of Pennsylvania* . . ., pp. 11–32.
[4] *The Civilian and Galveston Gazette*, Dec. 2, 1843, p. 2, col. 4.

were "laborious, persevering, and eager to accumulate," with the reputation of being very successful;[5] and in 1851 a Texas newspaper praised
the Germans of Austin County as "intelligent, industrious, and thrifty."[6]
Perhaps the most important and influential reference to the prowess of
German farmers in Texas was contained in the writings of Frederick
Law Olmsted, who, in the mid-1850's, contrasted the intensive, diversified, free-labor farming practices of the Germans with the careless,
casual methods, often involving slave labor, of southern Anglo-Americans.[7] A few years later, in 1858, another writer complimented the
Texas Germans for being "a thrifty and industrious people, rapidly accumulating property and adding to the productive wealth of the country. Their settlements are compact, fences well built, and farms in good
order."[8] By the outbreak of the Civil War, the idea was well-estab-
lished that German farmers in Texas were something special.

Observers in the post-bellum period continued the chorus of praise,
beginning in 1866, when one Anglo-American, speaking of the German
settlements near San Antonio, was moved to note that

. . . the more settled and thrifty appearance of the country indicated our
approach to the German settlement of New Braunfels . . . This whole region . . . is settled very largely by old country Germans, and they have left
their impress of industry, order and economy on this section, as they have
always done wherever they have found a home in the new world.[9]

His sentiments were echoed by an English traveler of the mid-1870's,
who observed in the same area the "well-fenced, well-cultivated fields,
such as the eye of even a New England farmer never rested upon."[10]
Another traveler was equally impressed, and added, "the more I see of
the Germans, the more I think of them. They almost invariably have
nice and happy homes, and always have something good to eat and
drink."[11] Similar comments can be found in many other contemporary

[5] Dispatch of William Kennedy to the Earl of Aberdeen, Galveston, September
9, 1844, published in Ephraim D. Adams (ed.), *British Diplomatic Correspondence Concerning the Republic of Texas—1838–1846*, p. 356.
[6] *The Texas Monument* (La Grange), July 30, 1851, p. 2, col. 1.
[7] Frederick Law Olmsted, *A Journey through Texas: or A Saddle-Trip on the
South-western Frontier.*
[8] J. De Cordova, *Texas: Her Resources and her Public Men . . .*, p. 221.
[9] H. H. McConnell, *Five Years a Cavalryman: or, Sketches of Regular Army
Life on the Texas Frontier, Twenty Odd Years Ago*, p. 38.
[10] Edward King, *The Great South: A Record of Journeys in Louisiana, Texas,
. . .*, p. 144.
[11] H. F. McDanield and N. A. Taylor, *The Coming Empire: or, Two Thousand
Miles in Texas on Horseback*, p. 193.

books, and even the editors of the *Texas Almanac* paid tribute to the alleged superiority of German farmers in the state.[12] The adjectives "thrifty," "prosperous," "successful," "industrious," and "frugal,"[13] were used repeatedly to describe the Germans.

Modern scholars have arrived at similar conclusions regarding the Texas Germans, generally on the basis of some of the nineteenth-century sources cited above. The geographer W. M. Kollmorgen wrote in the 1940's concerning Texas that: "German settlements to this day carry on a rather diversified form of agriculture. On comparable soil, traditional cotton farmers who have never raised much besides cotton and corn have reproduced a landscape similar to that prevailing in the older cotton states."[14] County historians have been even more enthusiastic, suggesting, for example, that "there can be no better citizens than the Germans,"[15] and "a thousand German farmers would be the best thing for this county."[16]

All of these references, from the earliest to the most recent, have one thing in common—they offer little factual basis for their claims of German agricultural distinctiveness and superiority in Texas. The reader is asked to accept the statements on faith, and the objective student of agricultural geography is hesitant to do so. Accordingly, the need for an objective appraisal based firmly in the factual becomes evident. The writer of the present study aspires to such a goal.

[12] "The Germans in Texas . . .," *Texas Almanac for 1872*, p. 76.

[13] Samuel N. Townshend, *Our Indian Summer in the Far West: An Autumn Tour of Fifteen Thousand Miles in Kansas, Texas, New Mexico, Colorado, and the Indian Territory*, p. 107; M. Whilldin (ed.), *A Description of Western Texas . . .*, p. 57; J. Burke, *Burke's Texas Almanac and Immigrant's Handbook for 1882*, p. 56; C. C. Gibbs, the Land Commissioner of Texas, as quoted in Kate H. Claghorn, "Agricultural Distribution of Immigrants," U.S. Industrial Commission Report, Vol. 15 (1901), p. 572; A. W. Spaight, *The Resources, Soil, and Climate of Texas. Report of Commissioner of Insurance, Statistics, and History*, pp. 68, 116, 329; George H. Sweet, *Texas . . . or the Immigrants' Hand-Book of Texas*, p. 39; "Report on the Cotton Production of the State of Texas . . .," in *Report on Cotton Production in the United States*, vol. 5 of [United States Census Office], Tenth Census, 1880, p. 104; (The South Western Immigration Company), *Texas: Her Resources and Capabilities . . .*, pp. 194, 227, 230, 239.

[14] Kollmorgen, "A Reconnaissance," p. 428.

[15] Victor M. Rose, *Some Historical Facts in Regard to the Settlement of Victoria, Texas, Its Progress and Present Status*, pp. 20, 63.

[16] Paul S. Taylor, *An American-Mexican Frontier: Nueces County, Texas*, p. 89; see also Hobart Huson, *Refugio: A Comprehensive History of Refugio County from Aboriginal Times to 1953*, vol. 2, p. 337.

Chapter Two

Nineteenth-Century Southern Agriculture and Its Expansion into Texas

Though the Germans constituted an important element in the settlement of Texas and are the focus of the present study, they were far exceeded numerically by southern Anglo-Americans, who were from the very beginning the dominant group in the occupation of the state. Agriculturally and otherwise, the southerners provided the matrix into which all other Texas settlers were placed, and a study of farming practices in the state can accomplish little if it ignores them. Whatever conclusions are drawn concerning the Germans must be based on a comparison with the southern Anglo-Americans, and therefore it is essential that the agricultural heritage of the larger group be investigated.

From the earliest years of settlement in the seventeenth century to the present time, agriculture in the southern states has differed from that of other sections of the country. Even more striking has been the contrast between the practices of the southern farmer and his counterpart-kinsman in northwestern Europe. By the year 1800, almost two centuries of contact with alien cultures in a unique physical and economic environment had emphasized these differences and contrasts. Southern agriculture was a blend of British, American Indian, and African contributions, mixed together in a land climatically quite different from that of the ancestral home of the Anglo-Americans who practiced it, a land which could produce in abundance many of the staples of the tropics. The future of southern agriculture at the beginning of the nineteenth century was enhanced by its position on the eastern rim of a vast, empty land into which it could spread. Expansion came suddenly, as though the long confinement in the narrow fringe of land along the Atlantic had built up an unbearable pressure, and in less than one century southern farmers spread over the lands to the west, carrying their agricultural way of life as far as the prairies of Texas.[1]

Still, despite many regional similarities, southern agriculture was not a homogeneous phenomenon spread evenly over the area south of the Mason-Dixon line. It was, rather, a conglomerate encompassing the extremes of great plantation owner and slave, wealth and poverty, but not lacking a middle ground of independent family farmers. The remarkable uniformity of ancestry that characterized the southern white population could not conceal intrasectional differences in the agriculture of the South. For this reason, it is desirable to investigate more closely the major source regions of the southern Anglo-American population of Texas.

Every state in the South contributed significant numbers of settlers, but there were some areas which overshadowed the others. Natives of the Upper and Gulf South were represented in roughly equal numbers, and two states, Tennessee and Alabama, together provided about one-fourth of the entire white population of Texas (Tables 1 and 2). Within Tennessee, the eastern and central portions of the state supplied the bulk of the emigration to Texas, while in Alabama the major source regions were the Tennessee River Valley in the north and, after 1850, the Black Belt.[2] To a lesser degree, the Piedmont of Georgia and the southwestern quarter of Mississippi were also notable as sources of Texas settlers. Many of the intraregional differences in southern agriculture could be found within these areas.

THE SYSTEM OF AGRICULTURE IN THE SOUTHERN SOURCE REGIONS

One major variable found within the structure of ante-bellum southern agriculture concerned the holding of slaves. To be sure, the range from rich to poor was not, as has often been pictured, one of sharply discernible classes, but rather a socioeconomic continuum, in which the gradation from poor white to large planter included a myriad of intermediate positions. Arbitrary though it may be, the division of this continuum on the basis of slaveownership, for the purposes of study, is both convenient and traditional. The settlers who came to Texas from Tennessee and the remainder of the Upper South were, as might be ex-

[1] The best general reference on the history of southern agriculture is Lewis Cecil Gray, *History of Agriculture in the Southern United States to 1860.*

[2] Charles S. Davis, *Cotton Kingdom in Alabama*, pp. 33, 43; Blanche H. Clark, *The Tennessee Yeomen 1840–1860*, p. 26.

TABLE 1

States of Origin of the Southern White Population of Texas, 1850

State of birth	Number	As a percentage of whites not born in Texas	As a percentage of total white population
Gulf South			
Alabama	12,040	11%	8%
Georgia	7,639	7%	5%
Mississippi	6,545	6%	4%
Louisiana	4,472	4%	3%
Upper South			
Tennessee	17,692	17%	11%
Kentucky	5,478	5%	4%
Missouri	5,139	5%	3%
Arkansas	4,693	4%	3%
Atlantic South			
North Carolina	5,155	5%	3%
South Carolina	4,482	4%	3%
Virginia	3,580	3%	2%
Texas	49,160	———	32%

Source: Seventh Census, 1850, p. xxxvi.

pected, mostly slaveless yeoman farmers.[3] Over four-fifths of the farmers in the Valley of East Tennessee were slaveless in 1860, and on the
Highland Rim in the middle portion of the state nearly 70 percent were
yeomen. Even in the Nashville Basin, slaveowners constituted well
under half of the total farmers.[4] In Alabama as a whole, less than one-
third of the white population belonged to the slaveholding class, but
in the more prosperous areas, the proportion was higher, as in the Tennessee River Valley in northern Alabama, where slaves constituted
one-half of the total inhabitants.[5] Statewide, Negroes made up 45
percent of the population, as opposed to less than 25 percent in Tennessee.[6]

[3] The term "yeoman" is used, reluctantly, for want of a better one. It suffers
from British connotations, and has been used by students of southern economic
history to designate both slaveless farmers and small slaveholders. In the present
study, it is used to identify middle-class family farmers who owned no slaves,
including landowners and landless alike.
[4] Clark, *Tennessee Yeomen*, pp. xxiii, 41–42.
[5] Davis, *Cotton Kingdom*, p. 43; Gray, *History of Agriculture*, vol. 2, p. 655.
[6] Gray, *History of Agriculture*, vol. 2, p. 656.

TABLE 2

States of Origin of the Southern Population of Texas, 1880

State of birth	Number	Whites: As a percentage of whites not born in Texas	As a percentage of total white population	Number	Negroes: As a percentage of Negroes not born in Texas	As a percentage of total Negro population
Gulf South						
Alabama	73,312	12%	6%	20,313	18%	5%
Georgia	47,168	8%	4%	14,239	12%	4%
Mississippi	50,146	8%	4%	12,689	11%	3%
Louisiana	26,204	4%	2%	11,768	10%	3%
Upper South						
Tennessee	72,724	12%	6%	10,434	9%	3%
Kentucky	29,229	5%	2%	4,892	4%	1%
Missouri	39,974	7%	3%	3,194	3%	1%
Arkansas	36,211	6%	3%	5,154	5%	1%
Atlantic South						
North Carolina	16,477	3%	1%	6,800	6%	2%
South Carolina	15,049	2%	1%	7,075	6%	2%
Virginia	14,546	2%	1%	14,482	13%	4%
Texas	591,161	——	49%	279,544	——	71%

Source: Tenth Census, 1880, I, 484–491.

The nonslaveholders were represented at one extreme of the spectrum by the oft-studied poor whites.[7] They probably existed in relatively small numbers and, in any event, contributed little to the settlement of Texas and so will be of little concern to the present study. The largest group of farmers in the ante-bellum period was composed of slaveless, middle-class yeomen. They were similar in many ways to their counterparts in the northern states and long suffered a surprising lack of attention from historians and historical geographers.[8] They were

[7] See, for example, Paul H. Buck, "The Poor Whites of the Ante-Bellum South," *American History Review*, 31 (1925), 41–54; and A. N. J. den Hollander, *De landelijke arme Blanken in het Zuiden der Vereenigde Staten.* Good descriptions of the poor whites are contained in the nineteenth-century works by George M. Weston, *The Poor Whites of the South*, and Frederick Law Olmsted, *A Journey in the Back Country.*

[8] The oversight has been corrected, largely through the work of A. N. J. den Hollander, "The Tradition of 'Poor Whites'," in *Culture in the South* (ed. by

the numerically dominant agriculturists in eastern and much of middle
Tennessee, the Piedmont pine forests of central Alabama, and the sandy
pine barrens adjacent to the coast. Nor were they absent in areas dominated economically by plantations, where they were found on the interfluves and even scattered in among the planters in the bottom lands.
The lower fringes of the yeoman class mingled with the destitute poor
whites, while the more prosperous mixed freely with the lower echelons
of the slaveowners.

On the same rungs and immediately above the yeomen on the southern economic ladder stood the small slaveholders, possessors of one to
a half-dozen or so Negroes.[9] In reality, they were little more than prosperous yeomen, differing only in that they had assistance in their farm
labor from a source other than the immediate family, and thus had an
investment in labor as well as land. The small slaveholder can hardly
be called a planter, given the usual implications of that title, for he generally worked alongside his Negroes in the field.

The remainder of the slaveholding Anglo-Americans, those owning
more than a handful of Negroes, should not be viewed as a homogeneous group, but they are placed together for the purposes of the
present study since attention is to be focused on yeomen and small
slaveholders. The gradation from holders of half a dozen slaves to
those owning hundreds was a smooth one, representing simply an up-
ward extension of the socioeconomic continuum of white southerners.[10]
In the source regions of Texas settlers, plantations were concentrated
in a number of select areas, generally those more favored by Nature,
including the Nashville Basin, the valley of the Tennessee River in
northern Alabama, and the Black Belt.

Throughout the South, among yeomen and planters alike, corn was
a crop of major importance, providing in various forms sustenance for

W. T. Couch); pp. 403–431, and Frank L. Owsley, *Plain Folk of the Old
South*.

[9] In the present study, slaveholders will be divided into two groups—those
owning one to five slaves and those possessing over five. This breaking point
was previously employed by Gray, *History of Agriculture*, vol. 1, p. 500.

[10] A good general reference on plantations is Paul S. Taylor, "Plantation
Agriculture in the United States: Seventeenth to Twentieth Centuries," *Land
Economics*, 30 (1954), 141–152. See also Merle Prunty, "The Renaissance of
the Southern Plantation," *Geographical Review*, 45 (1955), 459–491. A description of the operation of a cotton plantation in the Black Belt can be found
in Weymouth T. Jordan, *Ante-Bellum Alabama: Town and Country*, Chapter
III.

the family and feed for the livestock, in addition to being a marketable item which could be sold for cash or bartered.[11] The production per capita was markedly higher in middle and eastern Tennessee than in Alabama, a fact which lends some support to the generalization that the Upper South produced surplus food crops for consumption in the plantation areas of the Gulf states (Table 3). The yeoman farmers of the Valley of East Tennessee raised large quantities of wheat, twice as

TABLE 3

Comparative Production of Selected Crops in the
Southern Source Areas, 1850
Per 100 Inhabitants

	Valley of East Tennessee	Middle Tennessee	Alabama
cotton, bales	0.1	26	73
corn, bushels	4940	6520	3726
wheat, bushels	289	130	38
oats, bushels	1256	753	384
rye, bushels	5	16	2
barley, bushels	0.1	0.6	0.5
tobacco, pounds	56	1782	22
hay, tons	16	9	4
white potatoes, bushels	99	113	32
sweet potatoes, bushels	240	272	710
hemp, tons	0	0.2	0

Sources: Seventh Census, 1850, pp. 421, 429–433, 573–574, 584–590; Lewis C. Gray, *History of Agriculture in the Southern United States to 1860*, vol. 2, p. 876. Gray used the following counties for the Valley of East Tennessee: Greene, Hamilton, Hawkins, Jefferson, Knox, McMinn, and Roane; for middle Tennessee: Giles, Lincoln, Maury, Rutherford, Williamson, and Wilson.

much as was produced in middle Tennessee and seven times the per capita average of the state of Alabama. Oats occupied a place of much greater importance than wheat in all of the major source areas of Texas settlers, and its cultivation was also most common in eastern Tennessee. Nowhere, however, did the small grains even approach corn in importance. In the better parts of Alabama and much of the remainder of

[11] Donald L. Kemmerer, "The Pre-Civil War South's Leading Crop: Corn," *Agricultural History*, 33 (1949), 236–238.

the Gulf South, cotton was the dominant cash crop, found on the farms of yeomen and planters alike, though it was of less importance in the Piedmont and pine barrens of Alabama. In middle Tennessee, it shared prominence with other cash products, but it was almost totally absent in the eastern third of the state. In the source areas of Texas settlers, tobacco attained major importance only in the Nashville Basin and Highland Rim of middle Tennessee, where it was produced by both yeomen and slaveholders.[12] A kitchen garden was found on nearly every farm, rich or poor, containing a variety of vegetables, such as turnips, tomatoes, peas, and watermelons, and often a few fruit trees. In Alabama and other states of the lower South, peaches and figs were the most frequently encountered orchard trees, while in eastern Tennessee apples were more widely grown.[13] Both the white and sweet potato were common, but the former appears to have been grown principally in the Upper South. In eastern and middle Tennessee over three times as many white potatoes were produced per capita as in Alabama, while the situation was exactly the reverse with sweet potatoes (Table 3). The ratio of white potatoes to sweet potatoes varied from 1:2½ in the Tennessee areas to 1:22 in Alabama, a difference perhaps understandable in light of the fact that white potatoes did not grow well in the hotter summer climate of the Gulf South.

In all parts of both Alabama and Tennessee, swine were by far the most numerous livestock, outnumbering people by over three to one in some areas. There were at least ten times as many swine per unit of population in the South as in the source regions of Texas German settlers in Europe (Table 4), and pork and bacon formed an integral part of the rural diet. On the Cumberland Plateau of middle Tennessee the production of pork for export attained major importance.[14] The ownership of cattle was almost universal, for virtually every farm family had at least a few head, and few households lacked milk and butter.[15] The mountainsides of eastern Tennessee long had been used as range for the small, hardy cattle typical of the region, and the adjacent Valley

[12] A good description of tobacco culture in middle Tennessee is contained in Harriette S. Arnow, "The Pioneer Farmer and His Crops in the Cumberland Region," *Tennessee Historical Quarterly*, 19 (1960), pp. 315–319.
[13] J. B. Killebrew and J. M. Safford, *Introduction to the Resources of Tennessee*, pp. 436–437.
[14] Harriette S. Arnow, *Flowering of the Cumberland*, pp. 221–223.
[15] *Ibid.*, p. 214.

TABLE 4

*Comparative Numbers of Selected Livestock
in the German and Southern Source Areas, 1850*
Per 100 Inhabitants

	Hannover	West-phalia	Electoral Hesse and Nassau	Valley of East Ten-nessee	Middle Ten-nessee	Alabama
Cattle	46	32	34	69	69	94
Swine	26	14	17	269	361	247
Sheep	95	27	44	86	90	48
Horses	10	7	5	29	32	17
Mules & Asses	?	?	?	4	12	8
Oxen	?	?	?	5	9	9

Sources: Seventh Census, 1850, pp. 421, 429–433, 573–574, 584–590; Lewis C. Gray, *History of Agriculture in the Southern United States to 1860,* vol. 2, p. 876 (Gray used the following counties for the Valley of East Tennessee: Greene, Hamilton, Hawkins, Jefferson, Knox, McMinn, and Roane; for middle Tennessee: Giles, Lincoln, Maury, Rutherford, Williamson, and Wilson); August Meitzen, *Der Boden und die landwirthschaftlichen Verhältnisse des preussischen Staates . . .,* vol. 7, pp. 730–731. The American data are for 1850; the German data for 1873.

served as a feeder area.[16] Yeomen of the pinelands of central and southern Alabama brought herds to sell at the Gulf ports.[17] As is generally the case, cattle were most numerous in the more densely populated rural areas, and large herds were found on the extensive unimproved acreage of many cotton plantations. This helps account for the markedly denser cattle population in Alabama as opposed to central and eastern Tennessee. Surprising as it may seem, sheep outnumbered cattle in both eastern and middle Tennessee, in contrast to Alabama where cattle were twice as numerous (Table 4).[18] Still, even in Tennessee, the ownership of sheep was not as widely diffused as that of cattle. The horse was the draft animal of most yeoman farmers,[19] especially in

[16] Killebrew, *Introduction to the Resources,* p. 435; Gray, *History of Agriculture,* vol. 2, p. 881.
[17] Frank L. and Harriett C. Owsley, "The Economic Basis of Society in the Late Ante-Bellum South," *Journal of Southern History,* 6 (1940), 43.
[18] Arnow, *Flowering of the Cumberland,* p. 223.
[19] *Ibid.,* p. 193.

eastern Tennessee, where they outnumbered mules and oxen by six or
seven to one. Mules were not used by the large majority of ante-bellum
yeomen, in part because they were more expensive than horses and had
to be purchased rather than raised.[20] Slaveowners in the Gulf South
made much greater use of the mule as a draft animal, presumably because this long-lived, durable beast could better endure the rough treat-
ment meted out by slaves, and possibly because it had greater heat resistance. The Nashville Basin of middle Tennessee was a major breeding area of mules for sale to planters in Alabama and other Gulf
states.[21] Rounding out the farm livestock were barnyard poultry, of
which the chicken was the universal and almost sole representative in
the South. In contrast to the European farmer of the same period, the
southern yeoman was a highly skilled hunter who added variety to his
dinner table by frequent forays after the wild game of forest, swamp, or
prairie.

The yeoman farmers generally raised most of their own food, but the
majority, particularly in middle Tennessee and Alabama, also produced
one or more items intended for sale. For the yeomen of the better areas
of the Lower South, cotton was the most common cash crop, while in
middle Tennessee, tobacco, hogs, and corn were also sent to market.
Even in the Valley of East Tennessee, where transportation difficulties
had long encouraged a less commercial outlook, some wheat, corn,
wool, and cattle were sold.[22] The yeomen of the Alabama Piedmont and
coastal pine barrens dealt mainly in corn and livestock as sources of
income.[23] The small slaveholders placed more reliance than the yeomen
on production for market, but in this respect both groups were overshadowed by the planters, who were, above all, highly commercialized
operators concerned primarily with a staple product. In most plantation areas, cotton was the cash crop, but in the Nashville Basin the
large slaveowners also marketed tobacco and blooded livestock. The
yeoman farmers of eastern Tennessee had perhaps the most diversified
agricultural system in the areas under consideration,[24] but elsewhere in
the state and in Alabama, contrary to what might be expected, diversity
seems to have been greater among the highly commercialized planters
than among yeomen or small slaveholders, though most attention was

[20] Robert B. Lamb, *The Mule in Southern Agriculture*, pp. 37, 83.
[21] Killebrew, *Introduction to the Resources*, p. 621.
[22] *Ibid.*, pp. 357, 432.
[23] F. and H. Owsley, "Economic Basis," p. 43.
[24] Killebrew, *Introduction to the Resources*, p. 433.

devoted to a single cash product. The food crops raised on many plantations in Alabama and the other Gulf states were not always adequate to meet requirements, and some food was imported from the nonplantation areas of the Upper South or purchased from local yeomen.

Another major difference between slaveholders and yeomen in the Texas source areas was in the scale of operation. In both Alabama and the eastern two-thirds of Tennessee, the majority of yeoman farmers owned from fifty to two hundred acres, a large holding by European standards but considerably less than the slaveowners, who most commonly fell in the two to five hundred acre class.[25] Similar differences could be detected in improved acreage and value of production, supporting the concept of yeomen as simply planters in miniature.

Scattered farmsteads were the dominant settlement form throughout the rural South, and most landholdings were contiguous units. On yeoman farms, the houses were usually modest log structures or, less commonly, of frame construction, and the farmstead was rounded out by small, makeshift stables, barns and storage sheds, the omnipresent spring or well house, smokehouse, corncrib, chicken coop, and sometimes a separate kitchen house, tobacco barn, or cotton shed.[26] Large animal quarters and storage structures were not needed, for the cattle and hogs remained out of doors throughout the year in the mild southern climate. In thinly settled areas, such as the pinelands of Alabama and the mountains of eastern Tennessee, the livestock were permitted to run semiwild on the open range. In the Nashville Basin and other of the better agricultural areas, however, population pressures had begun to restrict the open range as early as 1800, though only one-third of the farms were completely fenced as late as 1870.[27] In any event, the fields in this land of excess timber were always enclosed, almost invariably by the Virginia-style worm fence.[28] The farmsteads of most

[25] Clark, *Tennessee Yeomen*, pp. 46, 49; F. and H. Owsley, "Economic Basis," pp. 38–40. The statistical methodology employed by Owsley and his students, including Clark, in obtaining these figures has been questioned by Fabian Linden, "Economic Democracy in the Slave South: An Appraisal of Some Recent Views," *Journal of Negro History*, 31 (1946), 140–189.

[26] Killebrew, *Introduction to the Resources*, pp. 354, 438; Harriette S. Arnow, *Seedtime on the Cumberland*, p. 272. A good illustration of a yeoman farmhouse can be found in Clement Eaton, *The Growth of Southern Civilization*, fig. 18 following p. 124.

[27] Killebrew, *Introduction to the Resources*, p. 358; Arnow, *Flowering of the Cumberland*, p. 215.

[28] Killebrew, *Introduction to the Resources*, pp. 363, 438; Arnow, "Pioneer Farmer," pp. 323–325.

slaveholders were actually little different from those of the yeomen, for the magnificent ante-bellum mansions associated in the popular mind with planters were limited to a few very large slaveowners. The majority dwelt in rather humble houses, which were often little more than glorified log cabins or unpretentious frame structures, and both education and social graces were often much less advanced or elaborate than has been commonly assumed.

Nineteenth-century American agriculture, and in particular that of the southern states, has been justifiably characterized as destructive and wasteful of soil and forest resources. In contrast to the better farmers of northwestern and Central Europe, even the best southern Anglo-American took more from the land than he gave back. Dunging was virtually unknown and concern for conservation still in the future. Intensive farming practices were not needed, for southerners generally had more land than they needed, and more was to be had just beyond the western horizon. Far less than half of the farm acreage in middle Tennessee was improved in 1850, while in Alabama and the Valley of East Tennessee, fully two-thirds of the farm land was unimproved.[29] For the most part, the farming practices of the slaveowners were on a plane with those of the yeomen, or perhaps even more extensive since their major investment was in labor rather than land, though the few progressive currents found in southern agriculture could usually be traced to the planters. It is not surprising, in view of such extensive use of the land, that productivity was rather low on the farms of yeomen and planters alike. About 1870 yields per acre in Tennessee were estimated at only twenty-three bushels for corn and fifteen bushels for wheat. Inadequate care for livestock is suggested by the loss of about thirty thousand sheep annually in the state.[30]

Farming equipment was not unlike that of Europe—the iron-tipped plows, hoes, wooden harrows, cradles, carts—which could be made and repaired at home or in local blacksmith shops. Some reapers and mowers could be found on farms in the Valley of East Tennessee, but in general southern farmers, yeomen and slaveowners alike, owned very little farm machinery, a trait which carried over well into the present century.[31]

Closely allied to this situation was the lack of locational stability of the southern farmers. At any time, a large part of the population was

---

[29] Seventh Census, 1850, pp. 429–433, 584–590.
[30] Killebrew, *Introduction to the Resources*, pp. 95, 96, 364.
[31] *Ibid.*, p. 355; Arnow, *Seedtime*, pp. 278–280.

on the move, and it was not uncommon for families to migrate more than once in a single generation. The roots which held them to any particular piece of land were shallow, and the result was a lack of appreciation for lasting improvements and conservational care of the land. The very appearance of their farmsteads suggested impermanence.

Major differences between yeomen and slaveholders were detected in land tenure. In selected counties of eastern and middle Tennessee, only 34 to 68 percent of the yeoman farmers owned their land in 1850, while in the pine barrens, Piedmont, and Black Belt of Alabama the range was almost identical, 32 to 67 percent.[32] In view of the fact that a great expanse of unoccupied land lay within reach to the west, the proportion of yeomen who owned their land at mid-century was surprisingly low. During ante-bellum times, the large majority of landless yeomen were either renters or squatters rather than sharecroppers. Among slaveholders, those who owned their land exceeded 80 percent in nearly all of the areas under consideration, and in many counties the proportion was as high as 90 and even 95 percent, presenting a great contrast to the yeomen.[33]

ANTE-BELLUM MIGRATION

The close of the War of 1812 marked the beginning of a particularly rapid westward expansion of the frontier, a movement which had, by the outbreak of the Civil War, brought large new areas within the pale of southern cultural and economic practices.[34] The factors which spurred emigration from the older areas of the South were varied and complex. Depletion of soil fertility had probably decreased the attractiveness of many areas, though the concept of a vast, sterile wasteland in the wake of the advancing southern frontier is not valid.[35] The periodic economic depressions that afflicted nineteenth-century America,

[32] Frank L. and Harriet C. Owsley, "The Economic Structure of Rural Tennessee, 1850–1860," *Journal of Southern History,* 8 (1942), 172–174; F. and H. Owsley, "Economic Basis," pp. 34–37.

[33] *Ibid.*

[34] An excellent brief summary of the course of southern settlement expansion is found in Frank Owsley, "The Pattern of Migration and Settlement on the Southern Frontier," *Journal of Southern History,* 11 (1945), pp. 147–176. See also W. O. Lynch, "The Westward Flow of Southern Colonists before 1861," *Journal of Southern History,* 9 (1943), pp. 303–327.

[35] See Avery O. Craven, *Soil Exhaustion as a Factor in the Agricultural History of Maryland and Virginia, 1606–1860,* and Kathleen Bruce, "Virginian Agricultural Decline to 1860: A Fallacy," *Agricultural History,* 6 (1932), 3–13.

notably the one beginning in 1837, characterized by low prices for agricultural produce, have frequently been mentioned as causes of rural migration. This so-called "safety-valve" theory is seemingly discredited, however, by the fact that land sales in southern frontier states increased with each *rise* in cotton prices in the ante-bellum period.[36] Another factor, not commonly recognized, was that older portions of the South, including the area of initial transmontane settlement in Tennessee, had in 1830 or 1840, by American standards at least, become overpopulated. An additional cause of emigration centered about the process of displacement of yeoman farmers by expanding plantations.

The search for logical social and economic explanations for nineteenth-century southern migration should not obscure what was, perhaps, a major factor: the irrational desire to move—which resulted from the prevailing mobility and lack of locational stability of the population—to move for the sake of moving. It was not difficult to find southerners among the migrants who had been reasonably prosperous and satisfied in their old homes, whose decision to seek new land farther west was based on little more than impulse. The empty land was there, friends and relatives had gone ahead, why not join them? Illogical migration of this sort sometimes brought settlers to new areas inferior to those from which they had departed. Such is human nature, that many imagined agricultural opportunities always to be better to the west, a myth finally shattered in a brutal fashion on the unfriendly expanses of the Great Plains.

POST-BELLUM MIGRATION

The Civil War wrought sudden, violent changes in southern society, but the long-range effect on agriculture was perhaps much less than might have been expected. The yeomen who survived the fearsome bloodletting, and it was they who were called upon to do most of the dying, were little affected by the southern defeat, and most returned to their farms and picked up where they left off. For those southerners who had owned slaves, a forced economic reorganization was necessary, but the transition produced a new order not greatly different from that which had fallen at Appomattox. Legally free, the Negro remained tightly bound by economic ties. Sharecropper huts replaced slave quarters, and the planter was freed from the obligation to feed and clothe his workers

---

[36] Douglass C. North, *The Economic Growth of the United States 1790–1860*, pp. 124, 128.

and care for them in their unproductive infancy and old age, but little else changed, and no one forgot his place in the social and economic order.

The continued movement westward of Anglo-Americans after the Civil War can best be thought of as merely the renewal of an ante-bellum phenomenon. The war itself and the devastation which was the unhappy lot of selected areas may have swelled the numbers of those moving west, but should not be regarded as prime causes. In fact, the war might best be thought of as a temporary hindrance to the westward expansion. War or peace, the southern farmer would have come to test his mettle on the fringes of the "Great American Desert."

THE AMERICAN SETTLEMENT OF TEXAS

The nineteenth-century movement into Texas of Anglo-Americans and, in the period before 1860, their Negro slaves, was almost predictable, for Texas lay astride the path of the rapid westward expansion of the southern frontier. The political situation before 1845 dictated that these settlers, in order to occupy Texas, had to go beyond the territorial limits of the United States, but Americans had proved in Upper Canada, and would prove again in California and the Canadian prairie provinces, that the attraction of new lands was much stronger than political ties. In fact, leaving the United States was a distinct advantage for persons who had debts or legal troubles.

A number of factors combined to funnel southern expansion toward Texas.[37] The inhospitable swamps of southwestern Louisiana and the rugged highlands of western Arkansas were not attractive to settlers, while at the same time the fertile prairies of Oklahoma and Kansas lay behind the supposedly permanent Indian frontier. West of the Indians lay the "Great American Desert" and beyond it the mighty Rockies. To the north, in Iowa and adjacent areas, was the domain of midwesterners, New Englanders, and European pioneers, its harsh climate repellent to the Gulf southerner and his staple crop. Relatively few were venturesome enough, in the first half of the nineteenth century, to cross the numerous obstacles and go on to Oregon and California. Only Texas remained; only there could the natural expansion of the South continue; only there could the planters and yeomen find the new homes and cotton lands they desired.

In 1820 Texas was a very sparsely inhabited land, with a total popu-

[37] Ray Allen Billington, *Westward Expansion: A History of the American Frontier*, pp. 471, 474, 481.

lation of about 3,000.[38] The Mexican inhabitants were concentrated
at the capital of San Antonio de Bexar, where 1,814 persons lived;
at Bahia (Goliad) with 600 population;[39] along the lower Rio Grande
in a few scattered settlements; and on the upper Rio Grande around
El Paso, which belonged to the major population center in New Mexico. Nacogdoches in East Texas, which in 1812 counted a population of about 1,000, had been almost completely abandoned as a
result of filibustering raids from Louisiana.[40] Anglo-American settlement was largely confined to scattered families in the area where the
Nacogdoches-Natchitoches road crossed the Sabine River[41] and to
the south bank of the Red River in far northeastern Texas, in a lo-
cality that was believed to lie in the Arkansas Territory.[42] Along the
San Antonio road from Nacogdoches to Bexar not a single settler
was to be found; only the ruins of two small communities destroyed
earlier by Indians and raiders from Louisiana. For all practical purposes, Texas in 1820 was an empty land, an unguarded, vulnerable
flank of Latin America.

Noting the emptiness of the province, the Mexican government
decided on a policy aimed at peopling Texas, to which end they
instituted the *empresario* system. Contracts were made with certain
individuals which called for the settlement of specified numbers of immigrants in tracts of land granted to these *empresarios* by the government. The first such contract was made with Moses Austin, an American who had acquired Spanish citizenship during an earlier residence
in Missouri. At his death, the contract was passed on to his son, Stephen
F. Austin, a man who properly has been called the "Father of Texas."[43]
Austin's colony lay in south-central Texas, including the valleys of the
lower Brazos and Colorado rivers, and its administrative center was
at San Felipe on the Brazos, founded in 1824 (Figure 1). Settlement
was begun in the early 1820's, and by the middle of the decade a census of the colony revealed a population of 1,800, including 443 slaves.

[38] Juan Antonio Padilla, "Texas in 1820," *Southwestern Historical Quarterly,*
23 (1919), 61.
[39] Mattie Austin Hatcher, *The Opening of Texas to Foreign Settlement, 1801–
1820,* pp. 356–357.
[40] Eugene C. Barker, *The Life of Stephen F. Austin,* p. 37.
[41] Hatcher, *The Opening of Texas,* p. 356.
[42] Rex W. Strickland, "Miller County, Arkansas Territory: The Frontier That
Men Forget," *Chronicles of Oklahoma,* 18 (1940), 12–34, 154–170; 19 (1941),
37–54.
[43] The best source on Austin and his colony, indeed, for all of pre-revolution-
ary Anglo-American settlement in Texas, is Barker, *Stephen F. Austin.*

FIGURE 1

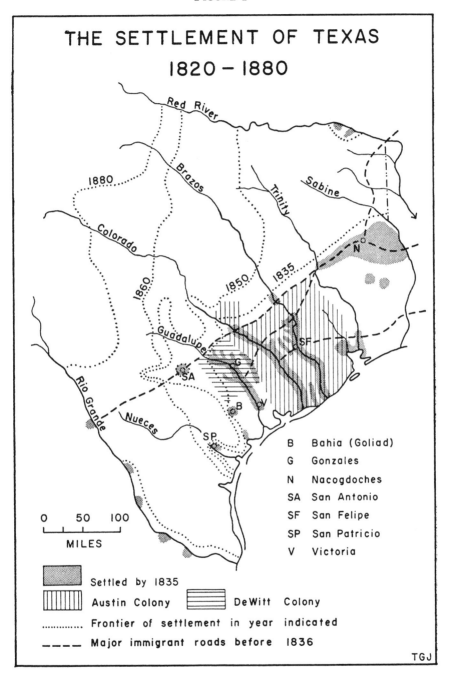

THE SETTLEMENT OF TEXAS
1820 – 1880

B   Bahia (Goliad)
G   Gonzales
N   Nacogdoches
SA   San Antonio
SF   San Felipe
SP   San Patricio
V   Victoria

0   50   100
MILES

Settled by 1835
Austin Colony   DeWitt Colony
.... Frontier of settlement in year indicated
– – – – Major immigrant roads before 1836

TGJ

In 1828 the total had risen to over 2,000, in 1830 to over 4,000, and
in 1831 to 5,665.[44] Settlers arrived in the colony both overland through
Louisiana and Arkansas and by sea from ports on the Gulf, principally
New Orleans. Austin received several other *empresario* grants from
the government, and the colony continued to grow throughout the
Mexican period.

The settlement was essentially riverine in character, and nearly
every land grant was rectangular in shape, with one of the smaller
sides fronting on a river or a smaller stream, reminiscent of the long
lots of New France. It is possible that this settlement form was diffused to the Spanish during their forty-year rule in Louisiana and
passed on intact to the Mexican rulers after independence. Two major
shoestring-shaped areas of settlement developed, one along the lower
Brazos and its tributaries and the other on the lower Colorado. A
smaller clustering developed near the mouth of the San Jacinto River
and along Buffalo Bayou. The settlers in Austin's colony were for
the most part yeoman farmers from Tennessee, Missouri, and Kentucky,[45] with the result that slaves formed a relatively small part of
the total population. In 1834 a Mexican official reported 9,000 people
in Austin's colony and the adjacent smaller colony of another *empresario*, of whom only 1,000 were Negro slaves.[46] The official atti-
tude of the government, though not enforced, was one of opposition
to slavery, and this may have discouraged large planters from coming
to Texas.[47] The slaveowners who did come were concentrated near
the mouths of the Brazos and Colorado, in the only major plantation
areas of the colony.

A second *empresario* who had some measure of success was Green
DeWitt, whose colony lay adjacent to Austin's on the west, in the valley of the Guadalupe River some distance inland from the coast. Settlement began in the mid-1820's, and it was reported in 1830 that 150
families lived in the colony, in a riverine pattern centered around
the capital of Gonzales.[48] The settlers were largely from Missouri,

[44] *Ibid.*, pp. 98, 149. The figures for 1828, 1830, and 1831 probably include
slaves.
[45] *Ibid.*, p. 149.
[46] Juan N. Almonte, "Statistical Report on Texas," *Southwestern Historical
Quarterly*, 28 (1924–1925), 198.
[47] Lester G. Bugbee, "Slavery in Early Texas," *Political Science Quarterly*,
13 (1898), 389–412, 648–668.
[48] See Ethel Z. Rather, "De Witt's Colony," *Texas State Historical Association Quarterly*, 8 (1904), pp. 95–192. Included is an excellent map depicting
the long-lot riverine settlement pattern.

Kentucky, and Tennessee, and the slave population was small. By 1834 the population had risen to some 900.[49]

Austin and DeWitt were the only *empresarios* who succeeded in introducing large numbers of Anglo-Americans into Texas. There were many others who had contracts and land grants, but they failed, in part because they lacked the momentum gained by Austin in his earlier start and in part because the land open to them was inferior to that granted to Austin and DeWitt. In addition, a law was passed in 1830 which forbade further settlement of Anglo-Americans in Texas, *except* in the Austin and DeWitt colonies.[50] Another *empresario*, Martín de León, succeeded in settling Mexicans in his colony on the lower Guadalupe River, below DeWitt's colony, around the town of Victoria in the 1820's,[51] and other *empresarios* brought Irish immigrants to the lower Nueces River at San Patricio in the 1830's. The Irish settlement numbered some 600 in 1834, while Victoria had about 300.[52]

Also in the Mexican period, unorganized Anglo-American immigration was occurring in eastern Texas, beyond the borders of the official colonies. For a time, an *empresario* was active in the Nacogdoches area, but the immigration to that area was composed primarily of squatters who entered Texas illegally, easily evading or ignoring the law prohibiting American immigration. When that law was repealed in 1834, a large-scale influx of American settlers began. In the summer, one Mexican official estimated that over 3,000 would enter Texas before the end of the year,[53] and it was reported that about 2,000 had landed at the mouth of the Brazos alone in January and February of 1835.

By the end of the Mexican period, there were probably about 30,000 Americans in Texas,[54] most of them in the Austin and DeWitt colonies and in the border region around Nacogdoches. Negro slaves comprised only 12 percent of the population and were concentrated in the plantations near the mouths of the Brazos and Colorado rivers.[55]

[49] Almonte, "Statistical Report," p. 198.
[50] Barker, *Stephen F. Austin*, pp. 296, 328.
[51] Mary V. Henderson, "Minor Empresario Contracts for the Colonization of Texas," *Southwestern Historical Quarterly*, 32 (1928), 5–6.
[52] Almonte, "Statistical Report," p. 186.
[53] *Ibid.*
[54] Eugene C. Barker, *Mexico and Texas 1821–1835*, p. 21.
[55] William R. Hogan, *The Texas Republic: A Social and Economic History*, pp. 21–22.

The bulk of the American population was still of the yeoman farmer class. The American-settled areas were essentially a series of shoe-stringlike strips along the lower courses of the rivers of south-central Texas, a loose clustering around Nacogdoches, the scattered cabins of squatters in southeastern Texas, and some small clusters on the Red River in the northeast.

Following the revolution of 1836, the immigration continued un-abated into the period of the Republic. The government of the newly independent state maintained the policy of granting free land to im-migrants, and in 1841, revived the *empresario* system to aid the settle-ment of frontier areas.[56] Following a drop in the early 1840's in re-sponse to Mexican raids,[57] a sharp rise in immigration occurred after 1843.[58]

Many of the immigrants during the period of the Republic were at-tracted to the older settled areas in south-central and southeastern Texas, where they expanded the settled areas up the river valleys far-ther to the interior and began to occupy the interfluves. The major area of expansion, however, was in eastern Texas to the north of the old San Antonio Road, which was cleared for settlement by the de-feat of the Indians in 1839.[59] Immigration during this period was largely unorganized, with the exception of the Peters Colony which brought settlers from Kentucky and Tennessee to the area around Dallas beginning in 1842[60] and two other *empresario* grants on the frontier, which, as will be discussed, were settled by Germans. Yeo-man farmers from Tennessee, Missouri, and Kentucky continued to come, but at the same time settlers from the Gulf South, primarily Alabama, were coming in ever-increasing numbers. Many of the Gulf southerners owned slaves, and the proportion of Negroes in the total population of Texas rose from 12 percent in 1835 to 27 percent in 1847. Immigration during the period of the Republic was the chief factor in the growth of the population to 142,000 in 1847, four times the total of 1835.[61]

Texas joined the United States in 1845, and the first fifteen years of statehood witnessed the greatest immigration in its history. The

[56] An excellent discussion of the public land policy of the Republic of Texas is contained in Seymour V. Connor, *The Peters Colony of Texas*, pp. 9–22, 111.
[57] Hogan, *The Texas Republic*, p. 14.
[58] Barnes F. Lathrop, *Migration into East Texas 1835–1860*, p. 61.
[59] Hogan, *The Texas Republic*, p. 14.
[60] Connor, *The Peters Colony*, p. 49.
[61] Hogan, *The Texas Republic*, pp. 9, 10, 21, 22.

population almost tripled from 1850 to 1860, reaching over 600,000 by the outbreak of the Civil War.[62] The settlers of this period were divided about equally between Gulf and Upper southerners (Table 1), with Tennessee and Alabama the leading contributors. The phenomenon that had begun in the 1820's continued, with the settlement of Texas accomplished in a leapfrog movement by settlers from states that were not adjacent. The Anglo-American population of Texas was sired by Tennessee and Alabama, not Arkansas and Louisiana, as should have been the case if the idea of the frontier settlement by people from areas adjacent to the east, which is still encountered occasionally in the literature,[63] were universally applicable. The remoteness of the source regions of Texas settlers was a result of the unusually rapid expansion of the southern frontier, which allowed large areas of Louisiana and most of Arkansas to be settled at roughly the same time as Texas. While some Tennesseans were coming to Texas, others were occupying Arkansas.

The immigrants settled almost exclusively in the eastern half of the state, creating a much denser population in the older settled areas, while at the same time they pushed the frontier westward in the northern portion of the state and partially filled the fertile Black Waxy Prairie (Figure 2). The major expansion of plantations took place in far northeastern Texas in the valleys of the Red River and its right-bank tributaries (Figure 3). The Cotton Belt had not reached its fullest westward expansion by 1860, contrary to an impression left by the late historian Walter Prescott Webb.[64] The Black Waxy Prairie, which held as much promise for the expansion of the slave-cotton economy as had the Black Belt of Alabama earlier in the century, was left to the yeomen from the Upper South to settle. Slavery and even cotton were largely alien to the Black Waxy Prairie in ante-bellum times, and in their stead was found a frontier crop economy reminiscent of the Midwest, in which wheat was dominant. The failure of the plantation system to occupy this fertile area can be explained in part by the absence of navigable streams, for water transport and plantations went hand-in-hand in the pre-railroad era.

Immediately after the Civil War, the influx of southerners into Texas

[62] Seventh Census, 1850, p. 504 and Eighth Census, 1860, volume on population, p. 486.

[63] The idea is expressed in Billington, *Westward Expansion*, p. 9.

[64] Walter Prescott Webb, *The Great Plains*, pp. 188–191. Webb's thesis is correct only if applied to state units, and then only if irrigated cotton is ignored.

FIGURE 2

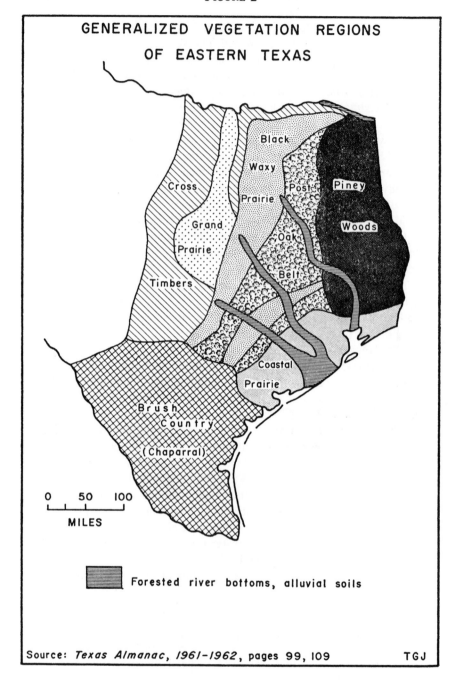

GENERALIZED VEGETATION REGIONS
OF EASTERN TEXAS

Black

Waxy

Cross

Prairie

Post

Piney

Grand

Woods

Prairie

Oak

Timbers

Belt

Coastal

Prairie

Brush
Country

(Chaparral)

0   50   100

MILES

Forested river bottoms, alluvial soils

Source: *Texas Almanac, 1961–1962*, pages 99, 109   TGJ

resumed. These new immigrants, like their predecessors, were about equally divided in origin between the states of the Upper and Lower South, though Alabama replaced Tennessee as the leading source region (Table 2). Southerners from the different states, both in the post-bellum period and earlier, concentrated in certain portions of Texas. The process of localization of immigrant groups is not difficult to understand. The forerunner, or true pioneer, selected a site—often by accident and certainly not always with the best judgment—found it to his liking, wrote to relatives and friends back in the source area, and thereby induced others to follow him. This process snowballed until a large-scale movement was underway. The result was that the source regions for settlers were often quite small areas, so that the population of one county in Tennessee or one small state in central Germany might be largely responsible for settling a particular county or adjacent counties in Texas. By this process, Tennesseans came to be dominant in the Black Waxy Prairie; Louisianans, mostly sugar planters and merchants, were the largest group in counties bordering the Gulf of Mexico; Georgians were concentrated in the plantation district of northeastern Texas; Alabamans occupied the inland counties east of the Tennesseans; and Mississippians located in compact areas in western south-central Texas[65] (Figure 3).

Post-war settlement succeeded in filling up the Black Waxy Prairie, and by 1880 the push into the semi-arid lands was well underway. Railroads aided the expansion westward, and at the same time stimulated settlement in previously thinly populated interfluvial areas of central Texas, where the railroads received extensive land grants. The total white population of the state rose from 421,000 in 1860 to 564,000 in 1870, 1,200,000 in 1880, and 1,750,000 in 1890,[66] with southern Anglo-Americans comprising the bulk of these numbers.

However, the pioneers of the South were not alone in their task of wresting Texas from the realm of Latin America. Many thousands of immigrants came directly from Europe, and among them Germans were by far the most numerous. A description of the Old World agricultural heritage of the Germans and an account of their settlement of Texas follows.

---

[65] Ninth Census, 1870, vol. I, pp. 372–373.
[66] Eighth Census, 1860, volume on population, p. 486; Ninth Census, 1870, vol. I, p. 64; Tenth Census, 1880, volume on population, p. 3; Eleventh Census, 1890, "Population, Part I," p. xcviii.

FIGURE 3

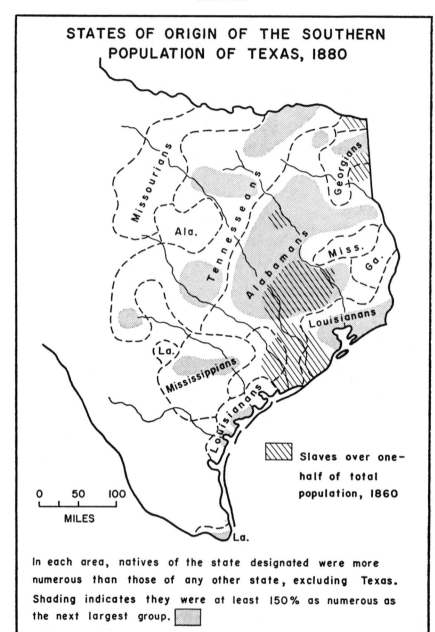

STATES OF ORIGIN OF THE SOUTHERN
POPULATION OF TEXAS, 1880

Slaves over one-
half of total
population, 1860

0   50   100
MILES

In each area, natives of the state designated were more
numerous than those of any other state, excluding Texas.
Shading indicates they were at least 150% as numerous as
the next largest group.

Source: U.S. Census of Population, 1880, pp. 528-531   TGJ

Chapter Three

Nineteenth-Century German Farmers and Their Emigration to Texas

T he history of German farmers has not been a happy one. In various parts of Central Europe, the semi-slavery of feudal times gave way to the bloodshed of peasant revolts, only to be followed by the widespread devastation wrought by the marauding armies of the Thirty Years' War, the raiders of Louis XIV of France, and the troop movements associated with other lesser conflicts. The nineteenth century dawned with more hope than its predecessors, brightened by edicts in Prussia and several other German states which outlawed the last vestiges of serfdom. Encouraging advances were being made in scientific agriculture through the work of Albrecht Thaer, Justus von Liebig, and others. In addition, the German countryside was destined to enjoy a half-century of uninterrupted peace following 1815. Still, there were serious flaws in the agricultural economy, some of long standing and others of more recent origin, which combined to produce the greatest outpouring of emigrants ever witnessed, before or since, in the troubled history of the German lands.[1] Over much of the remainder of Europe the story was the same.

The German emigrant farmers were attracted to many countries. Some moved eastward into the vast Slavic domain in Europe; others chose Latin America, primarily southern Brazil, Argentina, and Chile; and still others settled in the far-flung British Empire, principally in Australia and Canada. The majority, however, chose the United States,

---

[1] The best general source on the history of German agriculture is by Theodor von Goltz, *Geschichte der deutschen Landwirtschaft.* Others used are Richard Krzymowski, *Geschichte der deutschen Landwirtschaft,* and Klaus Ekkehart, *Deutsche Bauerngeschichte.*

FIGURE 4

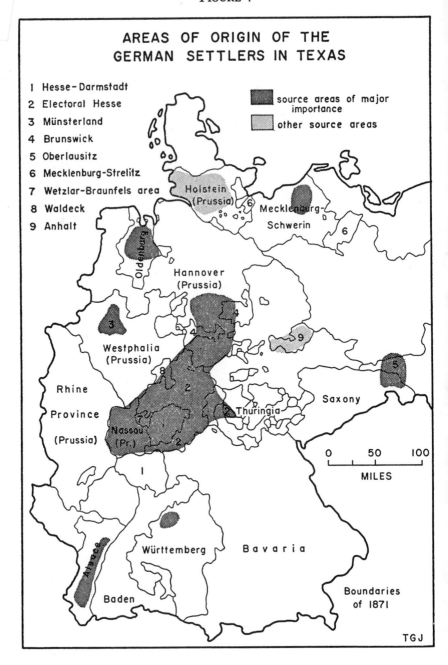

AREAS OF ORIGIN OF THE
GERMAN SETTLERS IN TEXAS

1 Hesse–Darmstadt
2 Electoral Hesse
3 Münsterland
4 Brunswick
5 Oberlausitz
6 Mecklenburg-Strelitz
7 Wetzlar–Braunfels area
8 Waldeck
9 Anhalt

source areas of major importance

other source areas

Holstein (Prussia)

Mecklenburg-Schwerin

Oldenburg

Hannover (Prussia)

Westphalia (Prussia)

Rhine Province (Prussia)

Nassau (Pr.)

Thuringia

Saxony

Württemberg

Bavaria

Baden

0   50   100
MILES

Boundaries of 1871

TGJ

and Texas received a share of them during the course of the century. Only minor portions of the German-speaking lands contributed significantly to overseas migration, and for this reason it is necessary to locate more exactly the source regions of the Texas settlers. Most of them came from the Middle and High German provinces of Nassau, Electoral Hesse, Upper Hesse-Darmstadt, Alsace, far western Thuringia, and the Heilbronn area of Württemberg, as well as from the Low German areas of Oldenburg, southern Hannover, Brunswick (Braunschweig), the Münsterland, and Mecklenburg.[2] The Wetterau, a region in Upper Hesse-Darmstadt to the north of Frankfurt-am-Main, was particularly noted as a source of Texas settlers.[3] Lesser numbers came from Holstein, Waldeck, Anhalt, and the right bank portions of the Prussian Rhine Province (Figure 4). In addition, many Wendish people from Saxon and Prussian Lausitz settled in Texas. Agricultural practices and rural settlement form differed considerably from one part of Germany to another in the last century, and in order to understand the farming heritage of the Texas Germans, attention must be directed primarily to the agricultural systems of the specific areas from which they came.

THE SYSTEM OF AGRICULTURE IN THE GERMAN SOURCE REGIONS

In most of Germany, farming was characterized by emphasis on small grains, improved pasture, and manure-producing livestock. In northwestern and north-central Germany, including Oldenburg, the Münsterland, and Mecklenburg, rye was the dominant grain, supplemented by oats, while farther to the south, particularly in Alsace, Hesse, and

---

[2] Information on the origins of Texas Germans can be found in Viktor Bracht, *Texas im Jahre 1848*, p. 148; Rosa Kleberg, "Some of my Early Experiences in Texas," *Texas State Historical Association Quarterly*, 1 (1898), 302; Oscar Canstatt, *Die deutsche Auswanderung, Auswandererfürsorge und Auswandererziele*, pp. 223–224; Julius Fröbel, *Aus Amerika: Erfahrungen, Reisen und Studien*, Vol. 2, p. 320; George C. Engerrand, *The So-Called Wends of Germany and Their Colonies in Texas and in Australia*, pp. 89 ff.; and Caroline von Hinueber, "Life of German Pioneers of Early Texas," *Texas State Historical Association Quarterly*, 2 (1899), 228. Additional information was obtained from the old ship lists, which often included the province and even village of origin of the emigrants.

[3] "Erinnerungen an die Trümmer der Adels-Colonie in Texas u.s.w.," *Der deutsche Pionier*, 1 (1869), 143–144; Canstatt, *Die deutsche Auswanderung*, pp. 223–224.

Nassau, wheat and barley increased in importance.[4] Winter cultivation of grains was not uncommon in any of the areas. The white potato,
an import from the New World that had gained widespread acceptance
in the eighteenth century, was found throughout the German lands,
but its significance was particularly great in the Wetterau area and
the remainder of Hesse and Nassau, where it was the principal food.
The potato was also a major crop in Alsace, Brunswick, and southern Hannover;[5] but in the provinces of northern and northwestern
Germany it was less important, though major advances in its cultivation were made in the Münsterland in the first half of the nineteenth
century.[6] Most German farmers, regardless of area, grew hay to supplement oats and barley as feed for their livestock, and two cuttings
were made each year in areas such as Hesse and Nassau.[7] Most farms
had both a garden, in which a variety of vegetables was raised, and a
small orchard with apples, plums, and pears. On the slopes bordering
the Upper Rhine Valley and the Rhine Gorge, in Nassau, portions of
Hesse, and Alsace, viticulture was widely practiced. In the vineyard
areas, wine was a common beverage, but elsewhere, in the remainder
of Germany, beer was preferred. Tobacco was raised in small amounts
in portions of Hesse, Nassau, and Alsace.[8]

Livestock played a vital role in the agricultural system, since a generous application of animal manure, not uncommonly supplemented
with human waste, was needed to provide high crop yields. In the infertile areas of "eternal rye culture" in northwestern Germany, where
in some instances this grain was planted on the same field for twenty
consecutive years, heavy dunging was vital. Liebig's advocacy of chem-
ical fertilizers had virtually no effect on the German peasant, and
even today the odor of dung heaps permeates the rural villages in
some areas. The importance of domestic animals was further heightened by the restrictions placed on hunting. The woodlands of Germany were rich enough in wild game, but since feudal times they had
been the domain of the nobility, and the hunt was confined to the leis-

[4] Wilhelm Müller-Wille, "Feldsysteme in Westfalen um 1860," *Deutsche
Geographische Blätter,* 42 (1939), 119–121; August Meitzen, *Der Boden und
die landwirthschaftlichen Verhältnisse des preussischen Staates . . .,* Vol. 7, pp.
346–347; "Deutschland," *Meyers Konversations- Lexikon,* Vol. 4, series of maps
following p. 876.
[5] "Deutschland," Vol. 4, maps; Meitzen, *Der Boden,* Vol. 7, pp. 346–347.
[6] Müller-Wille, "Feldsysteme in Westfalen," p. 122.
[7] Meitzen, *Der Boden,* Vol. 7, p. 210.
[8] *Ibid.,* Vol. 7, p. 222; *Meyers Lexikon,* Vol. 4, maps.

ure hours of the privileged. As a result, the peasants had not retained the hunting skills of their distant ancestors. Cattle were found on most farms in all parts of Germany, though they were more numerous in provinces such as Hannover, with over forty-five head per one hundred population in the early 1870's, and less so in other areas, including Hesse, Nassau, and Westphalia which had about thirty-three per one hundred[9] (Table 4). Milk, butter, and cheese all were important in the rural diet. There were more swine in northern Germany, notably in Hannover and the Münsterland, than in the south, particularly in Alsace, where they were less numerous and pork was not as significant as a food. In contrast, sheep were much more common in Hesse, Nassau, and Hannover, where they out-numbered cattle, while in the Münsterland and all of Westphalia they had declined in importance since the 1700's.[10] Exceptional was the farmer who possessed a horse to serve as a draft animal, for there were only five horses per one hundred population in Hesse and Nassau in the 1870's, and ten for each one hundred in Hannover.[11] More common was the ox, though many farmers lacked even this sturdy beast, relying instead on the family milk cows to pull the plow. Chickens were by far the most numerous barnyard poultry, with geese and ducks in important secondary roles.[12]

A great deal of variety was encountered in the rural settlement form in the different areas contributing emigrants to Texas.[13] In northwestern Germany, including the Münsterland, Oldenburg, and Holstein, the farmsteads were dispersed or situated in loose clusterings called *Drubbel* or *Weiler*, which were often insular in a surrounding heath. The houses[14] in these areas, and in Mecklenburg and portions of southern Hannover as well, combined living quarters, stalls, barn and storage rooms under one roof—the so-called *Einheitshaus*—represented

---

[9] Meitzen, *Der Boden*, Vol. 7, pp. 730–731.

[10] *Ibid.*, Vol. 7, pp. 730–731.

[11] *Ibid.*

[12] *Ibid.*, Vol. 7, pp. 682–683.

[13] Among the better general sources on settlement form are Rudolf Martiny, "Die Grundrissgestaltung der deutschen Siedlungen." *Petermanns Mitteilungen Ergänzungsheft No. 197;* Adolf Helbok, *Deutsche Siedlung, Wesen, Ausbreitung und Sinn*; Werner Radig, *Die Siedlungstypen in Deutschland*; and *Westermanns Atlas zur Weltgeschichte*, Part II, "Mittelalter." The best English source is Robert E. Dickinson, "Rural Settlement in the German Lands," *Annals of the Association of American Geographers*, 39 (1949), 239–263.

[14] For good general sources on German house types, see Wilhelm Müller-Wille, "Haus- und Gehöftformen in Mitteleuropa," *Geographische Zeitschrift*, 42 (1936), 121–138; August Meitzen, *Das deutsche Haus*; and the map by A. Haberlandt in *Illustrierte Völkerkunde*, Vol. 2, Part 2, following p. 176.

principally by the type known as the Lower Saxon House. In the other major source areas, the farmsteads were grouped in compact, irregular villages called *Haufendörfer*, except in Mecklenburg, where the villages displayed linear (*Strassendorf*) or circular (*Rundling*) patterns. The farmstead in Upper Hesse, Nassau, Alsace, and parts of Brunswick and southern Hannover, was composed of a series of separate buildings situated around three sides of a central courtyard, with a wall and gate facing the street, a type generally referred to as the Middle German or Frankish farmstead (*mitteldeutsches Gehöft*). In the Wetterau area, so notable as a source of Texas settlers, it was not uncommon to find structures of an individual holding arranged on only two sides of the courtyard, with the third side bordered by the buildings of an adjacent farmstead.[15] In most of the areas under consideration, and particularly in Hesse, Nassau, and Alsace, construction was of the half-timbered or *Fachwerk* style, in which a framework of wooden beams was filled in with brick or wattling.

In all areas, the garden plot was located adjacent to the farmstead, while the fields lay some distance away. In the farm-village areas as well as the regions of dispersed or loosely clustered farmsteads, each peasant usually had a number of separate small fields scattered over the countryside, often considerable distances apart. In most of the areas under consideration, the *three-field system*, a remnant of feudal times, still existed: the farmers owned land in each of three major enclosed divisions or *Gewanne*, one of which was generally left fallow and served as pasture. Within the separate *Gewanne* there were no fences, and each was planted in a single crop by all farmers having land there. By the nineteenth century, many local modifications of this system had developed, creating an extremely complex situation. Even in northwestern Germany, where the three-field system was never established, each farmer's land was usually split up into a number of nonadjacent plots.[16] In none of the source areas of Texas settlers were operational farm units with wholly contiguous lands common.

As a rule, farms were rather small throughout Germany, but in some overpopulated areas they attained grotesque miniaturization, especially in the source regions of Hesse, Nassau, Alsace, and Württemberg, where fragmentation was encouraged by the surviving tradition

[15] Kurt Ehemann, *Das Bauernhaus in der Wetterau und im SW-Vogelsberg,* Forschungen zur deutschen Landeskunde, Vol. 61, pp. 54–55, map no. 1 at back of book.

[16] Müller-Wille, "Feldsysteme in Westfalen," pp. 121–124.

of Roman Law, by which land was divided equally among all heirs.[17] Conditions were different in Hannover, the Münsterland, and other north German areas where land descended to one heir, who was obliged to buy out the others. Many farms were not large enough to support the families which toiled upon them, and additional income was often obtained by means of various household industries.

For much of the nineteenth century, German farmers operated on a semisubsistence level, and were interested primarily in feeding their own families. The surplus was taken to the nearest market village to be sold. The important subsistence element was a key factor in maintaining the diversity of crops and livestock found on each farm. Only in the vineyard regions and the market gardening areas found near many cities was agriculture highly commercialized. Between about 1860 and 1880, however, German farmers became much more market-oriented, particularly in response to the expanding urban markets of Central Europe. Although most farmers continued to produce much of their own food, concern had shifted to the supply of urban consumers. With the cash they received for their produce, the German farmers acquired a taste for factory-made goods and other physical evidences of a higher standard of living.

In most agricultural areas of Germany, the land was worked quite intensively, becoming almost gardenlike in the more thickly-populated regions. The intensity was achieved chiefly through heavy application of human and animal labor, inasmuch as capital was in limited supply. Virtually all work was done by the individual families, and it was not unusual to see women and children working in the fields, a phenomenon still observable in the German countryside. They accomplished their tasks using time-tested implements—the wooden plow, the scythe, and the sickle. The intensive application of labor was generally rewarded by a productivity that was high by nineteenth-century standards, a necessity if hunger was to be avoided on the small farms.

In western Germany, including most of the source regions of Texas settlers, many farmers owned their land, in contrast to Mecklenburg and most of the remainder of the provinces east of the Elbe and Saale rivers, where large estates were the rule and the peasants little better off than their serf ancestors. Ownership was the dream if not the heritage of the German farmer. Whether tenant or owner, the peasant com-

[17] Eugen Jäger, *Die Agrarfrage der Gegenwart,* Vol. 2, p. 111; Vol. 3, p. 60.

monly occupied land that his ancestors had tilled for centuries, and he expected that his descendants would continue to live in the same place and enjoy the benefits of whatever improvements he made. This locational stability of the population encouraged a striving for permanence, which manifested itself best, perhaps, in the solid, enduring farmstead structures.

NINETEENTH-CENTURY RURAL EMIGRATION

The causes of rural emigration were extremely complex, and any brief attempt to outline them necessarily oversimplifies the situation. Some areas responded to adverse conditions with massive outpourings of their population while other areas, similarly affected, did not. Still, it will contribute to the understanding of the emigration of German farmers to Texas to consider some of the factors which encouraged them to leave their homeland.

The most important causes were economic and took a number of different forms. The accelerating fragmentation of farms in over-populated areas had reached a critical level. The famous economist Friedrich List, among others, realized that a crisis was at hand in 1842, and he pleaded for changes in the inheritance laws and for con-solidation and enlargement of the holdings.[18] In addition, over much of northern and eastern Germany, where the law provided for a single heir, those not inheriting land were finding it increasingly difficult to find a place, however humble, in economic life. To this gradual worsen-ing of conditions was added, in 1845, a potato blight which ravaged not only parts of Germany, but much of northwestern Europe as well. Potato harvests continued to be bad in 1846 and 1847,[19] and the blight struck again in an exceptionally severe manner over much of Ger-many in 1851–1854.

Overpopulation and crop failures were not the only contributing factors. Another major force at work in Gemany during this period was the trend toward industrialization, and by the 1850's, mechanized factory production had advanced to the point where it was compet-ing with and undermining home industry, thus depriving many farm-ers of a much needed supplementary source of income.[20]

[18] Friedrich List, *Die Ackerverfassung, die Zwergwirtschaft und die Aus-wanderung*, pp. 9–10, 15–17.

[19] J. H. Clapham, *The Economic Development of France and Germany, 1815–1914*, p. 137.

[20] Canstatt, *Die deutsche Auswanderung*, p. 28.

The revolutions in Germany in 1848 were carried out for the most part by nonagricultural elements in the population. As a result, the failure of the revolutionary cause was more influential in encouraging emigration among better-educated, city-dwelling Germans, and did not worsen rural conditions significantly in most areas. There were a number of small "Latin" farming settlements established overseas by men of the "Forty-Eighter" class, and it is true that politically discontented Germans served as organizers of some of the numerous groups which recruited emigrants in the rural areas, but in general the revolutions have probably been overemphasized as a cause of migration. More important, though doubtlessly less inspiring, was the desire to escape the required years of military service.

The massive emigration of the period ending in the late 1850's was followed by about a decade during which the numbers leaving Germany dropped markedly. The lot of the German farmer had improved considerably. The crop failures of the late 1840's and early 1850's did not recur, and the increasing degree of commercialization in agriculture held promise of a better future. Starvation was no longer recurrent in the German countryside, having been replaced in the hierarchy of worries by concern for market prices.

To the dismay of the German farmer, his attainment of a higher plateau of economic existence was soon endangered by a flood of cheap imported agricultural produce on the European market, grown on the new farm lands of America and Australia, inexpensively produced on a large scale and transported by the technology of the burgeoning mechanical age—greatly improved farm machinery, the railroad, the ocean-going steamship. Prices began to fall in the late 1870's and continued to decline through the 1880's and 1890's, scarcely affected by hastily constructed tariff walls. Unable to mechanize effectively because of the small size of their fields, German farmers were obliged to shift from cash grains to the production of goods better suited to their small-scale, intensive system—dairy and poultry products, fruit and vegetables, and feeder livestock. Adding to the economic distress of the German farmer were higher taxes, a rising cost of living, and increased costs of production, which, when coupled with falling prices, resulted in a steady rise in farm debt. German agriculture had entered its second crisis period of the century, one which brought about an even larger outpouring of emigrant farmers than the first, an exodus that reached its peak in the early 1880's.

Unlike their predecessors of the 1840's and 1850's, these emigrants

were not fleeing in the face of hunger and misery, but rather seeking
to maintain the higher standard of living to which they had so recently
become accustomed. They went not as pioneers prepared to subdue
the wilderness on the frontiers of the world, but as secondary settlers
expecting to continue as commercial farmers. They did not undertake
a dangerous journey in sailing ships to lands largely unknown, but
rather were carried swiftly and safely by steamship and railroad to
destinations of proven desirability.

THE GERMAN SETTLEMENT OF TEXAS, 1831–1860

Texas differed from all other southern states, except Missouri, in that
it received large numbers of German immigrants. The attention of
the German farmer was drawn to Texas by a great volume of literature that was, for the most part, full of praise. As might be expected,
such books not infrequently emanated from persons who were involved financially in Texas colonization, and the result was an uneven
contest between enthusiasm and objectivity. Other writers, catering
to the booming market for emigrant guidebooks, did not let their igno-
rance of Texas hinder them from publishing books about the area. In
1842 an organization in Germany devoted to overseas colonization
reported concerning Texas that "nowhere does the German race prosper better than here, where are united all the advantages of the tropics
with the comforts of the temperate zones."[21] One German writer in
1845 labeled Texas the "paradise of North America,"[22] while another
placed its soils "among the most fertile in the world."[23] In the mind
of the German farmer, Texas became a land of milk and honey, its
name synonymous with hope for a new and better life. Texas had its
detractors in Germany,[24] but their criticisms went largely unheard in
the din of approval and praise for this supposed earthly paradise.

The movement of Germans to Texas properly may be said to have
begun in the year 1831, for although there were a few Germans living
there prior to that date, their presence did not attract fellow country-

[21] (Verein zum Schutze Deutscher Einwanderer in Texas), "Akten der Cen-
tral-Verwaltung des Vereins zum Schutze Deutscher Einwanderer in Texas be-
treffend," records preserved in the archives at Schloss Braunfels, Hesse. The
translation is taken from John A. Hawgood, *The Tragedy of German America,*
p. 145.
[22] Johann H. S. Schulz, *Die deutsche Ansiedlung in Texas . . ..* p. 25.
[23] Carl von Solms-Braunfels, *Texas . . .,* p. 12.
[24] The critics often maintained that the climate of Texas was unhealthful. See,
for example, J. E. Wappäus, *Deutsche Auswanderung und Colonisation,* p. 49.

men to join them. It was in 1831 that Friedrich Ernst, a native of Oldenburg, received a grant of land from the Mexican government, lying
within the Austin colony in the valley of Mill Creek in present-day
northwestern Austin County (Figure 5). Here Ernst established his
farm.[25] He found the land much to his liking and wrote an enthusiastic
letter to a friend back in Germany, describing his new home in glow-
ing terms. The letter was published in a newspaper in Oldenburg and
also in a book describing travels in Texas,[26] and had a considerable
effect. In the years that followed, a small stream of German immigrants settled near Ernst in the area between the lower Brazos and
Colorado rivers, founding a number of German rural communities in
Austin, Fayette, and Colorado counties.[27] Ernst himself laid out a
townsite on his property in 1838, and it grew slowly to become the
village of Industry. Ernst's wife estimated that several hundred Germans settled in the area around Industry from 1838 to 1842.[28] The
immigration of the 1830's and early 1840's came principally from
the Low German areas of Oldenburg, the Münsterland in Westphalia,
and to a lesser extent Holstein,[29] though it was reported also that natives of Mecklenburg, East Prussia, Brandenburg, Posen, Silesia, West
Prussia, and Pomerania also settled in the area between the lower
Brazos and Colorado rivers by 1848[30] (Figure 4). Elsewhere in Texas,
Germans could be found only in small numbers scattered among the
American inhabitants.

The original impetus provided by Friedrich Ernst was the key factor in the early development of German settlement in Texas, but still,
the German element in the state might have remained relatively small
and insignificant had it not been for the work of the Verein zum
Schutze deutscher Einwanderer in Texas,[31] a society composed of

[25] The reader's attention is directed to several articles by Rudolph Leopold
Biesele that deal with Ernst's settlement: "The First German Settlement in
Texas," *Southwestern Historical Quarterly*, 34 (1930–1931), 334–339 and "Industry: The First German Settlement in Texas," *Deutsch-Amerikanische Geschichtsblätter*, 32 (1932), 523–528.

[26] Detlef Dunt, *Reise nach Texas* . . ., pp. 4–16.

[27] The best general source on these settlements is Rudolph Leopold Biesele,
The History of the German Settlements in Texas 1831–1861, pp. 42–52. See
also (Cat Spring Agricultural Society), *The Cat Spring Story*.

[28] Louise Stöhr, "Die erste deutsche Frau in Texas," *Der deutsche Pionier*,
16 (1884), 374.

[29] Kleberg, "Some of My Early Experiences," p. 302; Hinueber, "Life of German Pioneers," p. 228.

[30] Bracht, *Texas im Jahre 1848*, p. 148.

[31] The Society for the Protection of German Immigrants in Texas, also called

FIGURE 5

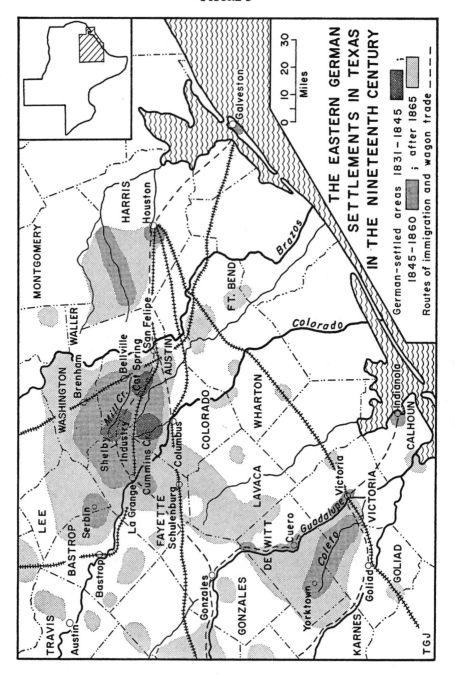

THE EASTERN GERMAN
SETTLEMENTS IN TEXAS
IN THE NINETEENTH CENTURY

German-settled areas 1831–1845 ;
1845–1860 ; after 1865
Routes of immigration and wagon trade ————

wealthy, titled Germans who were interested in overseas colonization for both economic and philanthropic reasons. These promoters hoped, by purchasing colonial lands and settling them with Germans, to realize a profit on their investment as land values increased with the development of the area, while at the same time to provide a safe and prosperous future for thousands of emigrants. After some consideration, Texas was chosen as the site for the colony.[32] The Verein obtained the right to settle Germans on a vast tract of land in west-central Texas known as the Fisher-Miller Grant (Figure 6).

The offer by the Verein to prospective emigrants was very attractive, and recruits were easy to find. Each unmarried man was to pay the equivalent of $120 and the head of each household $240, while each agreed to cultivate at least fifteen acres for three years and to occupy his house for the same period. In return for this, the Verein promised (1) free transportation to the colony, (2) free land in the colony (160 acres for a single man and 320 acres for a family), (3) a free log house, (4) provisions and all goods necessary to begin farming, supplied on credit until the second successive crop had been harvested, and (5) numerous public improvements, such as the construction of roads, mills, cotton gins, hospitals, schools, churches, orphan asylums, and even the canalization of rivers. All this the Verein proposed to do with a total capital of only about $80,000, apparently convinced that huge profits would be realized by keeping ownership of one-half of the land in the colony.

Under the supervision of Prince Carl von Solms-Braunfels, and later of the Baron von Meusebach, the Verein went about the task of colonization. Beginning in 1844, German emigrants were sent by sailing ship to Galveston, and thence to Indianola, the Verein port on Matagorda Bay. It was soon realized that the land obtained for colonization lay too far from the coast to be settled immediately, and as a result, New Braunfels[33] (Comal County, 1845) and Fredericksburg[34]

---

the Mainzer Adelsverein, the Adelsverein, or simply the Verein. Hereinafter it will be referred to as the Verein.

[32] Biesele, *History of the German Settlements*, pp. 66–110, is the best general source on the activities of the Verein.

[33] For information on New Braunfels, see Hermann Seele, *A Short Sketch of Comal County, Texas;* Biesele, *History of German Settlements,* pp. 111–138; and Rudolph L. Biesele, "Early Times in New Braunfels and Comal County," *Southwestern Historical Quarterly,* 50 (1946–1947), 75–92.

[34] The most valuable source on Fredericksburg is Robert Penniger (ed.), *Fest-Ausgabe zum 50-jährigen Jubiläum der Gründung der Stadt Friedrichsburg.*

Figure 6

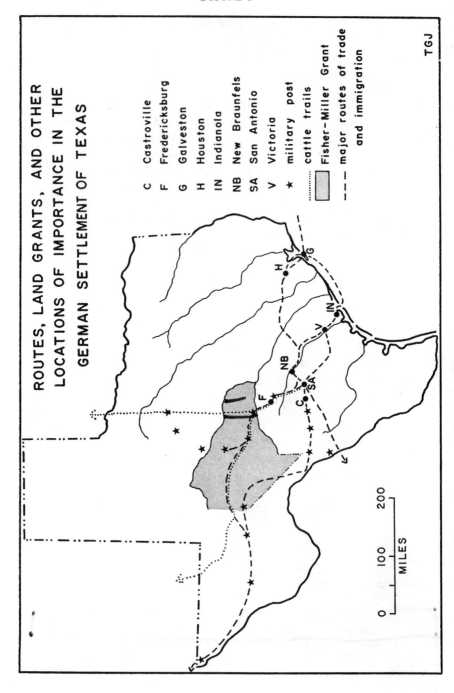

ROUTES, LAND GRANTS, AND OTHER LOCATIONS OF IMPORTANCE IN THE GERMAN SETTLEMENT OF TEXAS

C Castroville
F Fredericksburg
G Galveston
H Houston
IN Indianola
NB New Braunfels
SA San Antonio
V Victoria
★ military post
▦ cattle trails
▨ Fisher–Miller Grant
- - - major routes of trade and immigration

0   100   200
MILES

TGJ

(Gillespie County, 1846) were founded to serve as way stations on the road to the grant.

The German immigrants brought by the Verein numbered 7,380 in the period from 1844 to 1846.[35] In the following year, 1847, the Verein went bankrupt, a victim of improper management and inadequate planning. Not the least among the factors leading to its collapse was the nature of the land in the Fisher-Miller Grant. The soils were mostly stony and infertile, and the precipitation was meager and unreliable. In addition, the grant was extremely isolated and was inhabited by warlike Comanche Indians. Incredibly, no one connected with the Verein had so much as set foot on the lands of the grant before 1847. Two noblemen who had been sent to Texas earlier to evaluate it as a location for the colony had confined their activities to the southeastern part of the republic, the characteristics of which they naively attributed to the whole of Texas. Only several minor settlements were founded by the Verein in the grant, all in 1847 on the Llano River, which was its southern border. Only one of these, named Castell, survived the first few years, and it exists still today as a small village (Figure 7). In addition, a group of German intellectuals not connected with the Verein founded an ill-fated utopian communal settlement in the same area, also in 1847.[36]

In fact, the members of the Verein learned to their embarrassment that they had not actually purchased the land in the grant, but only the right to settle people there. Even this settlement right proved nonexistent when it was discovered that Fisher and Miller, who sold these rights to the Verein, had forfeited the grant before the sale took place by their failure to settle anyone there in the time period specified by the government of Texas. However, in the early 1850's the titles of German immigrants to land in the defunct grant were recognized by the state government, which legally owned the area.

Thousands of the Germans brought by the Verein were strewn out along the immigrant road from Indianola to Castell when the company collapsed. Most of them settled along the axis of this road without reaching the grant, while others remained in the port cities or scattered among the German settlements farther to the east in Texas. No further penetration was made into the grant, and most Germans sold whatever rights to land they had there, without ever having set

---

[35] John O. Meusebach, *Answer to Interrogatories . . .*, pp. 15–16.
[36] Louis Reinhardt, "The Communistic Colony of Bettina," *Texas State Historical Association Quarterly,* 3 (1899), 33–40.

FIGURE 7

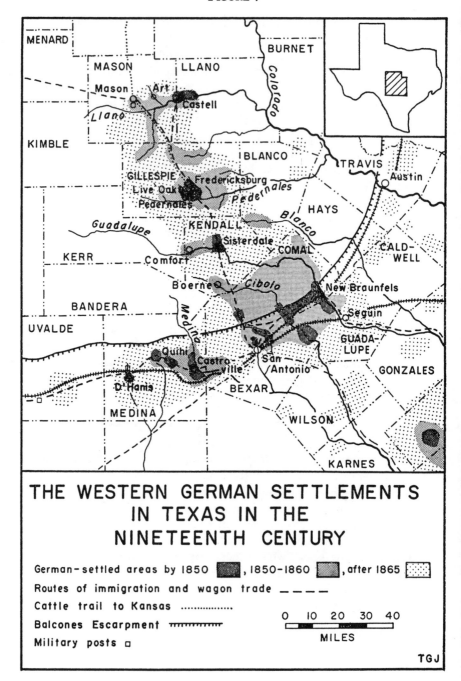

THE WESTERN GERMAN SETTLEMENTS
IN TEXAS IN THE
NINETEENTH CENTURY

foot upon it. The grant had acted as a great magnet, but its "power" was cut off before the Germans reached it.

That the majority of the settlers brought to Texas came from Nassau, southern Hannover, Upper Hesse-Darmstadt, Electoral Hesse,[37] Brunswick, far western Thuringia, Waldeck, and the Heilbronn area of northern Württemberg (Figure 4) is understandable, for it was there that the recruiting campaign of the Verein was focused. This in turn was a reflection of the places of residence of the noblemen who composed the Verein. It is reported with some exaggeration that in Hesse in the 1840's *"Geh mit ins Texas"* ("go with us to Texas") was heard as frequently as *"Guten Tag."*[38]

A second major colonization effort involving the settlement of German-speaking people in Texas reached fruition in 1844, when the *empresario* Henri Castro founded the town of Castroville on his land grant west of San Antonio[39] (Figure 7). Castro's activities continued over the next few years and resulted in the establishment of several additional settlements, creating a major German core area in Medina County. Castro brought a total of 2,134 settlers to Texas,[40] most of whom came from Alsace,[41] with lesser numbers from Swabia, German Switzerland, Baden, and the Münsterland.[42] Included also in the total were some French immigrants from Lorraine and the Franche Comté.[43]

The economic demise of the Verein and the end of colonizing activities by Henri Castro, both of which occurred in the late 1840's, did not halt or even diminish the flow of Germans to Texas. For about a decade after 1847, the annual numbers of German immigrants remained high. They came on their own initiative, attracted by books and letters written by their fellow countrymen and friends in Texas, and they chose to settle in the same general areas as their predecessors,

---

[37] Bracht, *Texas im Jahre 1848*, p. 148.

[38] Canstatt, *Die deutsche Auswanderung*, pp. 223, 224.

[39] The best source available on the Castro Colony is Julia Nott Waugh, *Castroville and Henry Castro, Empresario*. See also Lorenzo Castro, *Immigration from Alsace and Lorraine: A Brief Sketch of the History of Castro's Colony*.

[40] Waugh, *Castro-ville*, p. 68. Lorenzo Castro, *Immigration*, p. 4, incorrectly gives the total as 5,200.

[41] Julius Fröbel, *Aus Amerika: Erfahrungen, Reisen und Studien*, Vol. 2, p. 320. Fröbel mentioned the concentration of Alsatians in Medina County and noted that they called themselves Germans. He described one of the settlements as being populated by Alsatians and Württembergers.

[42] Bracht, *Texas im Jahre 1848*, p. 148.

[43] Lorenzo Castro, *Immigration*, p. 6.

thus strengthening the German belt and its three major nodes: between
the lower Brazos and Colorado rivers, between New Braunfels and
Fredericksburg, and in Medina County. For the most part they came
from the same German states as their predecessors, but there were
added numbers from the right bank of the Prussian Rhine Province,[44]
Saxon and Prussian Lausitz, and the eastern provinces of Prussia.
Among these immigrants were small but influential numbers of well-
educated refugees from the revolutions of 1848 who founded several
"Latin" farming settlements in the state.[45]

There are various estimates of the numbers of German-speaking
persons settled in Texas during this period, though in using them it
should be borne in mind that exotic elements in a population are
often overestimated (Table 5). One contemporary observer reported
that 7,161 Germans arrived in Galveston from Bremen alone in the
period from 1841 through 1846, with 3,388 in the latter year. In 1846
a total of about 8,000 Germans arrived in Galveston, with over 4,000
in the last three months of the year.[46] From the middle of October,
1845, to the end of April, 1846, it is said that 5,247 Germans arrived
in Texas, in thirty ships.[47] Not all of the immigrants went directly
from Europe to Galveston, and many stopped first at other American
ports. For example, the Deutsche Gesellschaft of New Orleans directed 7,634 Germans to Texas in the period from 1847 to 1861.[48]
The United States Census enumerated 8,266 persons of German birth
in 1850[49] and 19,823 a decade later,[50] figures which are probably too

---

[44] Bracht, *Texas im Jahre 1848*, p. 148.

[45] For descriptions of several of these communities, see A. Siemering, "Die
lateinische Ansiedlung in Texas," *Der deutsche Pionier*, 10 (1878), 57–62, and
Adalbert Regenbrecht, "The German Settlers of Millheim (Texas) before the
Civil War," *Southwestern Historical Quarterly*, 20 (1916–1917), 28–34. The
term "Latin farmers" designates educated, intellectual persons who had not
practiced agriculture prior to their emigration. Such communities were not uncommonly utopian in concept.

[46] Franz Löher, *Geschichte und Zustände der Deutschen in Amerika*, pp. 272,
273.

[47] Bracht, *Texas im Jahre 1848*, p. 243.

[48] John Hanno Deiler, *Geschichte der Deutschen Gesellschaft von New Orleans*, pp. 54–84. The statistics were taken from the records of the society.

[49] [United States Census Office], *Seventh Census, 1850*, p. xxxvii.

[50] *Population of the United States in 1860; Compiled from the Original Returns of the Eighth Census . . .*, Vol. 1, p. 490. The figure includes only persons
born in Germany. The total given in the census was 20,553, which included
Austrian-born.

FIGURE 8

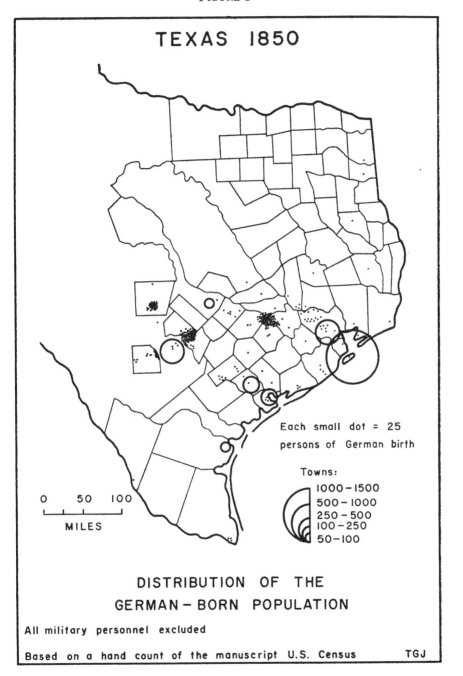

TEXAS 1850

Each small dot = 25
persons of German birth

Towns:

1000-1500
500-1000
250-500
100-250
50-100

0   50   100
MILES

DISTRIBUTION OF THE
GERMAN - BORN POPULATION

All military personnel excluded

Based on a hand count of the manuscript U.S. Census   TGJ

TABLE 5

*Estimates of the Size of the German Element
in Ante-Bellum Texas*

Year	Total white population	Estimated number of Germans[a]	Germans as a percentage of total white population
1844[b]	250,000*	10,000*	4% *
1845[c]			10% *
1845[d]		20,000*	
1846[e]	150,000	30,000*	20% *
1848[c]	180,000	25,000* to 30,000*	17% *
1850[d]	154,000	33,000*	20% *
1856[f]		20,000+	
1857[g]		35,000 to 40,000	
1860[h]	421,000	24,000+	6% +

* Estimate felt to be too high; +too low.
[a] The estimates include German-born and natives of German-born parents.
[b] Heinrich Berghaus, "Der Freistaat Texas," in *Allgemeine Länder-und Völkerkunde,* Vol. 6, pp. 367, 370.
[c] Viktor Bracht, *Texas im Jahre 1848,* pp. 102–103.
[d] Moritz Tiling, *History of the German Element in Texas from 1820–1850,* pp. 53, 54, 125.
[e] Franz Löher, *Geschichte und Zustände der Deutschen in Amerika,* p. 355.
[f] "Germans in Texas," *New York Daily Tribune* (January 4, 1856), p. 3, col. 4.
[g] Frederick Law Olmsted, *A Journey Through Texas . . .,* p. 428.
[h] Rudolph L. Biesele, *The History of the German Settlements in Texas 1831–1861,* pp. 62, 164.

low, an opinion shared by contemporary observers.[51] Their value in estimating the size of the German-speaking element is diminished by a lack of allowance for American-born children of the German immigrants and by the exclusion of Alsatians.

The large-scale immigration of Germans continued through the mid-1850's and resulted in the establishment of many new settlements. Around New Braunfels, Germans expanded quickly to the south and east in the fertile Black Waxy Prairie of eastern Comal County and adjacent portions of western Guadalupe and northeastern Bexar counties. At the same time, Germans began pushing westward up the val-

[51] Frederick Law Olmsted, *A Journey through Texas . . .,* p. 428, commented on the unreliability of the census of 1850 in determining the nativities of Texans.

FIGURE 9

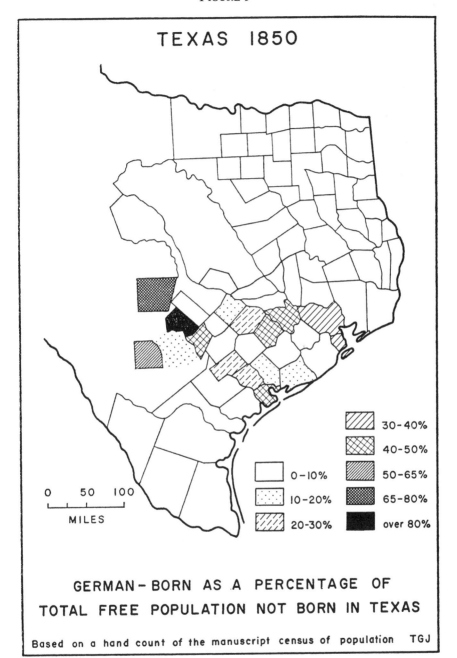

TEXAS 1850

▨ 30-40%	
▨ 40-50%	
☐ 0-10%	▨ 50-65%
⦂ 10-20%	▨ 65-80%
▨ 20-30%	■ over 80%

0   50   100
MILES

GERMAN - BORN AS A PERCENTAGE OF
TOTAL FREE POPULATION NOT BORN IN TEXAS

Based on a hand count of the manuscript census of population   TGJ

leys which penetrate the Balcones Escarpment into the Hill Country
of western Comal County and northern Bexar County. Farther to the
west, German settlement progressed in the areas of present-day Kendall County, where Boerne was founded in the Cibolo Valley and
Comfort and Sisterdale in the valley of the upper Guadalupe River[52]
(Figure 7). From Fredericksburg, Germans spread out to occupy
many of the fertile stream valleys in the Hill Country of Gillespie
County and reached northward to settle the valleys of the Llano River
and its tributaries in southeastern Mason County,[53] in the vicinity of
the older settlement of Castell; while to the east of Fredericksburg,
Germans settled the southern and western parts of Blanco County.

Many of the German immigrants who arrived at Indianola and pro-
ceeded inland along the routes to the interior found the lands of the
lower Guadalupe River attractive and settled there without going on
further to their original destinations at New Braunfels, Fredericksburg,
and Castroville. The result was the establishment of a large area of German settlement in DeWitt, Victoria, and Goliad counties. One major
concentration grew up in the valley of Coleto Creek, a right-bank
tributary of the Guadalupe[54] (Figure 5).

Other Germans, both during the period of the Verein and after-
wards, sought to reach New Braunfels by traveling overland from Galveston rather than going on by sea to Indianola. This route took them
through the older German-settled areas between the lower Brazos and
Colorado rivers, and many of them settled there without reaching their
intended destination. They, together with Germans from the older settlements, founded a number of new farming communities in this area
before the Civil War, expanding the German-settled region north-

[52] C. Hugo Clauss, "Boerne und das Cibolo-Thal in Kendall County,"
Schütze's Jahrbuch für Texas . . . für 1882, p. 29. Guido E. Ransleben, *A Hun-
dred Years of Comfort in Texas*. Still better is Ferdinand H. Lohmann, *Comfort
. . . Festschrift zur fünfzig-Jahr Jubelfeier der Ansiedlung*; see also *Diamond
Jubilee Souvenir Book of Comfort, Texas* . . . . About Sisterdale, see Siemering,
"Die lateinische Ansiedlung." Considerable description of life in Sisterdale, to-
gether with an illustration, is found in Samuel W. Geiser, "Dr. Ernst Kapp, Early
Geographer in Texas," *Field and Laboratory*, Vol. 14, No. 1 (1946), pp. 16–31.
See Biesele, *History of German Settlements*, pp. 139–177, for a general discus-
sion of these settlements.
[53] For the German settlement in the Llano River Valley, see two pamphlets
published by the Methodist Church, Llano District: *Kurze Beschreibung des 75.
Jubiläums und Geschichte der Llano-Gemeinde*, and *A Century of German
Methodism in the Llano River Valley of Texas, 1852–1952*.
[54] W. T. Eichholz, "Die deutschen Ansiedlungen am Colletto," *Schütze's
Jahrbuch für Texas . . . für 1884*, pp. 83–86.

NINETEENTH-CENTURY GERMAN FARMERS

ward into Washington County and across the Colorado River into southern Fayette County.[55] Along the same route, Germans began occupying the western portions of Harris County, to the east of the Brazos River near Houston (Figure 5).

There was one other major addition to the eastern end of the German belt in the pre-Civil War period. In 1853 and 1854, about 600 Wends from Saxon and Prussian Lausitz settled in sandy-soiled post oak country between the lower Brazos and Colorado rivers, to the west of Friedrich Ernst's original settlement.[56] They founded the town of Serbin, in present-day southern Lee County, and spread quickly into adjacent parts of northern Fayette County.

Many German immigrants in the ante-bellum period settled in the cities and towns of Texas rather than in rural areas. Galveston, because of its function as port of entry for immigrants, acquired large numbers of Germans beginning in the 1840's. Observers made various estimates of the size of Galveston's German population, which, however, must be used with caution. According to one traveler, Galveston had 3,500 persons of German birth or descent in 1854, roughly one-third of the total population,[57] and other estimators variously placed the proportion at one-fourth to one-half in the ante-bellum period.[58] A hand count of the censuses of 1850 and 1860 indicates that there were 1,088 and 1,613 persons of German birth in the city, respectively.[59] In Houston Germans had begun to settle in the late 1830's, and by 1840 there were some 75 German families and single men there,[60] and the county as a whole had 121 German voters.[61] In 1852 F. Kapp estimated that Houston was two-fifths German,[62] while

Biesele, *History of German Settlements*, pp. 52–65.

[56] The most scholarly work on the Wends in Texas is Engerrand, *The So-Called Wends*, pp. 89–156. See also Anne Blasig, *The Wends of Texas*.

[57] Olmsted, *A Journey through Texas*, pp. 424, 428.

[58] Friedrich Kapp, "Die Geschichte der deutschen Ansiedelungen des westlichen Texas und dessen Bedeutung für die Vereinigten Staaten," *Atlantische Studien von Deutschen in Amerika*, 1 (1853), 173. Ottomar von Behr, *Guter Rath für Auswanderer nach den Vereinigten Staaten von Nord Amerika mit besonderer Berücksichtigung von Texas . . .*, p. 88; Löher, *Geschichte und Zustände*, p. 353.

[59] Ralph A. Wooster, "Foreigners in the Principal Towns of Ante-Bellum Texas," *Southwestern Historical Quarterly*, 66 (1962–1963), 209, 210.

[60] Moritz Tiling, *History of the German Element in Texas From 1820–1850*, pp. 48–49.

[61] Gustav Dresel, *Houston Journal: Adventures in North America and Texas, 1837–1841*, p. 108.

[62] F. Kapp, as quoted in Tiling, *History of the German Element*, p. 129.

in 1858 another observer counted 1,500 Germans in a total population of 6,000.[63] The census revealed 425 German-born persons in Houston in 1850 and 816 in 1860.[64] The port of Indianola had 450 Germans in a total population of 1,200 in 1858,[65] while an observer in the mid-1850's estimated it to be one-half German.[66] The city of San Antonio gained large numbers of Germans from the Verein and Castro colonies, as well as from the later immigration. By 1850 a visitor estimated that its population was two-fifths German,[67] while a traveler in the mid-1850's placed the number of Germans in the city at 3,000, or one-third of the total population.[68] A hand count of the manuscript censuses revealed that 412 persons of German birth, 12.6 percent of the total free population, resided in San Antonio in 1850, while one decade later the figure was 1,477 and the percentage 19.3.[69] The state capital, Austin, also received many Germans, with the number of German-born rising from 60 in 1850 to 255 in 1860.[70]

Small towns along the route from Indianola to New Braunfels also acquired numbers of Germans, including Victoria, which reportedly had 800 Germans in a total population of 1,500 in 1858,[71] Cuero (which was also called Deutsche-Settlement), Gonzales, which had about 50 Germans in 1854 in a total population of 1,000,[72] Goliad, and Seguin.[73] Lesser numbers of Germans were found in Bastrop, La Grange, Columbus, and even San Felipe, the cradle of Anglo-American settlement in Texas.[74]

POST-BELLUM GERMAN IMMIGRATION

By 1860 the German element in Texas may well have exceeded 30,000 in number. The Civil War brought a temporary halt to the German immigration, but after 1865 the influx resumed. The Deutsche Gesellschaft of New Orleans reportedly directed 14,204 Germans to Texas

[63] Peter August Moelling, *Reise-Skizzen in Poesie und Prosa* . . . , p. 354.
[64] Wooster, "Foreigners in . . . Texas," pp. 209, 210.
[65] Moelling, *Reise-Skizzen*, p. 356.
[66] Olmsted, *A Journey through Texas*, p. 254.
[67] F. Kapp, as quoted in Tiling, *History of the German Element*, p. 129.
[68] Olmsted, *A Journey through Texas*, pp. 160, 428.
[69] Wooster, "Foreigners in . . . Texas," pp. 209, 210.
[70] *Ibid.*
[71] Moelling, *Reise-Skizzen*, p. 359.
[72] Olmsted, *A Journey through Texas*, p. 237.
[73] Bracht, *Texas im Jahre 1848*, p. 147.
[74] *Ibid.*

in the period from 1865 to 1886,[75] but most immigrants came entirely on their own initiative. An observer in 1871 noted a very considerable immigration of Germans through Galveston in the previous six months, most of whom were farmers heading to the interior of Texas to settle.[76] From 1881 through 1885, 5,106 Germans departed from Bremen alone for Galveston.[77] As had been the case before the war, the newly arrived Germans were attracted to those portions of south-central Texas where their fellow countrymen were to be found. The eastern end of the German belt received the bulk of these immigrants, due in part to the added impetus provided by the collapse of the plantation system. Many plantation owners divided their holdings into small farms and either sold or leased them to immigrants.[78] The extensive acreage in unimproved land that had characterized ante-bellum plantations was of major importance in providing settlement locations for the Germans, while sharecropping ex-slaves occupied the land that had been cultivated in pre-war days. In addition, railroad companies settled many Germans on the interfluvial lands they had been granted for building lines through south-central Texas.

The influx of Germans into the eastern end of the German belt continued through the 1870's, 1880's, and into the 1890's (Table 6). As had been the case in ante-bellum times, a large proportion of the immigrants were farmers, though the percentage of the German element engaged in agriculture was considerably lower than for the native-born Americans (Table 7).

After about 1870 a notable spreading out occurred, accomplished both by second-generation Germans from the older settled areas and by new immigrants.[79] The spread was given considerable impetus by the land disposal practices of the railroads. The dominant direction of the spread of German settlement was to the north, and in most cases, Germans settled together rather than dispersing among the Anglo-Americans, though they did often settle with Czechs. In many county histories for this area, mention is made of German settlers coming from

---

[75] Deiler, *Geschichte,* pp. 92–102.

[76] George H. Sweet, *Texas . . . or the Immigrants' Hand-Book of Texas,* p. 65.

[77] E. Philippovich (ed.), *Auswanderung und Auswanderungspolitik in Deutschland,* p. 427.

[78] See, for example, Paul C. Boethel, *History of Lavaca County,* p. 105.

[79] J. G. Meyer, "Die Colonie Neu Baden in Robertson County," *Schütze's Jahrbuch für Texas . . . für 1883,* p. 157. See also Irene T. Allen, *Saga of Anderson,* p. 122.

FIGURE 10

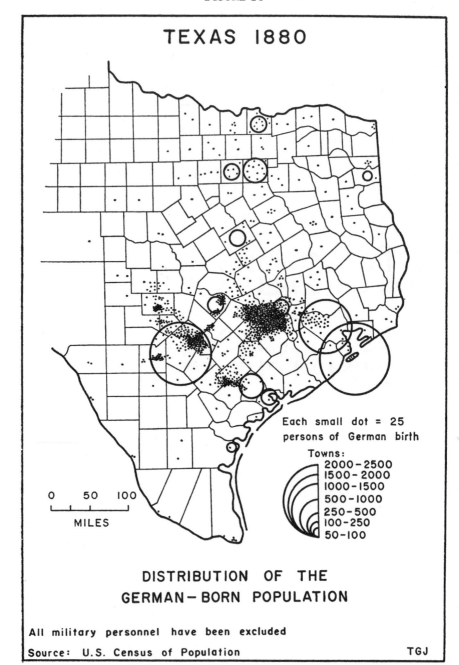

TEXAS 1880

Each small dot = 25
persons of German birth

Towns:
2000-2500
1500-2000
1000-1500
500-1000
250-500
100-250
50-100

0   50   100
MILES

DISTRIBUTION OF THE
GERMAN-BORN POPULATION

All military personnel have been excluded

Source: U.S. Census of Population   TGJ

TABLE 6

The Size of the German Element in Post-Bellum Texas

Census year	Born in Germany	Natives with both parents born in Germany	Natives with only one parent born in Germany	Total German stock	German stock as a percent of total white population
1870[a]	23,985	17,000		41,000	7.3%
1880[b]	35,347	40,650	10,483	86,480	7.2%
1890[c]	48,843	52,909	23,510	125,262	7.2%
1900[d]	48,295	70,736	38,241	157,272	6.5%

[a] Ninth Census, I, 338–339. The figure for natives of German parentage is an estimate derived from the following equation:

$$\frac{\text{number of German-born}}{\text{number of foreign-born}} = \frac{x}{\text{number of persons having foreign-born parent(s)}}$$

From the result, 40,784, was subtracted the number of German-born, all of whom presumably had German-born parents.

[b] Tenth Census, I, 493, 679, 690.

[c] Eleventh Census, vol. I, Population Part I, pp. 607, 686, 691, 694, 702.

[d] Twelfth Census, vol. I, Population Part I, pp. 733, 814, 822, 830.

TABLE 7

Percentage of All German-Born and Native Americans over Ten Years of Age Employed in Agriculture in Post-Bellum Texas

Census year	German-Born	Native Americans White	Negro
1870	43%	74%	
1880	57%	72%	
1890	55%	66%	68%

Source: U. S. Census, 1870, I, 758; 1880, volume on population, p. 847; 1890, Population Part II, pp. 472, 474, 490, 492, 612, 613.

counties further south in the period after 1865.[80] At the same time, a smaller expansion from the eastern end of the German belt to the south

[80] See, for example, Lillian S. St. Romain, *Western Falls County, Texas,* pp. 106–107; George W. Tyler, *The History of Bell County,* pp. 295–296.

FIGURE 11

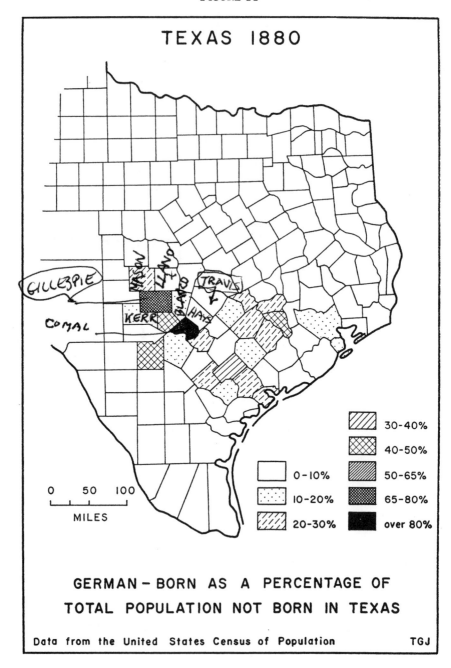

Data from the United States Census of Population   TGJ

into the previously avoided coastal prairies took place. Promotional activities of railroads, coupled with the rise of rice cultivation in some areas, attracted the Germans southward, into Fort Bend and Wharton counties.[81] The expansion also affected a number of other counties, and continued well into the twentieth century. Farther to the west, a spreading out movement took place on a smaller scale from the old Verein core area, first within Kendall, Comal, Gillespie, and Mason counties and later into the adjacent counties of Kimble, Bandera, Kerr, Blanco, Menard, and McCulloch.

In the last quarter of the century, numerous isolated German settlements began to dot northern and western Texas, established by Germans from both the older settlements in the state and from the American Midwest.[82] These were developed too late to be of concern in the present study.

The net result of nineteenth-century German immigration into Texas was the creation of a broad, fragmented belt of German settlement extending across the interior south-central portion of the state. The major features of this belt had been established by 1850, and subsequent immigration and natural population growth served simply to strengthen and expand it.

Thus the farmers of Germany and the South occupied the soil of Texas, bringing with them divergent agricultural traditions. Attention will now be directed to the meeting of these two traditions and the resulting changes made during the course of the nineteenth century.

[81] Clarence R. Wharton, *History of Fort Bend County*, pp. 223–225, discusses the influx of Germans from counties farther to the north.

[82] For a discussion of several of these colonies, see Albert M. Schreiber, *Mesquite Does Bloom.*

. . . . *Chapter Four* . . . .

Germans in the Cotton Kingdom: The Eastern End of the German Belt, 1831–1885

I n the more eastern of the German settlements in Texas, including the area of original colonization between the lower Brazos and Colorado rivers, the rural economy and physical environment are quite unlike those of the western portion of the German belt, and different systems of agriculture arose in these two areas. The German immigrant farmers who came to the eastern settlements found themselves in a cultural and physical milieu hardly comparable to that encountered by their more western kinsmen, for they were unmistakably in the Cotton Belt, though certainly on its western fringe. The Verein and Castro colonies, on the other hand, were situated largely in an area where livestock ranching became dominant. For this reason, the changing nineteenth-century agriculture of the two areas will be considered separately.

SAMPLE COUNTIES IN THE EAST

The use of the manuscript schedules of the United States censuses of 1850 through 1880 to provide a statistical framework for the study of the eastern German settlements has been confined mainly to Austin and Waller counties. The latter was established as a separate county in the 1870's, and prior to that time was largely a part of Austin County. The small number of farms in 1850 necessitated the inclusion of census returns from adjacent Fayette County for that year only. In addition, some use was made of the manuscript census for DeWitt County in 1860, though these figures were not included in the averages for the sample area.

The manuscript census schedules were used in the following man-

ner. The desired data, including the names of the farmers, were copied
from the agricultural schedules. Then, consulting of the population
schedules, which were fortunately arranged in the same order as those
for agriculture, produced information about the birthplace of each
farmer and his race. For 1850 and 1860, an additional step was necessary, a step by which the schedules of slave population were used to
ascertain the number of Negroes owned by each farmer. No sampling
was done for the first two census years under consideration; but for
1870, 50 percent of the farms were recorded and for 1880, 20 percent,
using approved sampling methods.[1] In all census years farms were discarded if the returns were in some way defective or if the farmer was
not German, southern Anglo-American, or Negro.[2]

[1] For a discussion of the sampling method see the Appendix.
[2] Defects in records were many and varied. In 1850 in Austin County, for
example, persons having nothing to do with farming were included in the agricultural schedules if they owned a horse. Incomplete schedules were rather
common, indicating that the census enumerator had no opportunity to talk to
the farmer in question, relying instead on whatever information could be obtained from a neighbor. In other cases the lack of completeness could obviously
be laid to the inefficiency of the enumerator. For 1880 when separate schedule
blanks were printed for northern and southern states, a few of the northern
schedule sheets, which omitted cotton, were used by mistake in Austin and
Waller counties. Farms recorded on such sheets were discarded unless the enumerator had the ingenuity to list cotton somewhere on the sheet. In the first three
census years used, the data for individual farms were recorded on both the front
and back side of the schedule sheet, providing some dangerous pitfalls for the
inexperienced user of the manuscript census. For example, some enumerators
used the front and back sides of separate sheets to record a single farm, in order
to avoid having to turn the sheet over. Usually such procedure was indicated
by the page numbers at the top of each sheet, but not always. In a few instances
it was impossible to find matching front and back sides, making use of the sheet
impossible.

The numbers of farmers in each group for the four census years were as
follows:

	1850	1860	1870	1880
German-born, no slaves	101	210	307	213
German-born, slaveowners	10	9	----	----
Natives, German-born father	----	----	----	17
Total Germans	111	219	307	230
Southern whites, no slaves	113	53	135	129
Southern whites, 1–5 slaves	80	44	{ ex-slave- }	----
Southern whites, over 5 slaves	83	95	} owners 68 {	----
Total southern whites	276	192	203	129
Negroes	----	----	287	139

For 1870 an effort was made to separate out all Anglo-Americans who had

Dominating the map of the sample counties is the Brazos River, which splits the area into an eastern portion, which became Waller County, and a western portion, the present-day Austin County. The bottom lands of the Brazos, comprising about one-eighth of the total area, were considered the best in the sample counties, and the fertile red alluvial soils were sought out quite early by slaveowners for their plantations. The bottoms were heavily timbered with such trees as the pecan, walnut, elm, and ash.[3] From both west and east, the similarly forested valleys of small tributary streams came to meet the Brazos. The most prominent physical feature of the area was an upland belt of post-oak forest, averaging about five miles in width, which extended across the county from northeast to southwest, perpendicular to most streams, forming the horizon from every eminence.[4] Its infertile soils were still but little under cultivation in 1880.[5] The rolling surface of the northern part of the county, comprising about half of the total area, was covered by a mosaic of forest and prairie, underlain by rich black soils that varied from waxy to sandy in composition.[6] The southern fringe of the county lay in the flat coastal prairie and was only sparsely settled by 1880. Taken as a whole, the county was about equally divided between forest and prairie,[7] with the agricultural population concentrated in the forested bottoms and the area of mixed vegetation with its fertile black soils. Fayette County, adjacent to Austin on the west, presented a similar pattern, with the alluvial bottom land of the Colorado River flanked on either side by small tributary stream bottoms and black-soiled areas with parklike vegetation. The area as a whole receives on the average about forty inches of precipitation annually, rather evenly distributed throughout the year. Nearness to the Gulf of Mexico makes the area vulnerable to hurricane activity in the late summer and early fall. Mean temperatures range from the low fifties in January to the mid-eighties in July, and the average growing season is

---

owned slaves in the ante-bellum period. German-born slaveowners and natives of German-born fathers were not present in numbers adequate to justify separate averages for them as groups.

[3] R. H. Loughridge (ed.), "Report on the Cotton Production of the State of Texas . . .," in *Report on Cotton Production in the United States . . .*, Part I, pp. 98, 102, 103.

[4] Martin M. Kenney, *An Historical and Descriptive Sketch of Austin County, Texas . . .*, pp. 1–3.

[5] Loughridge (ed.), "Report on the Cotton Production of the State of Texas," pp. 102–103.

[6] *Ibid.*, p. 102.

[7] Kenney, *Historical and Descriptive Sketch*, p. 1.

in excess of eight months.[8] In the summer, which is the dominant season, high temperatures combine with high relative humidity to produce hot, sultry conditions and uncomfortable sensible temperatures. Winters are mild, and intrusions of warm, humid air from the Gulf of Mexico are frequent, though occasional invasions of polar air cause lows in the twenties. According to the classification system devised by W. Köppen and G. T. Trewartha, the area has a humid subtropical climate.[9]

The choice of the Austin-Waller area as a sample is a most appropriate one as far as the nature of the population is concerned, for within its borders lay San Felipe, capital of the Austin Colony and the first Anglo-American settlement in Texas, as well as Industry and Cat Spring, two of the oldest German communities in the state. In the bottomlands of the Brazos and the lower reaches of its tributaries, was found the principal concentration of plantations, just as in adjacent Fayette County they were situated in the Colorado River bottoms. Away from the rivers, on the upper reaches of tributary streams and around the fringes of small prairies and openings were found the Anglo-American yeoman farmers and their German counterparts. To the east of the river, in what became Waller County, Anglo-Americans and Negroes were dominant in the population, while to the west, in Austin County, Germans were the largest single group. In actual count, German-born numbered over 750 in 1850,[10] increasing to about 2,700 in 1890,[11] after which the influx diminished. If the American-born children of German parents were included, the size of the German element in the Austin-Waller area reached about 4,000 in 1870.[12] In the first census year, 1850, German-born farmers were only about half as numerous as those born in the southern United States, but ten years later the immigrants were already in the majority and by 1880 German farmers outnumbered the white southerners by roughly two to one.

The German immigrants of the 1830's and early 1840's came prin-

---

[8] Climatic figures taken from *Texas Almanac, 1961–1962*, pp. 71–75.

[9] Glenn T. Trewartha, *An Introduction to Climate*, p. 235.

[10] Based on a hand count of the 1850 manuscript census of free population schedules. The Germans living around Industry were, for some reason, included in Fayette County, but their numbers have been added to the total for Austin County.

[11] [United States Census Office], Eleventh Census, 1890, Report on Population, Part I, pp. 657, 660, 663.

[12] Based on a hand count of the 1870 manuscript schedules of the census of population.

cipally from Oldenburg, the Münsterland, and Holstein,[13] but as the century progressed, they were joined by a large contingent from Mecklenburg, smaller numbers from Anhalt and Saxony, and a scattering of Germans from all of the eastern provinces of Prussia[14] (Table 8; Figure 4). To generalize, it may be said that the bulk of the immigrants came from northwestern and north-central Germany.

TABLE 8

Origins of the German-Born Farmers in
Austin County, 1870

State or Province	Percentage of German-born farmers	State or Province	Percentage of German-born farmers
Mecklenburg	15%	Bavaria	1%
Oldenburg	6%	Brunswick	1%
Saxony	5%	Saxe-Meiningen	1%
Anhalt	5%	Saxe-Weimar	1%
Baden	2%	Hamburg	1%
Württemberg	2%	Hannover	0.3%
Lippe-Detmold	2%	Bremen	0.3%
Hesse	2%	unspecified Prussia[a]	54%

Source: Manuscript census schedules of agriculture and population.
[a] Includes Westphalia (the Münsterland) and Holstein. It probably also includes some natives of Hannover, Electoral Hesse, and Nassau, for these states were annexed by Prussia in 1866.

In the early decades of settlement, the Upper South provided the largest share of the southern Anglo-Americans in Austin and adjacent counties, and in 1850 Tennesseans were still the largest single group (Table 9). In the thirty years that followed, however, southern immigration came mainly from the Gulf South, and by 1880 Alabamans alone accounted for well over one-third of all southern white farmers in Austin and Waller counties.

---

[13] Rosa Kleberg, "Some of My Early Experiences in Texas," *Texas State Historical Association Quarterly*, 1 (1898), 302; Caroline von Hinueber, "Life of German Pioneers of Early Texas," *ibid.*, 2 (1899), 228.
[14] Viktor Bracht, *Texas im Jahre 1848*, p. 148.

TABLE 9

Origins of the Southern White Farmers in
the Eastern Sample Counties

State	Percentage of all white southern farmers born in:	
	1850	1880
Alabama	4%	36%
Georgia	10%	8%
Mississippi	3%	7%
Louisiana	2%	3%
Florida	0%	2%
Gulf South	19%	56%
Tennessee	22%	6%
Kentucky	14%	4%
Missouri	3%	1%
Arkansas	2%	0%
Upper South	41%	11%
North Carolina	15%	11%
Virginia	13%	2%
South Carolina	8%	6%
Maryland	1%	0%
Atlantic South	37%	19%
Texas	2%	13%

Source: Manuscript census schedules of population and agriculture, Austin and Fayette counties, 1850; Austin and Waller counties, 1880. The inclusion of Fayette County for 1850 alone did not cause the percentages to be much different, since the origins of its southern population were very similar to those of the southerners in Austin County.

Negroes constituted an important element in the population all during the period of study. They first appeared independently as farmers in the statistics in 1870, at which time about 30 percent of all agriculturists in Austin County were colored, a deceptively low proportion in view of the fact that Negroes made up about two-fifths of the total population.[15] The discrepancy is explained by the practice of several census enumerators of listing old plantation units as single farms rather than as separate sharecropper farms. As a result the

[15] [United States Census Office], Ninth Census, 1870, I, 64–66.

produce of some Negro farms was listed under the names of white landowners instead of being credited to the ex-slaves who did the actual farming.

CROPS

Corn

The most universal crop of the southern United States was, without question, corn. It was found in the field and on the table of the humblest yeoman and the richest planter, and there were few meals where it was not present in some form. Southerners brought the crop to the Austin Colony in the early 1820's and found that it thrived in the fertile soil and hot, humid climate of the Brazos valley. For European immigrants, however, it was a new, unfamiliar crop that was virtually absent in nineteenth-century Germany. The speed and degree of German acceptance of corn is, therefore, a little surprising (Table 10). The family of F. Ernst, founder of Industry, depended on corn as the mainstay of their diet in the early years of settlement,[16] and its importance is further illustrated by the two-day journey in search of seed corn undertaken by one of the settlers in the German community of Cat Spring after the rampaging Mexican army had destroyed his crop as it stood in the fields in the spring of 1836.[17] Cornbread was adopted by the Germans as a major part of their diet from the very first,[18] and one immigrant in Austin County reported in a letter to incredulous friends and relatives back in Germany that the strange dish actually tasted all right.[19] Though the absolute dependence on corn decreased somewhat as the pioneer stage passed, the grain maintained the important place it had attained in the German crop association. Virtually all immigrant farmers raised corn in the 1850–1880 period, though in lesser amounts than the Anglo-Americans, and in the latter year it accounted for about 36 percent of the total cultivated acreage of the Germans, virtually the same as the 39 percent for south-

[16] Hinueber, "Life of German Pioneers," pp. 229, 231.
[17] Kleberg, "Some of My Early Experiences," p. 170.
[18] In addition to the sources already cited, see Louise Stöhr, "Die erste deutsche Frau in Texas," *Der Deutsche Pionier*, 16 (1884), 373; a letter written by Ernst contained in Detlef Dunt, *Reise nach Texas, nebst Nachrichten von diesem Lande . . .*, p. 12; and Gustav Dresel, *Houston Journal: Adventures in North America and Texas, 1837–1841*, pp. 75, 80.
[19] F. W. Luhn, "Bericht des Farmers F. W. Luhn aus Holstein über seine Erfahrungen in Texas . . .," *Jahrbuch der Neu-Braunfelser Zeitung fuer 1925*, p. 40. The original version was a sixteen page pamphlet published in 1849.

TABLE 10

Eastern Counties: Production of Corn, Cotton, and Tobacco, by Origins of the Population

| ITEM | YEAR | GERMANS | | SOUTHERN ANGLO-AMERICANS | | | | |
		German-born, no slaves	All Germans[a]	no slaves	Southern whites 1–5 slaves	over 5 slaves	All southern whites	NEGROES
Corn, bushels per farm and percentage of farms reporting	1850	237(94%)	263(94%)	345(93%)	592(99%)	1303(100%)	723(97%)	———
	1860	198(90%)	204(89%)	391(75%)	446(77%)	1538(94%)	1028(85%)	———
	1870	256(98%)	———	340(93%)[b]	884(97%)[c]		528(94%)	138(97%)
	1880	263(100%)	257(100%)	———	———	———	285(98%)	131(96%)
Cotton, bales per farm and percentage of farms reporting	1850	3.2(64%)	4.3(64%)	5.5(35%)	14.1(41%)	38.8(80%)	23.8(50%)	———
	1860	7.4(83%)	7.7(83%)	7.1(57%)	13.4(66%)	73.6(91%)	47.8(76%)	———
	1870	6.4(98%)	———	7.7(94%)[b]	16.4(97%)[c]		10.7(95%)	3.3(100%)
	1880	7.7(99%)	7.5(98%)	———	———	———	7.3(94%)	4.9(99%)
Tobacco, percentage of farms reporting	1850	31%	29%	2%	1%	0%	1%	———
	1860	5%	5%	2%	0%	2%	2%	———
	1870	6%		0%[b]	0%[c]		0%	0%
	1880	4%	3%				1%	0%

Compiled from the manuscript schedules of the United States Census. The sample counties were: 1850, Austin and Fayette; 1860 and 1870, Austin; 1880, Austin and Waller. The sample taken within the counties was 100 percent for 1850 and 1860; 50 percent for 1870; 20 percent for 1880.

[a] For 1850 and 1860, a few German-born slaveowners were included; in 1880, a small number of native-born farmers of German-born fathers was included.

[b] The figure for 1870 was obtained using those farmers in the sample who had had no slaves in 1860.

[c] The figure for 1870 was obtained using those farmers in the sample who had owned slaves in 1860.

erners. In the same year the respective average acreages in the crop were fifteen and seventeen, with the Negroes behind at less than ten acres.

Cotton

If the corn was the staff of southern life, cotton was its major medium of extraregional exchange. Planters from the Gulf South and middle Tennessee brought the crop to south-central Texas quite early, and five hundred bales were exported from the lower Brazos River area as early as 1828.[20] It was well suited to the fertile bottom lands and rich prairies of the eastern counties, and the 250-day growing season allowed ample time for it to mature. German immigrants adopted cotton almost immediately upon arrival, in spite of a total lack of familiarity with it, and apparently they felt no qualms about raising it in competition with slaveholders in the same area (Table 10). It was among the crops found on F. Ernst's farm at Industry even in the early 1830's,[21] and it was planted in the second year of settlement by the Germans at Cat Spring in the summer of 1835,[22] only to be destroyed during the revolutionary disturbances of the following spring.[23] By the 1840's and 1850's, the culture of cotton by the Germans settled between the lower Brazos and Colorado rivers was being cited as proof that free-labor farmers could successfully compete with slaveowning planters.[24] In the mid-1850's, Frederick Law Olmsted observed in a characteristic overstatement that German farmers near San Felipe "all cultivated cotton, and some had very extensive fields of excellent promise."[25] In fact, in ante-bellum times cotton was raised by a much higher percentage of Germans than of slaveless Anglo-Americans (Table 10). By 1856 it was reported that cotton was the chief cash crop of the Germans in Austin County,[26] and after the Civil War,

[20] William R. Hogan, *The Texas Republic: A Social and Economic History*, p. 16.

[21] Ernst letter in Dunt, *Reise nach Texas*, p. 12.

[22] From the diary of Robert Kleberg, as quoted in: [Cat Spring Agricultural Society], *The Cat Spring Story*, p. 138.

[23] Rosa Kleberg, "Some of My Early Experiences," p. 170.

[24] Ferdinand von Herff, *Die geregelte Auswanderung des deutschen Proletariats mit besonderer Beziehung auf Texas*, translation by Arthur Finck, Jr., M.A. thesis, University of Texas, Austin, 1949, p. 67; and *Neu-Braunfelser Zeitung*, January 28, 1853, p. 1, col. 6.

[25] Frederick Law Olmsted, *A Journey through Texas: or, A Saddle-Trip on the Southwestern Frontier*, p. 358.

[26] [Cat Spring Agricultural Society], *The Cat Spring Story*, p. 165.

when competition from the large planters ceased, it was universally accepted by the Germans as the heart of their crop economy. They became, first and foremost, cotton farmers, and their other commercial agricultural activities declined accordingly.[27] The minutes of the meetings of the German agricultural society at Cat Spring in Austin County are filled with references to the culture of cotton.[28] Approaching Cat Spring in 1876 one traveler observed that numerous piles of cotton bales in the farmyards helped create the false impression from a distance that the settlement was one of considerable size.[29] The German immigrants of the post-Civil War period adopted cotton immediately upon arrival,[30] including those who settled in isolated folk islands such as New Baden in Robertson County.[31] However, there is some indication as late as 1880 that cotton was not so important among the German farmers of the Coleto settlements and Guadalupe River Valley in Victoria County.[32]

Tobacco

Anglo-Americans from the Upper South, presumably those from Tennessee and Kentucky, introduced tobacco into south-central Texas in the 1820's. The crop was not unknown in Germany, for contrary to some popular belief it can be raised in areas with rather severe winters, and the rural male population of Central Europe had acquired a taste for pipe tobacco well before the beginning of the nineteenth century. Still, it was much more common in southern Anglo-America, where it served, in some areas, as the main cash crop in the place of cotton. Tobacco had lost its plantation-slave connotations by the close of the eighteenth century and was widely raised by yeomen in parts of the Upper South. The large number of Tennesseans among the ante-bellum southern white farmers in the eastern sample counties would lead one to expect that they might have been engaged in rais-

[27] W. A. Trenckmann, *Austin County: Beilage zum Bellville Wochenblatt* . . ., p. 8.
[28] [Cat Spring Agricultural Society], *Century of Agricultural Progress 1856–1956*, pp. 6, 23–24, 32, 36, 51.
[29] H. F. McDanield and N. A. Taylor, *The Coming Empire: or, Two Thousand Miles in Texas on Horseback*, p. 30.
[30] Loughridge (ed.), "Report on the Cotton Production of the State of Texas," p. 104.
[31] J. G. Meyer, "Die Colonie Neu Baden in Robertson County," *Schütze's Jahrbuch für Texas . . . für 1883*, pp. 146–160.
[32] Loughridge (ed.), "Report on the Cotton Production of the State of Texas," p. 107.

ing this crop, but surprisingly, tobacco culture was dominated by the German immigrant farmers instead (Table 10). The founders of Industry and Cat Spring were cultivating it in the 1830's, making cigars, and selling them in San Felipe and Houston,[33] and by the late 1840's there was a German cigar factory at Columbus in Colorado County.[34] The success of F. Ernst and R. Kleberg, the earliest of the German tobacco planters in Austin County, apparently influenced other Germans in the vicinity to try the crop, for by 1850 almost one-third of the slaveless Germans in Austin and Fayette counties reported tobacco, as opposed to only 2 percent of the American yeomen and less than 1 percent of the slaveowners. Ernst himself reported two thousand pounds of tobacco in 1850, while other Germans produced lesser amounts ranging from thirty to one thousand pounds.[35] German domination of tobacco culture, as well as their cigar-making, was recognized by the *Texas Almanac*[36] and other similar publications.[37] The attraction of tobacco raising to the Germans can perhaps be explained by its suitability to a small-scale operation with a great deal of intensive care, conditions under which the Germans felt they had an advantage in the competition with slaveholders. When it became apparent that the Germans could successfully compete in cotton as well, tobacco suffered a decline. It occupied a place of little importance by 1880.

Potatoes

In northern and northwestern Germany, the source region for the bulk of the immigrants in the eastern settlements, the white potato was not as important in the agricultural system and diet as it was farther south

[33] Friedrich W. von Wrede, *Lebensbilder aus den Vereinigten Staaten von Nordamerika und Texas . . .*, p. 132; and Rosa Kleberg, "Some of My Early Experiences," pp. 171–172. See also Hinueber, "Life of German Pioneers," p. 230. Other references to German tobacco culture in the eastern settlements can be found in Bracht, *Texas im Jahre 1848*, p. 58; Carl von Solms-Braunfels, *Texas, Geschildert in Beziehung . . .*, pp. 13–14; and W. Steinert, *Nordamerika vorzüglich Texas im Jahre 1849 . . .*, p. 134.

[34] "Fragmente aus Briefen," *Allgemeine Auswanderungs-Zeitung* No. 8, February 21, 1848, p. 115. The letter printed was written by a German farmer, Eduard N——s, who had settled near Columbus.

[35] Manuscript census schedules of agriculture and population, Fayette County, Texas, 1850.

[36] *The Texas Almanac for 1870*, p. 182. The statement was repeated in the 1872 edition, p. 29.

[37] [Houston and Texas Central Railway Company], *Texas the Best Land for the Emigrant*, p. 6.

in Germany. Still, the crop was well-known throughout Central Europe, and it is reasonable to expect that it might find a place in the crop association of the German immigrants. The sweet potato, on the other hand, was completely unknown in the German lands, while in the southern source regions, it was very important. The Anglo-Americans, particularly those from middle and eastern Tennessee, also raised the white potato, though its position was in all cases secondary to the sweet potato.

As had been the case with corn and cotton, the adoption of the sweet potato by the Germans was both rapid and widespread[38] (Table 11). One immigrant reported that, in a baked form, it had become one of his favorite dishes,[39] and another even wrote that he preferred them to the white variety.[40] The rapid acceptance was probably due in part to the belief held by many that the white potato was not suited to the warm climate,[41] and the adoption was facilitated by the great similarity in outward appearance of the two kinds of potatoes. The differences in planting procedures apparently presented no problem, for one German settler described the method of transplanting sweet potato sprouts quite accurately in a letter dated 1847.[42]

The culture of the white potato was not neglected, however, by either Germans or southerners (Table 11). One settler in the German community of Cummins Creek in Colorado County reported in 1844 that potatoes were being raised as winter vegetables, harvested in March,[43] and another in Austin County wrote that the white potato grew very well in Texas.[44] Others complained, however, that the warm climate made the storage of potatoes impossible, resulting in an eight-month period each year in which none were available.[45] The German agricultural society at Cat Spring did much to promote the cultivation of the white potato, and its members discussed various methods for improving yields of the crop.[46] In 1850 the ratio of white to sweet

---

[38] See, for example, Dresel, *Houston Journal*, pp. 75, 80.

[39] Luhn, "Bericht des Farmers F. W. Luhn," p. 40.

[40] *Allgemeine Auswanderungs-Zeitung*, No. 11, March 13, 1848, p. 168.

[41] Georg M. von Ross, *Des Auswanderers Handbuch* . . ., p. 287. See also Friedrich Schlecht, *Mein Ausflug nach Texas*, p. 151.

[42] *Allgemeine Auswanderungs-Zeitung*, No. 11, March 13, 1848, p. 168.

[43] Kuno Damian von Schütz, *Texas: Rathgeber für Auswanderer nach diesem Lande* . . ., p. 203.

[44] Luhn, "Bericht des Farmers F. W. Luhn," p. 37.

[45] [Cat Spring Agricultural Society], *The Cat Spring Story*, p. 161.

[46] [Cat Spring Agricultural Society], *Century of Agricultural Progress*, pp. 7, 47, 49, 95–96, 98.

TABLE 11

Eastern Counties: Production of Potatoes, by Origins of the Population

ITEM	YEAR	GERMANS		SOUTHERN ANGLO-AMERICANS				NEGROES
		German-born, no slaves	All Germans[a]	Southern whites no slaves	1–5 slaves	over 5 slaves	All southern whites	
Sweet potatoes, bushels per farm and percentage of farms reporting	1850	62(75%)	61(76%)	117(68%)	127(75%)	379(80%)	207(73%)	------
	1860	40(63%)	40(63%)	51(55%)	53(36%)	228(63%)	153(55%)	------
	1870	37(76%)	------	99(62%)[b]	162(68%)[c]		121(64%)	38(52%)
	1880	36(56%)	36(56%)	------			102(33%)	36(17%)
White potatoes, bushels per farm and percentage of farms reporting	1850	19(50%)	19(52%)	24(34%)	30(53%)	45(60%)	34(47%)	------
	1860	18(60%)	18(61%)	16(60%)	17(64%)	32(72%)	25(67%)	------
	1870	17(75%)	------	21(44%)[b]	26(44%)[c]		23(44%)	9(14%)
	1880	26(71%)	26(70%)	------			20(16%)	20(3%)
Ratio of white potatoes to sweet potatoes	1850	1:5	1:5	1:10	1:6	1:11	1:9	------
	1860	1:2	1:2	1:3	1:2	1:6	1:5	------
	1870	1:2	------	1:7[b]	1:10[c]		1:8	1:16
	1880	1:1	1:1	------			1:11	1:11

Compiled from the manuscript schedules of the United States Census. The sample counties were: 1850, Austin and Fayette; 1860 and 1870, Austin; 1880, Austin and Waller. The sample taken within the counties was 100 percent for 1850 and 1860; 50 percent for 1870; 20 percent for 1880.

[a] For 1850 and 1860, a few German-born slaveowners were included; in 1880, a small number of native-born farmers of German-born fathers was included.

[b] The figure for 1870 was obtained using those farmers in the sample who had had no slaves in 1860.

[c] The figure for 1870 was obtained using those farmers in the sample who had owned slaves in 1860.

potatoes among the Germans was about 1:5, as opposed to 1:10 for
Anglo-Americans, and by 1880 the German ratio approached 1:1,
while that of Anglo-Americans and Negroes remained about 1:10
(Table 11). Clearly, the German dietary heritage reasserted itself
during this period, and as various difficulties associated with the raising of white potatoes in the humid subtropical climate were overcome,
the production rose steadily at the expense of sweet potatoes. In the
Coleto settlements near Victoria, the Germans even specialized in the
raising of white potatoes, possibly because more of the settlers there
came from the areas of major importance in west-central and southern
Germany. They were encouraged by the two harvests that were possible each year, one in May and June and the other shortly before
Christmas, and their produce, which exceeded $50,000 in value each
year by 1880, was sold in San Antonio and other nearby towns.[47]

Gardens

Frequent references to the Germans in the eastern settlements having
kitchen gardens with a great variety of vegetables are scattered through
the literature of the period. F. Ernst of Industry, who had been head
gardener to the Grand Duke of Oldenburg, found time to begin a garden after the first few difficult years were over, and his production of
vegetables was noted by several travelers.[48] Other observers, too numerous to mention, reported gardens in virtually all German settlements that were visited.[49] The agricultural society at Cat Spring encouraged garden cultivation and regularly ordered seed from Washington, D.C., and from Germany.[50]
    Persistently in the accounts of Texas travelers of the mid-nineteenth
century and even in the works of modern scholars one encounters
statements to the effect that German farmers devoted more attention

[47] W. T. Eichholz, "Die deutschen Ansiedlungen am Colletto," *Schütze's Jahr-
buch für Texas . . . für 1884*, p. 86. See also Julius Schütze, "Meine Erlebnisse in
Texas," *Texas Vorwaerts*, February 1, 1884, p. 2, cols. 2–4; and W. G. Kingsbury, *Beschreibung von Süd-, West- und Mittel-Texas . . .*, p. 10.
    [48] Hinueber, "Life of German Pioneers," pp. 229, 231; Dunt, *Reise nach
Texas*, p. 94; Wrede, *Lebensbilder*, p. 132.
    [49] See, for example, Adalbert Regenbrecht, "The German Settlers of Millheim
(Texas) before the Civil War," *Southwestern Historical Quarterly*, 20 (1916–
1917), 30; Alwin H. Sörgel, *Für Auswanderungslustige! . . .*, p. 53; Schütz, *Texas*,
p. 203; Steinert, *Nordamerika vorzüglich Texas*, p. 65; and Peter August Moelling, *Reise-Skizzen in Poesie und Prosa . . .*, p. 359.
    [50][Cat Spring Agricultural Society], *Century of Agricultural Progress*, pp. 8, 9,
16, 24, 123.

to vegetable gardening than did the Anglo-Americans.[51] This alleged neglect on the part of the native inhabitants was variously attributed to their laziness[52] and dislike for fresh vegetables![53] Frederick Law Olmsted reported German farmers near Houston being ridiculed by the local Anglo-Americans for eating raw cucumbers.[54] Several writers went so far as to claim that Germans introduced vegetable gardening into Texas.[55] These reports of Anglo vegetable neglect were doubtlessly exaggerated, and it is significant that all but one of the contemporary statements came from the pens of German writers, the exception being Olmsted, who lost no love on white southerners. Unfortunately, the census manuscripts were of little help in comparing gardening activities, for the enumerators were inconsistent in reporting peas and beans, which might have served as useful standards of comparison. It is perhaps noteworthy that a greater percentage of German farmers reported both white and sweet potatoes, though the difference was often not great. Germans may well have devoted more attention to their kitchen gardens than did the Anglo-Americans, but there is no conclusive proof. The fact remains that most southern whites did have gardens. Fresh vegetables were traditionally an important part of their diet, and it is not particularly surprising that they offered none to travelers. Only the Negroes appear to have neglected the culture of vegetables. No support whatever could be found for the claim that Germans introduced gardening into the state.

A better argument might be made for German domination of commercial or market gardening in nineteenth-century Texas. As early as 1844, the British consul in the Republic noted that many German immigrants had turned to market gardening for their livelihood,[56] and

---

[51] See, for example, Ottomar von Behr, *Guter Rath für Auswanderer nach den Vereinigten Staaten von Nord Amerika mit besonderer Berücksichtigung von Texas* . . ., p. 85; Heinrich Ostermayer, *Tagebuch einer Reise nach Texas im Jahr 1848–1849* . . ., pp. 148–149; Steinert, *Nordamerika vorzüglich Texas*, p. 210; *Der Auswanderer nach Texas* . . ., pp. 48–49; and Dunt, *Reise nach Texas*, p. 92.

[52] Solms-Braunfels, *Texas*, p. 13.

[53] Behr, *Guter Rath für Auswanderer*, p. 85.

[54] Olmsted, *A Journey through Texas*, p. 374.

[55] Bracht, *Texas im Jahre 1848*, pp. 48–49; Ulysses P. Hedrick, *A History of Horticulture in America to 1860*, p. 361.

[56] Dispatch of William Kennedy to the Earl of Aberdeen, Galveston, September 9, 1844, published in: Ephriam D. Adams (ed.), *British Diplomatic Correspondence Concerning the Republic of Texas—1838–1846*, p. 356.

the two major port cities of the period, Galveston and Indianola,[57] were both supplied with fresh vegetables by German farmers living in the vicinity. The same was true of Houston, where German market gardeners were active as early as 1839.[58] On Galveston Island, many of the German gardens were only about one acre in size,[59] and they lay for the most part on the outskirts of the city, where the houses were more widely spaced.[60] The German gardeners at Indianola reportedly supplied the town with fresh vegetables all year round.[61]

In nineteenth-century Germany, market gardening was well developed—as, for example, in the source region of Westphalia, including the Münsterland, where all the large towns were surrounded by farms of this type.[62] In southern Anglo-America, however, market gardening was apparently not common, probably due in part to the sparsity of large towns and cities, particularly in Tennessee and Alabama, the two major contributors of Texas settlers. In light of the German heritage of market gardening in Europe and the documentation of their endeavors of this sort in Texas, it would seem logical to conclude that they surpassed the southerners in this respect. It should be remembered, however, that Germans formed a large part of the population of Galveston, Indianola, and Houston, and their domination of market gardening there thus would not be unexpected. In Austin County which was, to be sure, too far from any large town to be a major truck farming area, only about one-tenth of the German farmers reported income from market gardens in 1860, as opposed to 20 percent of the Anglo-Americans.[63]

Orchards

Orchards were part of the agricultural heritage of both Germans and southerners, and usually consisted of a small number of fruit trees in the kitchen garden. The Germans in Austin County were raising

[57] George H. Sweet, *Texas . . . or the Immigrants' Hand-Book of Texas*, p. 63; Olmsted, *A Journey through Texas*, p. 254.
[58] Samuel W. Geiser, *Naturalists of the Frontier*, p. 116.
[59] Alwin H. Sörgel, *Neueste Nachrichten aus Texas . . .*, p. 8.
[60] Ostermayer, *Tagebuch einer Reise*, p. 181.
[61] Olmsted, *A Journey through Texas*, p. 254.
[62] August Meitzen, *Der Boden und die landwirthschaftlichen Verhältnisse des preussischen Staates . . .*, vol. 2, p. 200.
[63] Manuscript census schedules of agriculture and population, Austin County, Texas, 1860.

peaches and figs as early as the 1830's,[64] and there was much discussion of tree crops among the members of the Cat Spring Agricultural Society.[65] One German in Washington County even engaged in mulberry-silk production,[66] though this was certainly unusual. Several references indicate that tree-culture was neglected by the Anglo-Americans in eastern Texas,[67] while frequent mention is made of orchards among the Germans.[68] Some modern scholars have credited the European immigrants, in particular F. Ernst of Industry, with being largely responsible for establishing orchardry in Texas.[69] Factual evidence is too fragmentary to support such claims. The census enumerators were lax in reporting the value of orchard products, making comparisons of dubious value, but perhaps it is significant that virtually the same proportion of Germans and southern whites in Austin and Waller counties listed orchards in 1880[70] (Table 12). It is possible that the lack of a tradition of locational stability among the southern Anglo-Americans resulted in the neglect of tree-culture, for orchards take years to establish, but there is no factual evidence to support this assumption. The very fact that Germans in the eastern settlements adopted fruit trees typical of the Gulf South, such as the peach and fig, suggests that orchards were rather common among the southerners, since otherwise diffusion would not have occurred so promptly. Mid-latitude fruits, including apples, pears, and cherries, did not thrive in the warm climate, and their culture was largely abandoned by the Germans.

Viticulture and Wine-Making

Vineyards were confined to a very small number of Germans in the eastern settlements (Table 12). This is not surprising, since most of

[64] Wrede, *Lebensbilder*, p. 132; Ottilie Fuchs Goeth, *Was Grossmutter erzaehlt*, p. 33.

[65] [Cat Spring Agricultural Society], *Century of Agricultural Progress*, pp. 5, 7, 10, 18, 41, 46, 85, 95.

[66] Albert Schütze, *Schütze's Jahrbuch für Texas ... für 1883*, p. 110.

[67] William A. McClintock, "Journal of a Trip through Texas and Northern Mexico in 1846–1847," *Southwestern Historical Quarterly*, 34 (1929–1930), 150–151, and Horace Greeley, as quoted in Sweet, *Texas ... or the Immigrants' Handbook*, p. 120.

[68] Regenbrecht, "German Settlers of Millheim," p. 30. See also footnotes 64 and 65.

[69] Hedrick, *History of Horticulture*, pp. 361–362.

[70] Manuscript census schedules of agriculture and population, Austin and Waller counties, 1880.

TABLE 12

Eastern Counties: Possession of Orchards, Wine-Making, and Processing of Hay, by Origins of the Population

ITEM	YEAR	GERMANS German-born, no slaves	All Germans[a]	SOUTHERN ANGLO-AMERICANS Southern whites no slaves	1–5 slaves	over 5 slaves	All southern whites	NEGROES
Orchards, percentage of farms reporting	1850	0%	0%	0%	0%	0%	0%	——
	1860	2%	2%	8%	0%	8%	6%	——
	1870	10%	——	6%[b]	12%[c]		8%	1%
	1880	17%	17%	——	——	——	26%	4%
Wine, percentage of farms reporting	1850	0%	0%	0%	0%	0%	0%	——
	1860	2%	2%	2%	0%	6%	4%	——
	1870	2%	——	0%[b]	0%[c]		0%	0%
	1880	1%	1%	——	——	——	1%	0%
Hay, tons per farm and percentage of farms reporting	1850	1.6(24%)	1.8(24%)	2.0(21%)	2.0(29%)	4.3(41%)	2.9(29%)	——
	1860	——(6%)	——(6%)	——(8%)	——(5%)	——(12%)	——(9%)	——
	1870	——(78%)	——	——(41%)[b]	——(50%)[c]		——(44%)	——(44%)
	1880	6.0(31%)	6.0(30%)	——	——	——	4.9(8%)	0(0%)

Compiled from the manuscript schedules of the United States Census. The sample counties were: 1850, Austin and Fayette; 1860 and 1870, Austin; 1880, Austin and Waller. The sample taken within the counties was 100 percent for 1850 and 1860; 50 percent for 1870; 20 percent for 1880.

[a] For 1850 and 1860, a few German-born slaveowners were included; in 1880, a small number of native-born farmers of German-born fathers was included.

[b] The figure for 1870 was obtained using those farmers in the sample who had had no slaves in 1860.

[c] The figure for 1870 was obtained using those farmers in the sample who had owned slaves in 1860.

the immigrants came from northern Germany, where the culture of the grape is impossible due to the cold climate, and beer is the major beverage. The few vineyards which were established often drew favorable comments from observers, who foresaw a great future for this agricultural specialty. It was reported, for example, that one German near Houston had planted seven thousand grapevines,[71] while a Rhinelander in Fayette County produced an average of a thousand barrels of wine each year,[72] and still another farmer allegedly introduced a species of German grape into Colorado County.[73] One German even exported vine clippings to France.[74] The meetings of the German agricultural society at Cat Spring occasionally contained discussions of viticulture,[75] and one of its members for many years raised Herbemont grapes.[76] Viticulture was almost totally lacking in the agricultural heritage of the southern Anglo-Americans, and only a very few reported wine in the census.

More common was the practice of making wine from wild grapes, principally the variety known as the Mustang, which was found in abundance in the valleys of the Colorado, San Antonio, and Guadalupe rivers and their tributaries. The *Texas Almanac* acknowledged the Germans as the leading wine-makers in the state,[77] and those settled on Coleto Creek, a tributary of the lower Guadalupe, received special mention.[78] In adjacent DeWitt County, eleven farmers, all of them Germans, reported wine in 1860, ranging in quantity from 1 to 280 barrels.[79] Nearby, wine-making from wild grapes was reported among the Germans around Gonzales.[80] The practice seems to have been

[71] Schütz, *Texas*, p. 204.
[72] A. J. Rosenthal, "Fayette County," *Schütze's Jahrbuch für Texas . . . für 1883*, pp. 42–43. The farmer, C. Niederauer, wrote an article entitled "Weinbau" which appeared on pp. 71–72 of *Schütze's Jahrbuch für Texas . . . für 1884*.
[73] M. Whilldin (ed.), *A Description of Western Texas . . .*, p. 26.
[74] [The South Western Immigration Company], *Texas: Her Resources and Capabilities . . .*, p. 113.
[75] [Cat Spring Agricultural Society], *Century of Agricultural Progress*, pp. 7, 15, 43, 68, 69, 71, 108, 116.
[76] *The Austin County Times*, July 10, 1886, p. 3, col. 3.
[77] *The Texas Almanac for 1870*, p. 89, repeated in the 1873 edition, p. 139.
[78] A. S. Thurmond, "Goliad County," *The Texas Almanac for 1867*, p. 111. German wine-making in the Coleto settlements is also mentioned in Eichholz, "Die deutschen Ansiedlungen," p. 86.
[79] Manuscript census schedules of agriculture and population, DeWitt County, 1860. For an additional reference to wine-making in DeWitt County, see Moelling, *Reise-Skizzen*, p. 362.
[80] Olmsted, *Journey through Texas*, p. 236.

more common in the lower Guadalupe Valley, including the Coleto settlements, than in the older eastern settlements between the lower Brazos and Colorado rivers, probably because the wild grapes were found in greater abundance and because more Germans from the wine-making areas of Hesse and Nassau had settled there.

The process of making wine from the wild Mustang grape was quite different from that associated with vineyard grapes, and involved the addition of extremely large amounts of sugar after the preliminary fermentation. Many German farmers were very secretive about the processes they used, and there surely were methods that died with those who practiced them. One German, however, left a detailed description of his wine-making art.[81]

Small Grains

Small grains had played key roles in German agriculture in Europe, similar to that played by Indian corn in southern Anglo-America, providing both bread and livestock feed. Rye and oats were of particular importance in the areas of northwestern and north-central Germany which supplied most of the emigrants for the eastern settlements. Among southern farmers, oats were widely grown, especially in eastern Tennessee, where wheat was also important, but rye was uncommon and barley virtually unknown.

It is not surprising that immigrants from the lands of "eternal" rye culture in Oldenburg and the Münsterland attempted to raise this grain in Texas, but to judge from the imperfectly-reported census returns, only a small measure of success was achieved (Table 13). In 1860, over one-eighth of the German-born farmers in Austin County mentioned rye as one of their crops, as opposed to only 4 percent of all southern whites. Difficulties with climate and disease, however, hampered rye production, and in the 1880's Germans in one part of the county complained that the crop did not grow one year in five and had never been raised successfully in the area.[82] Even less success was obtained with wheat (Table 13). The Cat Spring Agricultural Society obtained from the United States Department of Agriculture samples of wheat from many varied parts of the world in an effort

[81] A. Weilbacher, "Zubereitung von Wein aus der Mustang-Traube," *Schütze's Jahrbuch für Texas . . . für 1884*, pp. 187–193.
[82] *The Austin County Times*, 1883, as quoted in [Cat Spring Agricultural Society], *The Cat Spring Story*, p. 160.

TABLE 13

Eastern Counties: Production of Wheat, Rye, and Oats, by Origins of the Population

		GERMANS		SOUTHERN ANGLO-AMERICANS				
		German-born, no slaves	All Germans[a]	Southern whites no slaves	1–5 slaves	over 5 slaves	All southern whites	NEGROES
ITEM	YEAR							
Wheat,	1850	0%	0%	0%	0%	0%	0%	----
percentage	1860	5%	5%	4%	0%	4%	3%	----
of farms	1870	0%	----	1%[b]	0%[c]		0%	0%
reporting	1880	1%	1%	----			1%	0%
Rye,	1850	0%	0%	0%	0%	0%	0%	----
percentage	1860	13%	13%	6%	2%	4%	4%	----
of farms	1870	9%	----	1%[b]	0%[c]		1%	0%
reporting	1880	7%	7%	----			0%	0%
Oats,	1850	1%	1%	4%	10%	9%	7%	----
percentage	1860	5%	5%	2%	7%	5%	5%	----
of farms	1870	0%	----	1%[b]	0%[c]		1%	0%
reporting	1880	15%	15%	----			21%	1%

Compiled from the manuscript schedules of the United States Census. The sample counties were: 1850, Austin and Fayette; 1860 and 1870, Austin; 1880, Austin and Waller. The sample taken within the counties was 100 percent for 1850 and 1860; 50 percent for 1870; 20 percent for 1880.

[a] For 1850 and 1860, a few German-born slaveowners were included; in 1880, a small number of native-born farmers of German-born fathers was included.

[b] The figure for 1870 was obtained using those farmers in the sample who had had no slaves in 1860.

[c] The figure for 1870 was obtained using those farmers in the sample who had owned slaves in 1860.

to find a suitable type;[83] but the reward of over twenty years of experiment was repeated rust or blight, and finally the crop was abandoned.
The presence of several grist mills in the German Coleto settlements
in DeWitt, Victoria, and Goliad counties suggests that wheat may
have fared better there.[84] Barley failed to get a foothold in the eastern
settlements in spite of a very early introduction by Germans in the
1830's,[85] and was almost never reported in the census returns (Table
14).

Of the four major small grains, only oats achieved long term success, and, somewhat surprisingly, its production seems to have been
slightly more common among Anglo-Americans than Germans (Table
13). On the other hand, the cultivation of sorghum, as a fodder crop
as well as a source of molasses, was largely limited to the Germans.
The failure of the Germans to produce small grains, notably rye and
wheat, in commercial quantities forced the importation of flour from
northern states[86] before the Civil War, at a cost of about eight dollars
for a barrel of two hundred pounds.[87]

Haymaking

Hay formed a vital part of agriculture throughout Germany, for winter stall-feeding of livestock was necessary in the colder climate. In
the southern United States it was much less essential, since livestock
were permitted to forage for themselves all year on the open range
in many areas. Still, it seems likely that more hay was made by southern
farmers than has generally been thought, particularly in eastern and
middle Tennessee, where the open range was considerably restricted
by the mid-1800's. In the ante-bellum period, in fact, the percentage
of Anglo-Americans reporting hay in the eastern sample counties was
about equal to that of the Germans (Table 12). Both groups took
advantage of the excellent possibilities offered by the scattered prairies
of Austin and adjacent counties for making hay from the native
grasses,[88] though several German writers pointed out that it was not

[83] [Cat Spring Agricultural Society], *Century of Agricultural Progress*, pp. 9,
13, 16, 17, 22, 45, 75, 81, 84, 86.
[84] The mills were at Yorktown and on Spring Creek in Victoria County, the
latter being wind-powered.
[85] Hinueber, "Life of German Pioneers," p. 230.
[86] Ostermayer, *Tagebuch einer Reise*, p. 57.
[87] Luhn, "Bericht des Farmers F. W. Luhn," p. 41.
[88] A notable exception was F. Ernst of Industry, who was apparently not
making hay in the mid-1830's (Dunt, *Reise nach Texas*, p. 13).

TABLE 14

Eastern Counties: Production of Barley and Ownership of Sheep and Swine, by Origins of the Population

ITEM	YEAR	GERMANS		Southern whites			SOUTHERN ANGLO-AMERICANS	
		German-born, no slaves	All Germans[a]	no slaves	1–5 slaves	over 5 slaves	All southern whites	NEGROES
Barley, percentage of farms reporting	1850	0%	0%	0%	0%	0%	0%	-----
	1860	1%	1%	0%	0%	1%	1%	
	1870	0%	-----	0%[b]	0%[c]		0%	0%
	1880	0%	0%	-----			0%	0%
Sheep per farm and percentage of farms reporting	1850	216(2%)	216(2%)	58(12%)	31(8%)	71(29%)	61(16%)	-----
	1860	101(7%)	110(8%)	70(9%)	39(18%)	59(18%)	55(16%)	
	1870	32(11%)	-----	44(4%)[b]	356(13%)[c]		231(7%)	0(0%)
	1880	38(15%)	37(14%)	-----			61(4%)	0(0%)
Swine per farm and percentage of farms reporting	1850	18(94%)	20(94%)	39(96%)	41(97%)	71(99%)	49(97%)	-----
	1860	12(85%)	12(85%)	33(92%)	35(89%)	74(95%)	54(93%)	
	1870	11(84%)	-----	20(80%)[b]	28(93%)[c]		22(84%)	7(76%)
	1880	9(91%)	8(90%)	-----			12(89%)	8(68%)

Compiled from the manuscript schedules of the United States Census. The sample counties were: 1850, Austin and Fayette; 1860 and 1870, Austin; 1880, Austin and Waller. The sample taken within the counties was 100 percent for 1850 and 1860; 50 percent for 1870; 20 percent for 1880.

[a] For 1850 and 1860, a few German-born slaveowners were included; in 1880, a small number of native-born farmers of German-born fathers was included.
[b] The figure for 1870 obtained using those farmers in the sample who had no slaves in 1860.
[c] The figure for 1870 obtained using those farmers in the sample who had owned slaves in 1860.

1. Thus did they live. The A. Fischer family and their limestone house at Live Oak Settlement, in the Hill Country of Gillespie County, toward the end of the last century (from the writer's collection of Texas Germania.)

2. A bit of transplanted Germany. The half-timbered, plastered Klingel-
hoefer house in Fredericksburg.

3. Two half-timbered houses. Above, a limestone house built by August Faltin at Comfort in Kendall County about 1857. At a later date the chimney was replaced by a wooden door (used with the permission of *Landscape,* edited by J. B. Jackson). Below, a *fachwerk* house, complete with casement windows, which stands on West Schubert Street in Fredericksburg.

4. A plastered and whitewashed Texas-German house, characteristic of many found in the town of Castroville in Medina County.

5. The meeting hall of the Austin County *Landwirthschaftlicher Verein* at Cat Spring. The building dates from the nineteenth century and houses an agricultural society that has been active since 1856.

6. Two typical larger stone houses without half-timbering built by the Hill Country Germans in the latter part of the nineteenth century. Above, a limestone house located on West Orange Street in Fredericksburg. Below, a fine sandstone house built by the Ellebracht family about 1870 in a pleasant valley called "Canaan" by the early settlers, in southeastern Mason County.

. Two other examples of German use of stone in construction. Above, the
turdy small house of limestone and half-timbering built by Ernst Flach at
'omfort in Kendall County, in the 1850's. Below, a splendid sandstone barn
uilt in the last century on the ranch of J. Brandenberger in southeastern
Iason County.

8. A German stone fence used to enclose a livestock pen on the old Anton Willmann ranch in Mason County.

needed in such a warm climate.[89] References to hay made from field crops and improved pastures began to appear in the minutes of the Cat Spring Agricultural Society in the late 1850's,[90] and the census returns of 1870 and 1880 suggest that Germans might have been devoting more attention to it than either Anglo-Americans or Negroes. A visitor in Cat Spring in the mid-1870's was struck by the rows of haystacks on the German farms.[91]

LIVESTOCK

Draft Animals

Horses were the major draft animals for both Anglo-Americans and Germans beginning quite early in the settlement history in the east. They were reported among the Germans at Cat Spring as early as 1835,[92] and in 1843 a Galveston newspaper mentioned the "fine herds of cattle, horses and hogs" of the German settlers between the lower Brazos and Colorado rivers.[93] By 1850 virtually all farmers in the area reported horses, a condition which persisted throughout the period under study (Table 15). This was not unexpected as far as the southerners were concerned, but for the Germans it represented a change from oxen, which had been the chief draft animal in Europe. Oxen were also quite common,[94] but they occupied a secondary position (Table 15). A yoke of five-to-six year-old work oxen could be purchased for thirty-five or forty dollars in the 1840's.[95] There was a sharp decline in the number of oxen between 1870 and 1880, in part because of the inadaptability of these slow beasts to farm machinery. The use of mules in the ante-bellum period was confined largely to slaveholding Anglo-Americans, but after the war the use of the mule began to be of importance among Germans and Negroes (Table 15). The mules in Austin and adjacent counties were presumably imported from breeding areas such as the Upper South, though no references to

---

[89] Schütz, *Texas*, p. 204; Luhn, "Bericht des Farmers F. W. Luhn," p. 33.

[90] [Cat Spring Agricultural Society], *Century of Agricultural Progress*, pp. 11, 18, 22.

[91] McDanield and Taylor, *The Coming Empire*, p. 30.

[92] Kleberg, "Some of My Early Experiences," pp. 170, 300. See also Dresel, *Houston Journal*, p. 75.

[93] *The Civilian and Galveston Gazette*, December 2, 1843, p. 2, col. 4.

[94] Oxen among the Germans in Austin County in the 1830's are reported in Kleberg, "Some of My Early Experiences," pp. 170, 300; and *The Civilian and Galveston Gazette*, December 2, 1843, p. 2, col. 4.

[95] Luhn, "Bericht des Farmers F. W. Luhn," p. 37.

TABLE 15

Eastern Counties: Possession of Draft Animals, by Origins of the Population

ITEM	YEAR	GERMANS		SOUTHERN ANGLO-AMERICANS				NEGROES
		German-born, no slaves	All Germans[a]	Southern whites — no slaves	1–5 slaves	over 5 slaves	All southern whites	
Horses per farm and	1850	3(95%)	3(95%)	6(96%)	8(99%)	15(100%)	9(98%)	----
	1860	4(95%)	4(95%)	5(92%)	6(100%)	11(97%)	8(96%)	----
percentage of	1870	4(98%)	4(98%)	6(91%)[b]	10(96%)[c]		7(92%)	2(83%)
farms reporting	1880	4(99%)	4(98%)	----		----	6(95%)	2(86%)
Oxen per	1850	4(62%)	4(63%)	6(68%)	7(85%)	11(97%)	8(82%)	----
farm and	1860	5(76%)	5(77%)	5(55%)	7(89%)	12(98%)	10(84%)	----
percentage of	1870	5(66%)	----	6(53%)[b]	8(81%)[c]		7(62%)	3(26%)
farms reporting	1880	4(15%)	4(14%)	----		----	4(30%)	3(27%)
Mules and asses	1850	1(21%)	1(22%)	1(17%)	3(28%)%	5(62%)	4(34%)	----
per farm and	1860	2(19%)	2(19%)	3(38%)	2(39%)	7(82%)	5(60%)	----
percentage of	1870	2(33%)	----	3(35%)[b]	4(68%)[c]		4(46%)	1(11%)
farms reporting	1880	2(46%)	2(45%)	----		----	3(35%)	2(18%)

Compiled from the manuscript schedules of the United States Census. The sample counties were: 1850, Austin and Fayette; 1860 and 1870, Austin; 1880, Austin and Waller. The sample taken within the counties was 100 percent for 1850 and 1860; 50 percent for 1870; 20 percent for 1880.

[a] For 1850 and 1860, a few German-born slaveowners were included; in 1880, a small number of native-born farmers of German-born fathers was included.

[b] The figure for 1870 was obtained using those farmers in the sample who had had no slaves in 1860.

[c] The figure for 1870 was obtained using those farmers in the sample who had owned slaves in 1860.

this were found. In general, the various groups of farmers in the eastern counties differed little in their choice of work animals (Table 16).

Cattle

It has been fairly well established that a herding economy moved west with the American frontier, occupying areas on the fringes of settlement. The activities of herder pioneers in the South have been written about at length,[96] and these accounts represent little more than an elaboration of an idea first expressed by Frederick Jackson Turner in the late nineteenth century.[97] Texas was no exception, for herding moved west with the southern Anglo-Americans, reaching its present location in western Texas in the latter half of the nineteenth century. The thesis proposed by Walter Prescott Webb[98] and his followers[99] that the range-cattle industry was born in South Texas is misleading in light of the fact that both Anglo-American and Spanish-Mexican herding practices originated far beyond the borders of Texas. Nor was the meeting place of these two herding traditions uniquely in Texas, for they mingled in California as well.

In the pre-Civil War period, herding on the open range was an important activity in much of eastern Texas, including the areas of German settlement between the lower Brazos and Colorado. Cowboys and roundups, branding and rustling—in short, all the elements of western ranching—were present and persisted until population pressure, increased competition from cotton, and fencing forced a curtailment in the 1860's.[100] Germans had settled so thickly at Cummins Creek in Colorado County by 1847 that the open range was becoming restricted even at that early date,[101] but in some localities it persisted until the 1860's. To allow livestock to run unattended on the open range was an entirely new economic undertaking for the Germans, alien to their European agricultural heritage, but no special skill was required to let livestock run semiwild, and they quickly adopted the practices of the Anglo-Americans. The mild climate allowed the cattle to forage for themselves all year, for they could find ample prairie grass from

---

[96] Frank L. Owsley, "The Pattern of Migration and Settlement on the Southern Frontier," *Journal of Southern History*, 11 (1945), 147–176.

[97] Frederick Jackson Turner, *The Frontier in American History*.

[98] Walter Prescott Webb, *The Great Plains*, pp. 207–215.

[99] Francis L. Fugate, "Origins of the Range Cattle Era in South Texas," *Agricultural History*, 35 (1961), 155–158.

[100] Trenckmann, *Austin County*, p. 8.

[101] *Allgemeine Auswanderungs-Zeitung*, No. 12, March 20, 1848, p. 181.

TABLE 16

Eastern Counties: Draft Animal Ratios and Value of Farm Implements and Machinery, by Origins of the Population

| ITEM | YEAR | GERMANS | | SOUTHERN ANGLO-AMERICANS | | | | NEGROES |
| | | German-born, no slaves | All Germans[a] | Southern whites | | | All southern whites | |
				no slaves	1–5 slaves	over 5 slaves		
Ratio of oxen to horses	1850	1:1.3	1:1.2	1:1.4	1:1.2	1:1.4	1:1.3	-------
	1860	1:1.0	1:0.9	1:1.7	1:1.1	1:0.9	1:1.0	-------
	1870	1:1.1	-------	1:1.9[b]		1:1.4[c]	1:1.6	1:2.0
	1880	1:5.9	1:6.4	-------			1:4.4	1:2.7
Ratio of mules and asses to horses	1850	1:12	1:11	1:29	1:9	1:5	1:7	-------
	1860	1:12	1:10	1:5	1:10	1:2	1:3	-------
	1870	1:5	-------	1:5[b]		1:3[c]	1:4	1:9
	1880	1:3	1:3	-------			1:6	1:7
Value of implements and machinery per farm	1850	$46	$51	$70	$ 97	$221	$125	-------
	1860	$71	$74	$61	$101	$387	$236	-------
	1870	$82	-------	$77[b]		$147[c]	$103	$29
	1880	$85	$83	-------			$ 60	$23

Compiled from the manuscript schedules of the United States Census. The sample counties were: 1850, Austin and Fayette; 1860 and 1870, Austin; 1880, Austin and Waller. The sample taken within the counties was 100 percent for 1850 and 1860; 50 percent for 1870; 20 percent for 1880.

[a] For 1850 and 1860, a few German-born slaveowners were included; in 1880, a small number of native-born farmers of German-born fathers was included.

[b] The figure for 1870 was obtained using those farmers in the sample who had had no slaves in 1860.

[c] The figure for 1870 was obtained using those farmers in the sample who had owned slaves in 1860.

February through November, and in the winter months of December and January they fed on the canebreaks and Spanish moss of the stream bottoms.[102] Germans began building up their herds in the 1830's,[103] and by 1840 some had as many as seventy-five to one hundred or more cattle.[104] A newspaper article several years later complimented their "fine herds" of cattle,[105] and in 1846 the Germans of Austin and Colorado counties were referred to as farmers and stock raisers.[106] In the same year, a traveler observed cattle scattered in groups on the prairie between Industry and another German settlement, Shelby.[107] It was not difficult to acquire reasonably large herds, due to rapid natural increase, and most of the immigrant settlers soon had many times the number of cattle they had owned in Germany (Table 17). In what may have been the prototypical Texas brag, a German-Swiss farmer in Austin County claimed he began in 1841 with a herd of 7 cattle which increased to 150 five years later, including 45 calves dropped in 1846 alone.[108] Another German suggested that a single cow and calf, which could be purchased for only ten dollars, could multiply in a decade to 40 head.[109] According to one German farmer who owned 30 head, cattle could be sold for five dollars each to a local slaughterhouse which extracted tallow for export to Europe.[110] The members of the German agricultural society at Cat Spring were requested in 1856 to file their brands with the secretary of the club, and it was recommended that all strange livestock be removed from the local prairies.[111] Manuscript census returns in the sample eastern counties indicate that both Germans and Anglo-Americans had fairly large herds of cattle by 1850, but a decline was evident in postwar days (Table 17). Farther to the southwest, German settlers around the port town of Indianola were reportedly engaged in

---

[102] *Ibid.*, No. 11, March 13, 1848, p. 168.
[103] Kleberg, "Some of My Early Experiences," pp. 170, 300; Hinueber, "Life of German Pioneers," p. 231; Dresel, *Houston Journal*, p. 75.
[104] S. S. B. Fields, George Freeman, and J. Hampton Kuykendall, tax lists for Fayette, Colorado, and Austin counties, 1840.
[105] *The Civilian and Galveston Gazette*, December 2, 1843, p. 2, col. 4.
[106] Sörgel, *Neueste Nachrichten*, p. 22.
[107] Wilhelm Hermes, "Erlebnisse eines deutschen Einwanderers in Texas," *Kalender der Neu-Braunfelser Zeitung fuer 1922*, p. 19.
[108] Sörgel, *Für Auswanderungslustige!* p. 52.
[109] *Allgemeine Auswanderungs-Zeitung*, No. 12, March 20, 1848, pp. 183, 184.
[110] Schütz, *Texas*, pp. 205–206.
[111] [Cat Spring Agricultural Society], *Century of Agricultural Progress*, pp. 5, 6.

TABLE 17

Eastern Counties: Possession of Cattle, by Origins of the Population

| | | GERMANS | | SOUTHERN ANGLO-AMERICANS | | | | |
| | | | | Southern whites | | | | |
ITEM	YEAR	German-born, no slaves	All Germans[a]	no slaves	1–5 slaves	over 5 slaves	All southern whites	NEGROES
Milch cows per farm and percentage of farms reporting	1850	9(96%)	11(95%)	19(94%)	25(99%)	41(99%)	28(97%)	———
	1860	11(97%)	12(96%)	16(91%)	21(95%)	27(95%)	23(94%)	———
	1870	9(99%)		9(80%)[b]	12(94%)[c]		10(84%)	3(44%)
	1880	7(98%)	7(98%)				6(82%)	3(45%)
Other cattle per farm and percentage of farms reporting	1850	15(89%)	18(89%)	34(90%)	53(99%)	90(97%)	57(95%)	———
	1860	45(92%)	47(92%)	63(81%)	91(82%)	99(87%)	87(84%)	———
	1870	25(87%)		174(50%)[b]	196(75%)[c]		184(59%)	6(11%)
	1880	17(92%)	19(91%)				21(72%)	4(33%)
Total cattle per farm	1850	23	28	51	78	130	83	———
	1860	54	56	72	99	118	101	4
	1870	31		119[b]	169[c]		138	
	1880	23	25				24	6

Compiled from the manuscript schedules of the United States Census. The sample counties were: 1850, Austin and Fayette; 1860 and 1870, Austin; 1880, Austin and Waller. The sample taken within the counties was 100 percent for 1850 and 1860; 50 percent for 1870; 20 percent for 1880.

[a] For 1850 and 1860, a few German-born slaveowners were included; in 1880, a small number of native-born farmers of German-born fathers was included.

[b] The figure for 1870 was obtained using those farmers in the sample who had had no slaves in 1860.

[c] The figure for 1870 was obtained using those farmers in the sample who had owned slaves in 1860.

livestock herding in the late 1840's.[112] In all cases, cattle raising was carried on in addition to crop farming, among both Germans and Anglo-Americans. It perhaps deserves mention that descendants of one of the original families in Cat Spring, the Klebergs, took over management of the famous King Ranch in southern Texas in the late nineteenth century and contributed greatly to its spectacular development.

Swine

Hogs were very common in the north German areas that supplied most of the immigrants in the eastern settlements, but, as was pointed out in the preceding chapter, they were even more common and many times as numerous in the source regions of southern settlers (Table 4 in Chapter II). It was to be expected that both groups would keep hogs in Texas, and such was the case (Table 14). They were quite numerous among the Germans as early as the 1840's,[113] and the census returns reveal an almost universal ownership of swine by both groups, with greater numbers on the farms of southern Anglo-Americans. Sows with six to eight piglets could be purchased for five dollars at mid-century,[114] and the natural increase was extremely rapid. They were allowed to run semiwild like the cattle, feeding on the mast of the various types of oak trees found in the forests of the eastern settlements, supplemented by corn. At local markets, pork sold for about five cents a pound.[115] The swine population declined on both German and American farms during the second half of the century, coincident with the disappearance of the open range.

Milk Cattle and Dairy Products

The census figures for "milch cattle" are of dubious value in assessing dairying activities, since every cow with calf, whether or not milked, was apparently enumerated under this heading (Table 17), but the figures for butter are quite helpful. They reveal that the percentage of Anglo-Americans and Germans reporting dairy products was about equal, and that in fact the native-born farmers made more butter per farm than the Germans (Table 18). Neither group reported much

[112] Ostermayer, *Tagebuch einer Reise*, p. 62.
[113] Schütz, *Texas*, p. 205; *The Civilian and Galveston Gazette*, December 2, 1843, p. 2, col. 4.
[114] Luhn, "Bericht des Farmers F. W. Luhn," p. 37.
[115] *Allgemeine Auswanderungs-Zeitung*, No. 11, March 13, 1848, p. 169.

TABLE 18

Eastern Counties: Production of Dairy Goods and Cash Value per Acre of Farm Land, by Origins of the Population

ITEM	YEAR	GERMANS		SOUTHERN ANGLO-AMERICANS				
		German-born, no slaves	All Germans[a]	no slaves	Southern whites 1–5 slaves	over 5 slaves	All southern whites	NEGROES
Butter, pounds per farm and percentage of farms reporting	1850	193(87%)	206(88%)	236(91%)	296(97%)	453(97%)	321(95%)	----
	1860	---(91%)	---(90%)	---(89%)	---(80%)	---(83%)	---(84%)	---(12%)
	1870	---(81%)	----	---(51%)[b]	---(72%)[c]		---(58%)	---(12%)
	1880	111(77%)	109(77%)	----			122(67%)	72(27%)
Cheese, percentage of farms reporting	1850	2%	2%	4%	1%	9%	5%	----
	1860	6%	6%	4%	0%	1%	2%	----
	1870	11%	----	1%[b]	0%[c]		1%	0%
	1880	1%	1%	----			0%	0%
Cash value of farm per acre of land	1850	$2.44	$2.51	$2.38	$3.53	$3.77	$3.40	----
	1860	$6.88	$6.30	$5.99	$7.27	$4.94	$5.10	----
	1870	$7.67	----	$5.63[b]	$5.14[c]		$5.31	?
	1880	$9.09	$9.28	----			$6.01	$6.62

Compiled from the manuscript schedules of the United States Census. The sample counties were: 1850, Austin and Fayette; 1860 and 1870, Austin; 1880, Austin and Waller. The sample taken within the counties was 100 percent for 1850 and 1860; 50 percent for 1870; 20 percent for 1880.

[a] For 1850 and 1860, a few German-born slaveowners were included; in 1880, a small number of native-born farmers of German-born fathers was included.

[b] The figure for 1870 was obtained using those farmers in the sample who had had no slaves in 1860.

[c] The figure for 1870 was obtained using those farmers in the sample who had owned slaves in 1860.

cheese, possibly because of the careless practices of the census enumerators (Table 18).

It was often maintained, in the literature of the time, that German farmers were the first to devote much attention to dairying in nineteenth-century Texas, a practice supposedly neglected by the Anglo-Americans.[116] One immigrant, for example, reported that even those native farmers who owned over a thousand head of cattle often had little or no butter and milk.[117] The census figures for butter production refute this claim and make it abundantly clear that milk products played an important role in the diet of both Germans and Americans. Only the Negro farmers of post-bellum times seem to have neglected dairying.

Milk cows were regarded as a necessity by most settlers. F. Ernst of Industry reportedly bartered over one thousand acres of his land for a dozen cows in the early 1830's in order that his family might have milk and butter.[118] In the following decade, a cow with calf could be purchased for only eight to ten dollars in Austin County, and milk and butter were reported plentiful.[119] Generally, pens were built for the purpose of milking. The calves were kept there all day, but the cows were allowed to run free, returning to their calves of their own accord in the evening. The calves were not allowed in the same pens until milking was completed early in the morning.[120]

Commercial dairying was uncommon in nineteenth-century Texas, and few farmers of either group practiced this specialty. Mention was made, however, of German dairymen near Galveston who provided the city with milk; and others near Indianola in the valley of the Guadalupe produced milk, butter, and cheese for that port town.[121] German farmers in Colorado County sold butter in the county seat of Columbus as early as 1847,[122] but they did not specialize in this product.

Poultry

Large flocks of poultry apparently were found on most farms in the

[116] Georg M. von Ross, *Der Nordamerikanische Freistaat Texas* . . ., p. 57. See also Schlecht, *Mein Ausflug nach Texas*, p. 105; and Ferdinand von Roemer, *Texas: Mit besonderer Rücksicht auf deutsche Auswanderung* . . ., p. 353.
[117] *Allgemeine Auswanderungs-Zeitung*, No. 12, March 20, 1848, p. 180.
[118] Stöhr, "Die erste deutsche Frau," p. 373.
[119] Luhn, "Bericht des Farmers F. W. Luhn," p. 37.
[120] Schlecht, *Mein Ausflug nach Texas*, p. 105.
[121] Ostermayer, *Tagebuch einer Reise*, pp. 57, 172.
[122] *Allgemeine Auswanderungs-Zeitung*, No. 12, March 20, 1848, p. 180.

eastern settlements. One German wrote in the mid-1840's that he had begun with eleven hens six weeks previously and now had forty chicks, with a total of seventy foreseeable in a few weeks, adding that hens laid all year round if fed corn.[123] Other Germans commented on the abundance of poultry and eggs,[124] and in the 1840's, hens could be bought for twenty-five cents each, ducks for fifty cents, and turkeys for a dollar.[125] One immigrant charged, with no factual basis, that Anglo-Americans only rarely kept poultry.[126] The census of agriculture did not enumerate poultry before 1880, but at that time nearly all white farmers, regardless of origin, reported some, though the Germans apparently had slightly more per farm and nearly twice as many eggs (Table 19). In the mid-nineteenth century, the city of Galveston was supplied with eggs by German farmers in the vicinity.[127]

TABLE 19

Poultry in Austin and Waller Counties, 1880,
by Origins of the Population

	Average number of poultry per farm	Average number of eggs produced per farm per year	Percentage of farms reporting poultry and eggs
German-born	40	136 dozen	99%
All Germans[a]	40	134 dozen	98%
Southern whites	32	78 dozen	92%
Negroes	14	36 dozen	74%

Source: Manuscript census schedules of agriculture and population.
[a] Includes a few natives of German-born fathers.

Sheep

Sheep were relatively unimportant in the rural economy of the German and Anglo-American source regions, though they were known to both groups. In the settlements between the lower Brazos and Colorado

[123] Sörgel, *Für Auswanderungslustige!* p. 52.
[124] Luhn, "Bericht des Farmers F. W. Luhn," p. 37; Schütz, *Texas*, p. 205; Dorus Kromer, *Die Amerikafahrt: Aus den Goldgräberjahren eines Schwarzwälder Bauernsohns,* p. 36.
[125] *Allgemeine Auswanderungs-Zeitung,* No. 11, March 13, 1848, p. 168.
[126] Schlecht, *Mein Ausflug nach Texas,* p. 93.
[127] Ostermayer, *Tagebuch einer Reise,* p. 57.

rivers, they were never very numerous, and the large majority of farmers owned none. Flocks were kept by some of the slaveowners and a few of the southern and German yeomen (Table 14).

DIVERSITY

Diversity of crops and livestock characterized the semisubsistence rural economy in the German source regions, as well as in eastern Tennessee and even in more market-oriented southern areas. There seems to be little justification for claiming a heritage of greater diversity for either group. Still, it has frequently been maintained that the crop-livestock association of the German farmers in the eastern settlements had more variety than that of the Anglo-Americans and Negroes,[128] and some very respectable scholars have added their voices to the chorus.[129] Little factual basis was found to back up this claim, for the reliance on cotton and corn was universal, both among Germans and non-Germans (Table 20). The only support for the hypoth-

TABLE 20

Percentage of Improved Acreage in Cotton and Corn, in Austin and Waller Counties, 1880, by Origins of the Population

	Percentage in corn	Percentage in cotton	Percentage in cotton and corn
German-born	36%	39%	75%
All Germans[a]	35%	39%	74%
Southern whites	39%	39%	78%
Negroes	36%	48%	84%

Source: Manuscript census schedules of agriculture and population.
[a] Includes a few natives of German-born fathers.

esis lies in the fact that many German farmers in the ante-bellum period had two cash crops—cotton and tobacco. In addition, Germans more frequently raised both white and sweet potatoes (Table 11). The overall picture, however, reveals little difference between the two

[128] Moelling, *Reise-Skizzen*, p. 367; Ostermayer, *Tagebuch einer Reise*, p. 109.
[129] Walter M. Kollmorgen, "A Reconnaissance of Some Cultural-Agricultural Islands in the South," *Economic Geography*, 17 (1941), 428; Hogan, *The Texas Republic*, p. 20; and [United States Immigration Commission], *Immigrants in Industry: Recent Immigrants in Agriculture*, Vol. 22, Part II, p. 377.

groups, and close scrutiny of the crops reported suggests that large slaveholders had a better claim to diversity than either of the yeoman groups under study. Only the Negroes lagged behind notably in diversity, which is not surprising in view of the economic pressures applied through the sharecropper system. Perhaps if the futile experiments with wheat and rye had succeeded, the Germans of the eastern settlements would have maintained a more diversified system, but, as it was, by 1880 at least they seem to have succumbed almost completely to emphasis on the duo of cotton and corn, a fact recognized by census workers in the massive study of cotton which accompanied the 1880 census.[130] As far as livestock was concerned, no significant differences were observable in the types kept by Germans and Anglo-Americans, but the Negroes once again were by themselves in a lower class.

Settlement Form

Pattern of Settlement

The Germans of the eastern settlements made no effort to establish farm villages in their new homeland, creating instead a typically dispersed American pattern. Many of the immigrants, particularly in the early period in the 1830's and 1840's when the settlement pattern was being shaped, came from the northwestern part of Germany, where scattered or loosely-clustered farmsteads were the rule. This heritage and the land policy of the Mexican and Republican governments, under which immigrants were given large grants, coupled with the pre-existence of a pattern of scattered farmsteads established by the southern settlers in the area, discouraged the creation of villages. Later emigration drew more heavily on farm-village areas such as Mecklenburg, Anhalt, and the eastern provinces of Prussia, but the cheapness of land in the eastern counties and the tradition of scattered farmsteads among both the southerners and earlier German settlers produced a strong centrifugal force which overpowered the farm village heritage of the later immigrants.

The various German settlements between the lower Brazos and Colorado rivers were little more than loose agglomerations of farms, with unpopulated areas between the various communities, similar in some ways to the *Drubbel* of parts of Oldenburg, but in fact almost identical to the settlements of Anglo-American yeomen. One observer in the mid-1840's described the German community of Cummins

[130] *Loughridge,* "Report on the Cotton Production of the State of Texas," p. 104.

Creek in northern Colorado County as extended, with open spaces between the individual houses,[131] while another wrote that the farms in the community were scattered about on numerous oak openings.[132] A traveler in the mid-1870's found the identical pattern at Cat Spring, which he described as "only a big assemblage of eighty acre farms, with their cozy cottages . . ."[133] These settlements generally grew up around the farm of a single pioneer German, such as F. Ernst of Industry. In time, several stores, a church or two, an inn, and the homes of nonagricultural persons would appear somewhere in the midst of the cluster of farms, and a small trading village would result. It was such a community, rather than a farm village, that Ernst had in mind when he laid out the site of Industry in 1838, for the lots were only 50 by 150 feet,[134] much too small for farmsteads.

In the postwar period, German immigrants played an important role in a major revision of the settlement pattern in the eastern counties. For a decade or so following the end of the war, the large plantations were subdivided by their owners and either sold or leased to small farmers. This process was well underway in Washington County by 1866, where ninety different pieces of land, totalling over ten thousand acres, were sold to Germans in a six-month period.[135] A German-language newspaper noted as late as 1871, however, that plantation owners were just beginning to realize that their large holdings must be broken up, and reported that one Anglo-American in northern Fayette County had sold land to six Germans, while still keeping a nice piece for himself.[136] The same procedure was noted in Lavaca County.[137] It seems likely that unimproved portions of the old plantations were sold to Germans and other immigrants, while Negroes remained on the improved land as sharecroppers. Other former slaveowners despaired completely of working with free Negro labor and disposed of all their land to whites.

Farm Structures

German immigrants were quick to adopt the American custom of build-

---

[131] Solms-Braunfels, *Texas*, p. 56.
[132] Schlecht, *Mein Ausflug nach Texas*, p. 86.
[133] McDanield and Taylor, *The Coming Empire*, p. 30.
[134] Rudolph L. Biesele, *The History of the German Settlements in Texas 1831–1861*, p. 46.
[135] J. H. Randle, County Clerk of Washington County, as quoted in *The Texas Almanac for 1867*, pp. 171–172.
[136] *Wöchentliche Texas Post*, January 1, 1871, p. 8, col. 4.
[137] Paul C. Boethel, *History of Lavaca County*, p. 105.

ing log cabins as temporary first dwellings,[138] for they were reported
in many of the eastern settlements,[139] even as late as the mid-1850's.[140]
Once the pioneer stage had passed, frame structures generally replaced
the log houses, which were sometimes demoted to the status of stalls
or chicken coops. Olmsted reported that the Germans in Austin County
in the mid-1850's "were engaged in enlarging and decorating their
houses,"[141] and one of the settlers of Millheim in the same county recalled in later years that most of the population of his community lived
in frame houses by 1856.[142] The temporary six-sided home built by
F. Ernst at Industry in the early 1830's and a stone house constructed
by a German in a nearby settlement[143] can be regarded only as unique
exceptions to the normal sequence. A traveler in 1876 commented on
the attractiveness of the farm houses around Cat Spring.[144]

The Germans made no effort to combine house, barn, stables, and
storage rooms under one roof, as had been the tradition in the homeland of many of the immigrants. The warm climate made such facilities unnecessary, since a minimum of winter feed was put up and
most livestock remained out-of-doors all year. Instead, the Germans
copied the farmsteads of the southern yeomen, which consisted of a
small, separately built barn and stable, modest storehouses, a well
house, a corncrib, a chicken coop, and generally a smokehouse. In the
1830's and 1840's, storehouses and stables were observed among the
German settlers,[145] and F. Ernst of Industry also had a smokehouse.[146]
The neat barns and stables at Cat Spring drew special comment from a
traveler in the 1870's.[147] On some farms in recently settled areas, out-
buildings were totally lacking.[148]

Fences and Fields

In ante-bellum days it was imperative to fence in fields and gardens, or

[138] Seymour V. Connor, "Log Cabins in Texas," *Southwestern Historical Quarterly*, 53 (1949–1950), 105.
[139] Kleberg, "Some of My Early Experiences," p. 299; Luhn, "Bericht des Farmers F. W. Luhn," p. 38; Dresel, *Houston Journal*, p. 75.
[140] Regenbrecht, "German Settlers of Millheim," p. 29.
[141] Olmsted, *A Journey through Texas*, p. 358.
[142] Regenbrecht, "German Settlers of Millheim," p. 29.
[143] Biesele, *History of the German Settlements*, pp. 45, 56.
[144] McDanield and Taylor, *The Coming Empire*, pp. 29, 30, 33.
[145] Dresel, *Houston Journal*, p. 75; Steinert, *Nordamerika vorzüglich Texas*, p. 130.
[146] Steinert, *Nordamerika vorzüglich Texas*, p. 130.
[147] McDanield and Taylor, *The Coming Empire*, p. 30.
[148] Kromer, *Die Amerikafahrt*, p. 36.

more accurately, to fence out livestock. The bulk of the land was open range, where herds of cattle and hogs ran loose to forage for themselves on the grasses of the small prairies and the mast of the oak forests. Not to fence would have been tantamount to including one's cropland as part of the open range. The Germans not only adopted the custom of open range, but also copied the types of fences used by Anglo-Americans to enclose their fields, most commonly the Virginia worm fence made of split rails.[149] At least one ingenious German, who settled near Indianola, had a fence consisting of closely spaced prickly pear cacti.[150] The references to Germans enclosing their fields are quite numerous, and some writers praised the fine condition of their fences.[151] Although one German settler in Austin County advised in the 1840's that, if money were available, eight or ten acres of natural prairie should be enclosed to prevent the time-consuming job of searching for livestock,[152] the use of the open range appears to have been universal among the Germans of the eastern settlements. Fences were also used to enclose pens for draft animals, poultry, hogs, milk cows, and calves.[153] The open range disappeared due to the expansion of culti-vated acreage, as well as the desire to improve breeds of livestock and provide improved pasturage. German members of the Cat Spring Agri-cultural Society joined farmers in much of the United States in search-ing for a suitable fencing material before the introduction of barbed wire solved the problem.[154]

SCALE OF OPERATION

Perhaps the most striking difference between German and Anglo-American farmers in the eastern ante-bellum settlements was the scale of operation. Whether the measure was size of farm, improved or unimproved acres, numbers or value of livestock, or quantity of corn

[149] Diary of Robert Kleberg, as quoted in [Cat Spring Agricultural Society], *The Cat Spring Story*, p. 138. See also *ibid.*, p. 57, and [Cat Spring Agricultural Society], *Century of Agricultural Progress*, pp. 5, 6, 7.
[150] Olmsted, *A Journey through Texas*, p. 254.
[151] Dresel, *Houston Journal*, p. 75; Steinert, *Nordamerika vorzüglich Texas*, p. 134; Kleberg, "Some of My Early Experiences," p. 170; Sörgel, *Für Auswanderungslustige!* p. 53; J. De Cordova, *Texas: Her Resources and Her Public Men . . .*, p. 221; and Whilldin, *Description of Western Texas*, p. 38.
[152] Luhn, "Bericht des Farmers F. W. Luhn," p. 39.
[153] Kromer, *Die Amerikafahrt*, p. 36; Luhn, "Bericht des Farmers F. W. Luhn," p. 39; Schlecht, *Mein Ausflug nach Texas*, p. 105.
[154] [Cat Spring Agricultural Society], *Century of Agricultural Progress*, pp. 7, 11, 16, 25, 49, 52, 59, 66, 86, 98.

TABLE 21

Eastern Counties: Farm Acreages, by Origins of the Population

ITEM	YEAR	GERMANS		SOUTHERN ANGLO-AMERICANS				NEGROES
		German-born no slaves	All Germans[a]	no slaves	Southern whites 1–5 slaves	over 5 slaves	All southern whites	
Average farm size, in acres	1850	175	250	321	356	937	554	------
	1860	169	208	299	537	3045	1712	------
	1870	183	------	318[b]	796[c]		532	?
	1880	183	182	------	------	------	260	58
Improved acres per farm	1850	19	21	24	44	107	56	------
	1860	26	29	30	49	225	130	------
	1870	33	------	50[b]	139[c]		80	28
	1880	43	42	------	------	------	42	26
Unimproved acres per farm	1850	156	228	295	309	830	492	------
	1860	143	179	269	489	2820	1581	------
	1870	150	------	268[b]	658[c]		452	?
	1880	141	140	------	------	------	218	32

Compiled from the manuscript schedules of the United States Census. The sample counties were: 1850, Austin and Fayette; 1860 and 1870, Austin; 1880, Austin and Waller. The sample taken within the counties was 100 percent for 1850 and 1860; 50 percent for 1870; 20 percent for 1880.

[a] For 1850 and 1860, a few German-born slaveowners were included; in 1880, a small number of native-born farmers of German-born fathers was included.

[b] The figure for 1870 was obtained using those farmers in the sample who had had no slaves in 1860.

[c] The figure for 1870 was obtained using those farmers in the sample who had owned slaves in 1860.

produced, the Germans invariably reported less (Tables 21, 22, 10, 15, 17). Their farms were miniatures of those of the southern yeomen, who in turn have been pictured as miniature planters. They formed a unique class of farmers which might best be called "small yeomen." During the 1830's and early 1840's, when land was free to immigrants, the Germans acquired quite large grants, some in excess of 4,000 acres.[155] Many found, however, that their grants lay in regions too remote for immediate settlement and instead purchased on credit small tracts in areas where settlement had already begun.[156] Still, by 1840, the average size of German landholdings in Austin, Colorado, and Fayette counties was in excess of 1,700 acres, almost the same as the average of 1,900 for all Anglo-Americans and considerably larger than the 700-acre holdings of slaveless American yeomen. One German owned as much as 4,600 acres of land.[157] Such figures are misleading, however, since only a small part of these enormous holdings was actually used for agricultural purposes. Shortly after 1840, the policy of awarding free land to new settlers was discontinued, and the Germans who arrived in the middle and latter part of the decade had to purchase their land, usually from other Germans who had come earlier. By 1850 German farms were only a little over half the size of those owned by slaveless Anglo-Americans, and there was little change by 1860 (Table 21). References to the small farms of the Germans are numerous.[158] Market gardens in the vicinity of Galveston often did not exceed one acre in size.[159] Accompanying the smaller size of farms was, as might be expected, a lower average cash value of farm, less use of farm labor, fewer livestock, a corresponding lower total value of livestock, and smaller amounts of corn. The largest scale of operation was found among the Anglo-American slaveholders.

In the period following the Civil War, the Germans apparently cut the gap in scale of operation and reached a level comparable to that of the Americans. They equalled the Anglos in value of farm production by 1870 and in improved acres and cash value of farm a decade later.

[155] Stöhr, "Die erste deutsche Frau," p. 373; *The Civilian and Galveston Gazette*, December 2, 1843, p. 2, col. 4.
[156] William Bollaert, *William Bollaert's Texas*, p. 276. See also *The Civilian and Galveston Gazette*, December 2, 1843, p. 2, col. 4.
[157] Tax lists for Austin, Fayette, and Colorado counties, 1840.
[158] De Cordova, *Texas*, p. 249; Olmsted, *A Journey through Texas*, pp. 359, 362; *The Civilian and Galveston Gazette*, December 2, 18•3, p. 2, col. 4; A. Dunlevy, "Colorado [County]," *The Texas Almanac for 1859 . . .*, p. 171; Ostermayer, *Tagebuch einer Reise*, p. 171.
[159] Sörgel, *Neueste Nachrichten*, p. 8.

TABLE 22

Eastern Counties: Value of Farm, Livestock, and Production, by Origins of the Population

| ITEM | YEAR | GERMANS | | | SOUTHERN ANGLO-AMERICANS | | | | |
		German-born no slaves	All Germans[a]	no slaves	Southern whites 1–5 slaves	over 5 slaves	All southern whites	NEGROES
Average cash value of farm	1850	$ 428	$ 629	$ 765	$1257	$ 3536	$1884	------
	1860	$1162	$1327	$1638	$3910	$15057	$8835	------
	1870	$1405	------	$1791[b]	$4102[c]		$2825	$393
	1880	$1664	$1690	------	------		$1563	$384
Value of livestock per farm	1850	$ 288	$ 325	$ 595	$ 876	$ 1659	$1003	------
	1860	$ 626	$ 667	$ 977	$1175	$ 2680	$1865	------
	1870	$ 398	------	$ 719[b]	$1523[c]		$ 994	$123
	1880	$ 283	$ 299	------	------		$ 318	$ 85
Average value of total farm production	1850	------	------	------	------	------	------	------
	1860	------	------	------	------	------	------	------
	1870	$ 894	------	$ 876[b]	$1785[c]		$1180	$377
	1880	$ 547	$ 533	------			$ 542	$313

Compiled from the manuscript schedules of the United States Census. The sample counties were: 1850, Austin and Fayette; 1860 and 1870, Austin; 1880, Austin and Waller. The sample taken within the counties was 100 percent for 1850 and 1860; 50 percent for 1870; 20 percent for 1880.

[a] For 1850 and 1860, a few German-born slaveowners were included; in 1880, a small number of native-born farmers of German-born fathers was included.

[b] The figure for 1870 was obtained using those farmers in the sample who had had no slaves in 1860.

[c] The figure for 1870 was obtained using those farmers in the sample who had owned slaves in 1860.

Comparative levels of cotton production were equal as early as 1860, and corn nearly so twenty years later, but Germans still had smaller farms and fewer cattle and hogs in 1880.

The initial tendency of Germans to operate on a smaller scale can be laid to two causes. First, most of them had expended whatever capital they possessed in paying for the long voyage from Europe, in contrast to the Anglo-Americans, who were able to move overland at a minimum of expense. Once the equalizing force of free grants was removed, the Germans had to purchase what land they could on credit or with whatever meager capital remained, and they were not in a position to buy as much land or livestock as the Anglo-Americans. The second contributing factor was simply that the Germans were accustomed to operating on a small scale in Europe, and their cultural heritage reasserted itself in the new homeland. For them, one hundred acres was a very large farm, four thousand acres a principality. As we have seen, F. Ernst of Austin County was so overwhelmed with the league of land granted to him that he traded over 1,000 acres, or roughly one-fourth of it, for some milk cattle.[160] The survival of the tradition of small-scale operation is perhaps best ascertained by the fact that Germans had, for the first three census years, less land under cultivation than the Anglo-Americans. They had ample acreage in which to expand their fields had they wished to do so, but they chose instead to leave over 80 percent of their land unimproved (Table 23). F. Ernst cultivated only a few acres, using a hoe, in the early years of settlement.[161] By the 1870's and 1880's, both economic and cultural supports for small-scale farms had given way and the Germans were moving into a position of equality with the Anglo-Americans.

MARKETS AND DEGREE OF COMMERCIALIZATION

German immigrant farmers in the eastern counties showed a strong interest in producing goods for sale as soon after initial settlement as possible. Cotton and tobacco were sent to market as early as the mid-1830's, and cattle were sold to local slaughter-houses in the following decade.[162] A journalist from Galveston visited the German settlements between the lower Brazos and Colorado rivers in 1843 and reported that the farmers "now raise every year twice as much as they con-

[160] Stöhr, "Die erste deutsche Frau," p. 373.
[161] *The Civilian and Galveston Gazette*, December 2, 1843, p. 2, col. 4.
[162] Schütz, *Texas*, p. 206.

TABLE 23

Eastern Counties: Improved Acreage as a Percentage of Total Farm
Size, by Origins of the Population

	1850	1860	1870	1880
Germans:				
German-born, no slaves	11%	16%	18%	23%
All Germans[a]	8%	14%	--------	23%
Southern Anglo-Americans:				
No slaves[b]	8%	10%	16%	--------
1–5 slaves[b]	13%	9%	17%	--------
Over 5 slaves[b]	12%	7%		
All southern whites	10%	8%	17%	16%
Negroes	--------	--------	?	45%

Compiled from the manuscript schedules of the United States Census. The
sample counties were: 1850, Austin and Fayette; 1860 and 1870, Austin; 1880,
Austin and Waller. The sample taken within the counties was 100 percent for
1850 and 1860; 50 percent for 1870; 20 percent for 1880.

[a] For 1850 and 1860, a few German-born slaveowners were included; in 1880,
a small number of native-born farmers of German-born fathers was included.

[b] For 1870, the southern Anglo-Americans were divided into groups on the
basis of slave ownership in 1860.

sume."[163] German attention to market gardening was discussed
previously.

Though a few steamboats plied the Brazos in ante-bellum times,[164]
most farm produce from the Austin County area was hauled overland
in ox-wagons to market at Houston[165] on an oft-traveled road of dubious quality, which ran from Houston to the Brazos at San Felipe,
and on through the German settlements to La Grange on the Colorado.
One traveler reported that the German farmers at Cummins Creek in
Colorado County had difficulty marketing their farm produce in the
late 1840's,[166] but all other indications are that it was no great problem.
Farther to the west, Germans settled in the lower Guadalupe valley
marketed their goods overland at Indianola and San Antonio,[167] and

[163] The Civilian and Galveston Gazette, December 2, 1843, p. 2, col. 4.
[164] Kenney, Sketch of Austin County, p. 19; Luhn, "Bericht des Farmers F. W.
Luhn," pp. 28–29.
[165] Roemer, Texas, p. 90; Schlecht, Mein Ausflug nach Texas, p. 59.
[166] Jakob Thran, Meine Auswanderung nach Texas unter dem Schutze des
Mainzer Vereins . . ., pp. 53–54.
[167] Ostermayer, Tagebuch einer Reise, p. 172; Eichholz, "Die deutschen Ansiedlungen," p. 86.

had the good fortune to be situated on a major transport route to the interior. In the 1870's, railroads reached most of the eastern German settlements, replacing the ox-wagons and providing a cheap, rapid means for marketing agricultural produce.

The most market-oriented ante-bellum group were doubtless the Anglo-American slaveowners, but among the yeomen it appears that the Germans operated on a much higher degree of commercialization. In 1850, roughly two-thirds of all slaveless Germans raised cotton, as opposed to only a little over one-third of all Anglo-American yeomen (Table 10), and a decade later, on the eve of the Civil War, 83 percent of the Germans and only 57 percent of the slaveless Americans produced cotton. In addition, the Germans were virtually alone in the culture of tobacco for market (Table 10). In post-bellum times, however, there was a sharp rise in the proportion of southern whites who reported cotton, coincident with a rapid increase in the percentage of Alabamans in the population of the eastern counties and a marked decrease in the percentage of Tennesseans (Table 9). By 1870 nearly all farmers, regardless of origin, were raising cotton, and the Americans had attained a position comparable to the Germans in the production of staples for market. The higher degree of commercialization among the Germans perhaps can best be understood in terms of their motivation for emigration. The one factor above all others which induced them to leave Europe was the desire to improve themselves economically, to attain a higher standard of living. To have perpetuated the semisubsistence economy they had known in Europe would not have achieved this goal. The Germans were willing to face the hazards of fluctuating market prices in an effort to better their material condition. Similar determination was apparently not found in most Anglo-American yeomen.

INTENSITY AND PRODUCTIVITY

Farming Methods, or Input of Labor and Capital

Few would disagree that the agricultural heritage of nineteenth-century Germans encompassed more intensive farming practices than that of their contemporaries in southern Anglo-America. There would be less agreement, however, as to whether this aspect of their heritage reasserted itself in the areas of overseas settlement.

Both contemporary observers and modern scholars[168] have com-

---

[168] Hogan, *The Texas Republic*, p. 20; Boethel, *History of Lavaca County*, p. 105.

mented on the alleged superiority of German farming methods in nine-teenth-century Texas. One writer complained after the Civil War that only Germans and other European immigrants devoted adequate labor and attention to farming in the state,[169] while another acknowledged the superiority of the Germans and Bohemians in picking cotton.[170] The Germans, it was reported, had less land, but "they generally culti-vate it properly."[171] More specific references concerning the practices of the Germans in the eastern counties are difficult to find. While it is true that F. Ernst at Industry was irrigating both his garden and fields in the early 1830's, this practice was apparently not widespread among the Germans.[172] In contrast, it is fairly well documented that Germans did not use dung on their fields,[173] in imitation of the Americans and in direct contradiction of a centuries-old practice in Europe. Indeed, dunging was an impossibility under the open-range system, for the live-stock were not kept stabled. Nor did the Germans feel obliged to pro-vide winter quarters or herders for their livestock, which doubtlessly contributed materially to the fact that 8 percent of the cattle owned by Germans in Austin and Waller counties in 1880 died, strayed, or were stolen during the year, a figure identical to that of Anglo-Americans and not significantly below the 10 percent reported by Negroes.[174] In addition, the ratio of improved acres to total land was not notably higher among the Germans than the Anglo-Americans, if such may be considered one measure of intensity (Table 23). Unfortunately, reports for expenditures on fertilizer in the 1880 census were so imperfectly recorded as to be of no value. A comparison of expenditures on fencing failed to reveal any major differences, except to point out the neglect by Negro farmers (Table 24).

There were, however, other ways in which the claim of greater in-tensity among the Germans seems to be verified. Beginning in 1860, for example, the Germans reported a greater value of farming imple-ments and machinery per farm than the slaveless Anglo-Americans (Table 16), a fact made even more significant by the smaller size of German farms. Attention to improved farming methods is further in-dicated by the greater prevalence among Germans of societies and

[169] "The Germans in Texas," *The Texas Almanac for 1872*, p. 77.
[170] Loughridge, "Report on the Cotton Production of the State of Texas," p. 161.
[171] De Cordova, *Texas*, p. 249.
[172] Dunt, *Reise nach Texas*, p. 94.
[173] *Ibid.*, p. 13; Schütz, *Texas*, p. 202; Roemer, *Texas*, p. 36.
[174] Manuscript census schedules of agriculture and population, 1880.

TABLE 24

Expenditures on Fencing in Austin and Waller Counties, 1880,
by Origins of the Population

Group	Average amount spent on fences in previous year	Percentage of farms reporting fence expenditures
German-born	$82.00	47%
All Germans[a]	$89.00	47%
Southern whites	$77.00	43%
Negroes	$23.00	15%

Source: Manuscript census schedules of agriculture and population.
[a] Includes a few natives of German-born fathers.

clubs devoted to agriculture. Such associations were quite numerous
in Germany by the 1840's, having first appeared in the late eighteenth
century,[175] and may be considered a part of the heritage brought to
Texas by the immigrants. In Westphalia alone, there were forty-two
agricultural clubs by 1843.[176] They were less common but by no means
absent in the source regions of southern settlers, for both Tennessee
and Alabama had a number of such organizations in ante-bellum
times.[177] Germans in Austin County founded one of the first agricultural
societies in Texas in 1856,[178] and the minutes of its meetings for the
first thirty years or so are filled with discussions and suggestions on how
to improve farming methods.[179] The United States Department of Agriculture listed no fewer than eleven such societies in the eastern German
settlements in the post-bellum period, far more than were found among
comparable numbers of Anglo-Americans[180] (Figure 12). In fact, there

[175] Meitzen, *Der Boden*, 3 (1871), 469–498; Theodor von Goltz, *Agrarwesen
und Agrarpolitik*, pp. 171–172.
[176] Meitzen, *Der Boden*, 3 (1871), 473, 477–478.
[177] Blanche H. Clark, *The Tennessee Yeomen 1840–1860*, Chapter 3, "Agricultural Organizations in Tennessee, 1840 to 1860," pp. 69–107; Weymouth T.
Jordan, "Agricultural Societies in Ante-Bellum Alabama," *Alabama Review*, 4
(1951), 241–253.
[178] See Arthur L. Schuette, "The German Settlers of Cat Spring and Their
Scientific Study of Agriculture," M.A. thesis.
[179] [Cat Spring Agricultural Society], *Century of Agricultural Progress*.
[180] [United States Department of Agriculture], "Agricultural and Horticultural Societies and Clubs," *Report of the Commissioner of Agriculture for the
Year 1867*, p. 399; *A Directory of . . . Organizations in the Interest of Agriculture
. . .*, pp. 75 ff.; *List of . . . Farmers' Clubs, and Agricultural, Horticultural, and*

was one such club for every three hundred farmers of German birth
in Texas in 1880, as compared to one for every five thousand American-born farmers. The membership of such clubs almost never contained a mixture of Germans and Anglo-Americans, and the German
language was used in the meetings. The tendency of Germans to establish clubs of various sorts, both in Europe and overseas, has often
been noted, and students of German culture even speak of a *Vereins-
wesen,* or "intense desire to band together."[181] Rural German areas in
Texas abounded with clubs devoted not only to farming, but also to
shooting, singing, literature, gymnastics, and mutual aid. Unfortunately,
few of the agricultural societies survived the nineteenth century, and
those which did, such as the Austin County (Cat Spring) Landwirthschaftlicher Verein, had become little more than formal excuses to get
together and drink beer. These societies were all nonpolitical in purpose, and Texas Germans steadfastly refused to join the Grange.[182]

Productivity, or Output

Intensity is closely related to productivity, a high value of the former
commonly leading to a corresponding high value of the latter. There is
some fairly substantial evidence that German farms were producing
more value per acre than the farms of Anglo-Americans, and their
farms reported a corresponding higher cash value per acre (Tables 18,
25). The comparative yields of cotton and corn, which would provide
perhaps the best measure of productivity, could be computed only for
1879, a year in which, unfortunately, a drought cut production back,
acting as an equalizer (Table 26).

FARM LABOR AND MACHINERY

Slavery

The characteristic which has perhaps become most closely identified
with ante-bellum German farmers in Texas was an absence of slaves.
Both contemporary observers and modern scholars have laid stress on

---

Pomological Societies . . ., pp. 57–58; and *List of Agricultural Societies and
Farmers' Clubs* . . ., pp. 55–56.
[181] Hans Meyer, *Das Deutsche Volkstum*, pp. 162–163.
[182] *Bastrop Deutsche Zeitung*, April 9, 1874, p. 1, col. 4. An exception appears
to have been a German chapter of the Grange, No. 1033, at Content, Colorado
County (Whilldin, *Description of Western Texas*, p. 32).

FIGURE 12

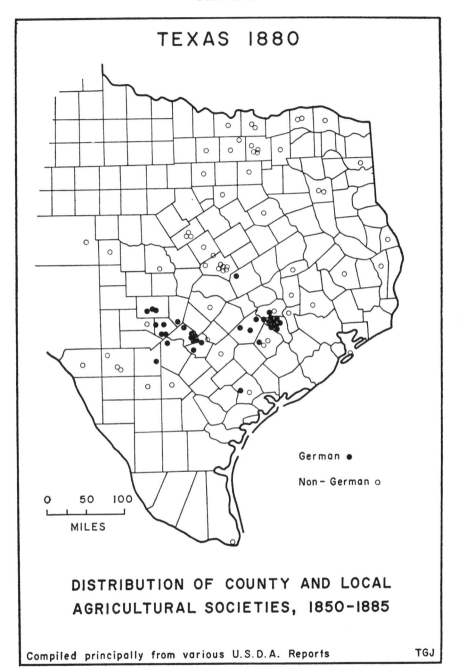

TEXAS 1880

German ●

Non − German ○

0   50   100

MILES

DISTRIBUTION OF COUNTY AND LOCAL
AGRICULTURAL SOCIETIES, 1850−1885

Compiled principally from various U.S.D.A. Reports   TGJ

TABLE 25

Value of Production per Acre in Austin and Waller Counties,
by Origins of the Population

| | Value of production per acre | |
Group	1870	1880
German-born	$4.89	$2.99
All Germans[a]	....	$2.93
Southern whites, no slaves in 1860	$2.75	....
Southern whites, slaveowners in 1860	$1.91	....
All southern whites	$2.22	$2.08

Source: Manuscript census schedules of agriculture and population.
[a] Includes a few natives of German-born fathers.
Figures for Negroes were excluded because acreage reports for them were too incomplete.

TABLE 26

Yields of Cotton and Corn in Austin and Waller Counties, 1879,
by Origins of the Population

Group	Cotton, bales per acre	Corn, bushels per acre
German-born	.45	17.3
All Germans[a]	.45	17.3
Southern whites	.42	16.9
Negroes	.39	13.6

Source: Manuscript census schedules of agriculture and population.
[a] Includes a few natives of German-born fathers.

the free-labor system found in the eastern settlements,[183] and there is no doubt that Germans were much less likely to own slaves than were the Anglo-Americans (Table 27). Much has been made of supposed German opposition to slavery in Texas, and the holding of Negroes has been pictured as offensive to their moral heritage.[184] In fact, the be-

[183] Olmsted, *A Journey through Texas*, pp. 140–142, 328, 358, 432; Traugott Bromme, "Der Freistaat Texas," Ch. IV in *Rathgeber für Auswanderungslustige* . . ., p. 251; and Hogan, *The Texas Republic*, p. 20.
[184] Solms-Braunfels, *Texas*, p. 14; Roemer, *Texas*, p. 28; Johann G. Büttner, *Briefe aus und über Nordamerika* . . ., Vol. 1, p. 212; Gilbert G. Benjamin, *The Germans in Texas*, p. 90.

TABLE 27

Slaveholding in the Eastern Sample Counties
by Origins of the Population

	1850 Percentage owning slaves	1860 Percentage owning slaves
German-born	9%	4%
Southern whites[a]	59%	72%

Source: Manuscript census schedules of population.

[a] The percentages for Anglo-Americans are not representative for Texas or the South as a whole, since the major plantation area in the Brazos River bottom was included.

lief was held among many Anglo-Americans in the 1850's that all Germans were "damned Dutch abolitionists." This image was acquired primarily as a result of a "statewide" convention of Germans held at San Antonio in 1854, at which a handful of Forty-Eighter intellectuals, who instigated and dominated the meeting, passed a mild abolitionist resolution.[185] The common German farmers had little to do with it. Also contributing to this image were written comments, primarily from the pen of Frederick Law Olmsted, praising the Germans of Texas for their free-labor economy.[186] Many Anglo-Americans heard the pronouncements of the 1854 convention, observed that few of their German neighbors owned slaves, and concluded that the Germans were an alien group bent on destroying the southern way of life. Nothing could have been further from the truth as far as the average German farmer in the eastern settlements was concerned. To call them abolitionists would be a serious misinterpretation of the facts.

Germans who owned Negroes were found as early as 1840 between the lower Brazos and Colorado rivers[187] and by 1850 there were twelve German slaveholders in Austin and Fayette counties, roughly one-tenth of all German farmers. Most owned fewer than five, but one German had fourteen and another twenty-seven.[188] Modern historians

[185] Rudolph L. Biesele, "The Texas State Convention of Germans in 1854," *Southwestern Historical Quarterly*, 33 (1929–1930), 247–261. See also Ada M. Hall, "The Texas Germans in State and National Politics, 1850–1865," M.A. thesis.

[186] Olmsted, *A Journey through Texas*, various pages.

[187] Tax lists of Austin, Colorado, and Fayette counties, 1840.

[188] Manuscript census schedules of population, Austin and Fayette counties, 1850.

and all but the most competent nineteenth-century observers[189] some-how overlooked them, and pronounced the Germans immune to the "peculiar institution." Olmsted, whose difficulty in finding Anglo-Americans who did not own slaves was exceeded only by his failure to locate Germans who did, "saw no negroes among them" in 1854.[190] Even though a smaller percentage of Germans owned slaves in 1860 than in 1850, the actual number of slaveowners had increased.[191] Not a single antislavery remark made by German peasant farmers in Texas could be found, such comments being confined to nonresident intel-lectuals and "Latin" farmers.[192]

It is fairly obvious that Germans in the eastern settlements were ac-quiring slaves and were doing so at an early date. While their free-labor heritage doubtlessly helps explain the fact that they were less likely to own Negroes, a more important factor was probably their meager capital resources.[193] Just as they were unable to buy as much land as the Anglo-Americans, so they were unable to buy slaves. Land owner-ship had priority, and most Germans exhausted their resources in that manner. Those Germans who did own slaves were, for the most part, the immigrants of the 1830's, who had longer to accumulate the neces-sary capital. It must also be kept in mind that Germans had to buy whatever slaves they had, unlike Anglo-Americans, many of whom in-herited slaves or acquired at no cost the offspring of Negroes already owned. Had slavery survived long enough for the Germans to acquire the needed capital, it is quite likely more of them would have bought Negroes.

The failure of the South as a whole to attract European immigrants in the ante-bellum period has been attributed by some scholars to the presence of slavery.[194] Even if the Germans were not morally opposed to slavery, it is conceivable that they might have avoided areas where

[189] Roemer, *Texas*, pp. 20, 199–201; Steinert, *Nordamerika vorzüglich Texas*, p. 129; De Cordova, *Texas*, p. 221; Karl von Sommer, *Bericht über meine Reise nach Texas im Jahre 1846*, pp. 74–75.

[190] Olmsted, *A Journey through Texas*, p. 358. In all fairness to Olmsted, it should be pointed out that he did include information supplied by a German in San Antonio to the effect that there were at least twelve German slaveowners in Texas, all of whom had immigrated prior to 1840 (p. 432).

[191] Manuscript census schedules of population, Austin County, 1860.

[192] Roemer, *Texas*, p. 28; Solms-Braunfels, *Texas*, pp. 39–40.

[193] De Cordova, *Texas*, p. 249.

[194] Max Hannemann, "Das Deutschtum in den Vereinigten Staaten, Seine Verbreitung und Entwicklung seit der Mitte des 19. Jahrhunderts," *Petermanns Mitteilungen Ergänzungsheft Nr. 224*, p. 20.

it was practiced in order not to place themselves in competition with Negro slave labor. There is, however, little or no factual evidence for such an opinion, because Germans settled in large numbers in Brazil and Missouri, in addition to Texas, where the institution was legal. Not one reference was found which suggested that ante-bellum German farm laborers had even the slightest difficulty finding work in Texas. Indeed, as will be discussed below, they seem to have been much in demand. A better explanation for the small numbers of European immigrants in the southern states is that by the 1840's, when the great mass emigrations of the nineteenth century began, the only desirable unoccupied lands in the South lay in Texas and Missouri, precisely the areas which attracted Europeans. In addition, the South lacked the large urban centers characteristic of the Northeast and, as a result, offered immigrants fewer opportunities for nonagricultural employment. The few cities which were found in the South, including New Orleans, St. Louis, and Galveston, did attract large numbers of Germans in ante-bellum times.

Hired Labor

Germans played a part in the hired labor market both as employers and employees. In the ante-bellum period, immigrants who had inadequate financial resources upon arrival quite commonly hired out as farm laborers until they had acquired enough money to begin farming on their own.[195] This also served as an apprenticeship period for the immigrants, during which they learned the basic procedures of the southern agricultural system. Not uncommonly, they worked for other Germans who had come to Texas earlier. German or Irish farm laborers could be hired at from eight to eighteen dollars per month plus room and board, usually much less than the twenty dollars or more needed to hire a Negro slave under the same terms.[196] In addition, the Germans had no qualms about doing certain kinds of farm work which southern tradition reserved for slaves. As a result, free laborers were much in demand and generally found only in the vicinity of German settlements.[197] One immigrant who arrived at Indianola early in 1852 reported that German farmers around Victoria, upon hearing of the arrival of his boat, went into town to waylay and employ the immigrants

[195] Luhn, "Bericht des Farmers F. W. Luhn," p. 35.
[196] From a Texas newspaper clipping of the mid-1850's, reprinted in Olmsted, *A Journey through Texas*, p. 513.
[197] De Cordova, *Texas*, p. 189.

before they moved inland. He was offered ten dollars per month plus room and board,[198] while fifty cents per day and board was offered in Austin County.[199] However, German farmers who were unable to find free laborers did not hesitate, if they had the funds, to rent slaves from their neighbors to perform such tasks as fencing and breaking new land.[200]

Labor conditions did not change notably after the Civil War, as the new immigrants continued to hire themselves out upon arrival. In 1880 German cotton laborers were reported in all of the eastern settlements, as well as in some non-German areas.[201] Farm wages were reported in the census returns for the first time in 1870, and from them it is apparent that comparable percentages of Germans and Anglo-Americans were employing laborers on their farms (Table 28). However, the average amount paid for labor was markedly lower among the Germans, indicating that they depended more on family labor than did the Anglo-Americans. It also appears that in later years a smaller percentage of Germans than either Anglo-Americans or Negroes hired themselves out as laborers (Table 29). Laborers in the post-bellum period were somewhat better rewarded for their work, receiving often five or six dollars per week, but the Negroes, now selling their own labor, had dropped from highest to lowest in the wage scale. Germans and Czechs were preferred as cotton pickers because they worked with more care than the ex-slaves.[202]

Agricultural Implements and Machinery

In the early years of settlement, the Germans in the eastern counties made out with only the barest minimum of farm tools, as is exemplified by F. Ernst of Industry, who used a hoe instead of a plow at first.[203] In letters back to Germany, some settlers advised their friends and relatives to bring various implements with them to Texas, since they were scarce. Still, plows could be had in Colorado County in the late 1840's for three to seven dollars, depending on the size,[204] a price within the

[198] Kromer, *Die Amerikafahrt*, p. 35.
[199] Regenbrecht, "German Settlers of Millheim," p. 29.
[200] Steinert, *Nordamerika vorzüglich Texas*, p. 135.
[201] Loughridge, "Report on the Cotton Production of the State of Texas," p. 161.
[202] *Ibid.*
[203] *The Civilian and Galveston Gazette*, December 2, 1843, p. 2, col. 4.
[204] *Allgemeine Auswanderungs-Zeitung*, No. 11, March 13, 1848, p. 169; No. 12, March 20, 1848, p. 183.

TABLE 28

Farm Wages in Austin and Waller Counties,
by Origins of the Population

	1870		1880	
	Average wages per farm	Percentage of farmers paying wages	Average wages per farm	Percentage of farmers paying wages
German-born	$125	34%	$ 84	24%
All Germans[a]	--------	--------	$ 89	24%
Southern whites, no slaves 1860	$276	32%	--------	--------
Southern whites, ex-slaveholders	$383	47%	--------	--------
All southern whites	$322	37%	$109	29%
Negroes	$110	6%	$ 22	13%

Source: Manuscript census schedules of agriculture and population.
[a] Includes a few natives of German-born fathers.

TABLE 29

Texas: Agricultural Laborers as a Percentage of Total Population
Engaged in Agriculture, by Origins of the Population

		Native Americans	
Census year	Germans[a]	Whites	Negroes
1870	27%	49%	
1880	19%	41%	
1890[b]	9%	16%	29%
1900[b]	33%	38%	49%

Source: Ninth Census, 1870, vol. I, p. 758; Tenth Census, 1880, vol. I, p. 847; Eleventh Census, 1890, "Population," Part II, pp. 612, 613; Twelfth Census, 1900, "Special Reports, Occupations," pp. 392–393.
[a] For 1870, 1880, and 1890, includes only German-born; for 1900 natives of German parentage also included.
[b] Includes only males.

reach of most newly arrived immigrants. As soon as a little capital was accumulated, the Germans acquired additional implements, including various machines which appeared on the market after mid-century, and by 1860 they reported a higher average value of farm implements and machinery than the southern Anglo-American yeomen (Table 24). One member of the agricultural society at Cat Spring bought a mowing machine in 1858, and by 1866 several others had also purchased them. The society had a special committee to buy and test new implements, and a mechanical planter and a sweep were obtained for this purpose. In 1873 a cash prize was offered to induce local artisans to design and build agricultural implements, and one year later it was announced that blacksmiths in the area would manufacture all cotton and corn planters in the future.[205]

LOCATIONAL STABILITY OF THE FARM POPULATION

The respective heritages of the Germans and southern Anglo-Americans would lead one to expect the European immigrants to have a greater tendency to remain settled in one place and establish firm ties with the land, and there are scattered reports which suggest that this may have been the case in Texas.[206] As early as 1843 an English-language newspaper in Galveston commented on the stability of the German farmers in Austin and Colorado counties, lauding the manner in which they "can commence a series of improvements, pursue them patiently for five, and even twenty years, to completion—the very converse of our Southern population, with whom all good must be realized within the year, or it is no good at all."[207] Less than a decade later another journalist wrote that Germans were displacing much of the Anglo-American population in Austin County by purchasing their land.[208] A similar displacement was observed underway in Gonzales County some sixty years later,[209] and it was largely in this manner that the German belt was steadily strengthened and expanded. In the valley of the lower Guadalupe River near Gonzales, a German immigrant observed late in 1848 that Anglo-Americans there had California gold fever and were offering their farms for sale quite cheap.[210] After the Civil War, the reluctance of Germans to sell land in Austin County was noted.[211] The evidence presented in support of the tradition of greater locational stability among the Germans is admittedly fragmentary and

[205] [Cat Spring Agricultural Society], *Century of Agricultural Progress*, pp. 15, 33, 35, 38, 49, 53, 60, 64, 65.
[206] Bracht, *Texas in Jahre 1848*, p. 107; Hogan, *The Texas Republic*, p. 11.
[207] *The Civilian and Galveston Gazette*, December 2, 1843, p. 2, col. 4.
[208] *The Texas Monument*, July 30, 1851, p. 2, col. 1.
[209] *Deutsch-Texanische Monats-Hefte*, Vol. 8, No. 5, July, 1903, p. 213.
[210] Ostermayer, *Tagebuch einer Reise*, p. 75.
[211] "Austin County," *Schütze's Jahrbuch für Texas . . . für 1883*, p. 120.

thin,[212] but it is perhaps significant that much of it came from the pens of Anglo-Americans and that no contradictory evidence was found.

TENURE AND INHERITANCE

Before the early 1840's, there was little difficulty involved in becoming a landowner in Texas since the government made free grants. For this reason the early German settlers in the east were able to acquire land immediately upon arrival. However, many of the grants were too remotely situated to allow occupancy, with the result that the Germans who owned them were forced to settle elsewhere and purchase small farms on credit.[213] The bullk of Anglo-Americans and Germans who settled in ante-belllum Texas came after the policy of free land grants had been discontinued, necessitating the purchase of land if tenancy was to be avoided. Land was bought either on credit or with money earned by serving as farm laborers or sharecroppers. One German immigrant in Austin County estimated in 1849 that three years as a hired farm hand were adequate to accumulate enough money to buy a farm. He figured that land in the county could be purchased for one to five dollars per acre, except in the bottoms where it was priced higher.[214] A German in the Cummins Creek settlement in Colorado County bought one hundred acres from an American for two hundred dollars in the late 1840's.[215]

In spite of the fact that Germans arrived with less capital resources, they had a much lower rate of tenancy than the native Americans. Even as early as 1850, 77 percent of the Germans were landowners as opposed to 69 percent for all Anglo-Americans,[216] and one American traveler several years later remarked on "the German tendency to invest in lands" in the eastern settlements.[217]

After the Civil War, the breakup of many of the plantations opened much land for settlement by German immigrants. The members of the

[212] An attempt was made to compare locational stability by matching names in the 1850 and 1860 census schedules. However, the English-speaking enumerators distorted the spelling of German names to the degree that matching was impossible.
[213] *The Civilian and Galveston Gazette,* December 2, 1843, p. 2, col. 4; Bollaert, *Bollaert's Texas,* pp. 275–276.
[214] Luhn, "Bericht des Farmers F. W. Luhn," pp. 35–36. See also Olmsted, *A Journey through Texas,* p. 359.
[215] Sörgel, *Für Auswanderungslustige!* p. 46.
[216] Manuscript census schedules of population, Austin and Fayette counties, 1850.
[217] Olmsted, *A Journey through Texas,* p. 429.

Cat Spring agricultural society in Austin County and the Turn Verein in Houston, fearing their countrymen would be trapped into permanent tenancy, sent letters to leading German newspapers in 1866, warning prospective immigrants not to make contracts of any kind with former slaveowners before coming to Texas.[218] The postwar immigrants were more likely to have funds to purchase land upon arrival than their antebellum predecessors had been, as is indicated by the ninety Germans who purchased land in Washington County shortly after the war ended.[219] Others rented land until they had saved enough money[220] or earned the needed cash as laborers. Whatever means they used to acquire land, the Germans continued to have a lower rate of tenancy than the Anglo-Americans (Table 30). The price for cultivated farms was

TABLE 30

Land Ownership in Austin and Waller Counties,
by Origins of the Population

Group	Percentage of farmers owning land, 1870	Percentage of farmers owning land, 1880
German-born	83%	86%
All Germans[a]	--------	85%
Southern Whites	71%	62%
Negroes	1%	25%

Source: Manuscript census schedules of agriculture and population.
[a] Includes a few natives of German-born fathers.

ten to twenty dollars per acre in Austin County in the early 1880's.[221] Of the farmers who did not own land, German tenants were much less likely to be sharecroppers than were native whites and Negroes (Table 31).

Few of the immigrants in the eastern settlements came from parts of Germany where division of land among all heirs was the tradition, and

[218] [Cat Spring Agricultural Society], *Century of Agricultural Progress*, pp. 32, 34.
[219] J. H. Randle in the *Texas Almanac for 1867, pp.* 171–172.
[220] A number of examples of post-bellum Germans who rented land initially, as well as some who bought farms upon arrival, are cited in A. Siemering, *Texas als Ziel deutscher Auswanderung . . .*, pp. 37–40. See also, Loughridge, "Report on the Cotton Production of the State of Texas," p. 104.
[221] "Austin County," *Schütze's Jahrbuch für Texas . . . für 1883*, p. 120.

TABLE 31

Tenure of Landless Farmers in Austin and Waller Counties, 1880,
by Origins of the Population

Group	Percentage renters	Percentage sharecroppers
German-born	66%	34%
All Germans[a]	69%	31%
Southern whites	43%	57%
Negroes	39%	61%

Source: Manuscript census schedules of agriculture and population.
[a] Includes a few natives of German-born fathers.

it is not surprising that single inheritance became the rule in Austin and adjacent counties, both among Germans and southerners. To be sure, some of the early immigrants who received over four thousand acres, had enough to split up among their children, but otherwise the landless offspring had to buy their own farms. Second-generation Germans in search of land contributed greatly to the northward and southward expansion of the German belt in the last quarter of the nineteenth century.

Chapter Five

Germans on the Rim of the Desert: The Western End of the German Belt, 1844–1885

In the mid-1840's the half of Texas west of the ninety-eighth meridian was still largely the unsettled hunting ground of wandering tribes of Plains Indians. The initial white occupation of this area was undertaken by thousands of German immigrants, who, under the original impetus provided by the Verein and Henri Castro, pushed the Texas frontier into the domain of the formidable Comanches. Here Germans were pioneers on the very forefront of westward expansion, not secondary settlers as they had been in much of the remainder of Anglo-America. Unlike their kinsmen farther east in Texas, who had settled in a region that was economically, socially, and environmentally a part of the South, these Germans occupied an untested land which was destined to belong in its entirety to neither South nor West.

THE NATURE OF THE LAND

German settlement in the West took place primarily in and on the fringes of the picturesque Texas Hill Country, to the north and west of San Antonio, a land of fertile basins and stream valleys interspersed by the accordant heights of eroded remnants of the Edwards Plateau.[1] Flanking the Hill Country, beyond the Balcones Escarpment which marks its eastern and southern border, are found the rolling expanses of the Gulf Coastal Plain. The first German footholds in the West were

---

[1] Good descriptions of the landforms in the Texas Hill Country are contained in W. T. Carter, *The Soils of Texas*, pp. 82 ff; and R. H. Loughridge (ed.), "Report on the Cotton Production of the State of Texas . . .," in *Report on Cotton Production in the United States*, pp. 135, 145, 148.

made near the escarpment, on the Coastal Plain where it meets the Hill Country, at Castroville in 1844 and New Braunfels in 1845.

If overall averages are considered, the western end of the German belt lies just on the humid subtropical side of the border with the semi-arid climates.[2] However, as is often the case in climatic transition zones, the averages are misleading, for in any given year the Texas Hill Country and the plains which border it may fall well within the area of semi-arid climates, and feel the hot, withering breath of the desert to the West. Average temperatures range from about 50° F. in January to over 80° F. in July and August, and the growing season is around 250 days. Perhaps the most outstanding characteristic of the climate is the un-reliability of precipitation. The figure for the average annual rainfall at Fredericksburg in Gillespie County, 27.5 inches, means very little when only 11 inches fall one year and 41 inches the very next, as happened in 1956 and 1957.[3] In the nineteenth century, two of the four census years used, 1859 and 1879, were marred by severe drought.[4] The wet years served only to convince the inhabitants that the dry ones were exceptional strokes of bad fortune, while in fact they were part of the normal course of climatic events, to be expected in such a transition zone. As was so often the case along the border of the semi-arid lands in North America, the settlers did not realize or would not admit that they were on the rim of the desert.

The soils in the western areas of German settlement varied from those of the valleys and basins of the Hill Country and the Black Waxy Prairie around New Braunfels, which were quite deep and fertile, to the stony, shallow soils or outcroppings of bare rock characteristic of the rugged, hilly interfluves.[5] The former were equal in fertility to any in the state, the latter nearly sterile and unsuitable for farming. The vege-tation cover found by the German settlers varied from the prairies, groves, and *galeria* forests of the Coastal Plain to the low, open forests of the Hill Country. Along the valleys of the rivers, which coursed the area from west to east, and their tributaries, were fine forests of mag-

[2] Climate data taken from *Texas Alamanac, 1961–1962*, pp. 71–75. The classi-fication system is that of Köppen and Trewartha, as outlined in Glenn T. Tre-wartha, *An Introduction to Climate*, p. 235.

[3] Taken from records in [State of Texas], the Office of the State Climatologist.

[4] The census enumerators often made notations on the margins of the agricul-tural schedules, such as "we had an extreme drought in 1879 . . ." (P. G. Temple, Gillespie Co.), and "a severe drought cut crops short in 1859" (D. P. Kinney, Blanco Co.). Some enumerators quoted long-time residents of the area to em-phasize the drought conditions (Mason County, 1880).

[5] Carter, *Soils of Texas*.

nificent cypress, pecan, and live oak trees, but elsewhere were found
only scattered mesquites, various types of small oaks, and junipers interspersed with coarse grasses. The openness of the forest and the
almost total lack of underbrush reminded one German observer of the
artificially planted woods of his homeland and presented an appearance
far removed from his European concept of a virgin forest. To seek
shade under the small, twisted, narrow-leafed mesquite tree was, in his
words, like trying to hold water in a sieve.[6] The savannalike woodland,
with its stunted trees, its xerophytic cacti and yucca, offered ample evidence of semi-aridity to even the untrained eye, but the warnings were
not heeded.

THE SAMPLE COUNTIES

Gillespie, Mason, and Llano counties were chosen to provide the statistical framework for the western German settlements, through the use
of the manuscript census schedules. They lie adjacent to one another
in the heart of the Hill Country and include in their collective population ample numbers of Germans and southern Anglo-Americans. In
1850 of these three only Gillespie County had been created, but it included within its borders all settled portions of what was to become
Mason and Llano counties. The Germans were still virtually alone on
the frontier in 1850, but by the following census year a balance had
developed in the population, in which Gillespie County was dominantly

TABLE 32

Germans in the Population of Gillespie, Llano,
and Mason Counties, 1870

County	Total population	German-born and natives of German percentage	German stock as percentage of total population
Gillespie	3,566	3,027	85%
Mason	678	360	53%
Llano	1,379	128	10%
Total	5,623	3,515	63%

Based on a hand count of the manuscript population schedules of the census.

[6] Ferdinand Roemer, *Texas: Mit besonderer Rücksicht auf deutsche Auswanderung*, pp. 143, 277–278.

German, Llano County largely southern Anglo-American, and Mason County divided about evenly between the two (Table 32). The agricultural schedules for Gillespie County in 1850 were incomplete, because the number of farms listed was considerably less than the total of persons designated as "farmers" in the population schedules. In fact, only thirty-six German farms were included. In order to obtain a larger and more meaningful number of German farmers, as well as to find some southern Anglo-Americans for purposes of comparison, the counties Comal, Guadalupe, and Hays were included in the averages for 1850. Comal County, in which New Braunfels was located, was almost entirely German, while Guadalupe contained both southerners and Germans and Hays was thinly settled almost exclusively by Anglo-Americans. Some use was made of the census schedules of Comal County in 1860, although the figures derived were not included in the averages for the sample area. The failure of the census enumerators, who were Germans, to list many of the Anglo-American farmers of Mason and Llano counties on the agricultural schedules in 1870 necessitated the inclusion of Blanco and Kerr counties, adjacent to Gillespie on the east and southwest, for that year only in order that adequate numbers of Anglo-Americans could be obtained for comparative purposes. These two counties were cast in the same mold as the other three. For 1850 and 1860, all of the usable farms on the agricultural schedules of the western counties were recorded, and in 1870 and 1880 a 50 percent sample was taken.[7]

For the western German settlements as a whole, the main source regions of the immigrants were Nassau, Upper Hesse-Darmstadt, Electoral Hesse, southern Hannover, the Upper Rhine Valley in Alsace, Brunswick, and the Heilbronn area of Württemberg, with smaller numbers from western Thuringia, Swabia, Saxony, and Waldeck (Figure

[7] The reader is referred to the Appendix for an explanation of sampling methods and the devices used to measure sampling error. The quality of the agricultural schedules for the western counties left much to be desired. The worst shortcoming was the omission of large numbers of farmers in 1850 and 1870, particularly in the latter year, when Mason and Llano counties were represented by unsatisfactory fragments. Gillespie and Comal counties for 1850 were also poorly done, and many farms in the immediate vicinity of Fredericksburg were left out, thus slighting one of the major areas of German settlement. In 1860 the enumerators failed to report crops in Mason, Llano, and other nearby counties, including Blanco, Kerr, San Saba, Bandera, and Medina, an omission not excusable by the drought of that year, since crops in adjacent Gillespie County were recorded. As a result, no figures could be presented for crop production among the Anglo-Americans for 1860.
The following table gives the number of farmers in each group according to

4). To these was added a scattering from the Rhine Province and eastern areas of Prussia.[8] The sample counties were fairly representative of the western settlements as a whole, as far as the specific German origins of the immigrants were concerned, with the exception of the Alsatians, who were found only in the Castro colony in Medina County, which was not included in the sample (Table 33). In contrast to German immigration farther east in Texas, the influx of settlers from Europe largely ceased before 1860 and did not resume after the Civil War.

There were a few scattered farms of Anglo-Americans near the junction of the Llano and Colorado rivers as early as 1850,[9] and in the same year, additional numbers of native-born settlers were found east of the Germans in Guadalupe and Hays counties. In general, however, southerners did not begin to occupy areas adjacent to the Germans until the latter part of the 1850's, over a decade after the founding of New Braunfels, Fredericksburg, and Castroville. By the eve of the Civil

---

their places of birth, indicates the sample counties used in each census year, and shows the percentage of farms in the agricultural schedules which were used:

Year	Sample counties	German-born	Natives of German-born fathers	All Germans	Southern Anglo-Americans, no slaves
1850[a]	Gillespie, Hays, Guadalupe, Comal	128	------	------	27
1860[a]	Gillespie, Mason,[c] and Llano[d]	376	------	------	173
1870[b]	Gillespie, Mason, Llano, Kerr, and Blanco	190	------	------	128
1880[b]	Gillespie, Mason, and Llano	289	69	358	347

a No sampling done.
b 50 percent sample taken.
c Formed from Gillespie and Bexar counties in 1858.
d Formed from Gillespie and Bexar counties in 1856.

[8] Viktor Bracht, *Texas im Jahre 1848*, p. 148; Wilhelm Hermes, "Erlebnisse eines deutschen Einwanderers in Texas," *Kalender der Neu-Braunfelser Zeitung fuer 1922*, p. 24; Lorenzo Castro, *Immigration from Alsace and Lorraine: A Brief Sketch of the History of Castro's Colony*, p. 6; Oscar Canstatt, *Die deutsche Auswanderung, Auswandererfürsorge und Auswandererziele*, pp. 223–224; "Erinnerungen an die Trümmer der Adels-Colonie in Texas u.s.w.," *Der deutsche Pionier*, 1 (1869), 143–144; Julius Fröbel, *Aus Amerika: Erfahrungen, Reisen und Studien*, Vol. 2, p. 320. Additional information was obtained from old ship lists.

[9] From information contained on a map drawn by H. Willke, found in *Instruction für deutsche Auswanderer nach Texas . . .*

TABLE 33

*Origins of the German-Born Farmers in Gillespie,
Llano, and Mason Counties, 1860*

State or province	Percentage of German-born farmers	State or province	Percentage of German-born farmers
Nassau	22%	Saxony	4%
Hannover	15%	Baden	1%
Hesse[a]	7%	Bavaria	1%
Brunswick	7%	Mecklenburg	1%
Württemberg	6%	Unspecified Prussia[b]	36%

Source: Manuscript census schedules of agriculture and population.
[a] Includes Hesse-Darmstadt and Electoral Hesse. It also includes the Schmal-kalden area of western Thuringia, the home of a number of Germans in the western settlements, which was at that time an outlier of Electoral Hesse.
[b] Includes the Wetzlar-Braunfels area of Hesse, which was an outlier of the Prussian Rhine Province. It contained the ancestral home of Prince Carl von Solms-Braunfels, and, as might be expected, supplied a significant number of the Verein immigrants.

War, Anglo-Americans dominated the population of Llano County and had also begun to settle in Blanco, Kerr, Bandera, and Uvalde counties, which flanked the German colonies on both east and west. Most of the immigration took place after 1865.

The southerners who settled next to the Germans in the western counties were mainly slaveless yeomen from the Upper South (Table 34). Tennesseans alone constituted nearly one-third of the southern white farmers in the sample counties in 1860, and no significant changes were detected in the post-bellum period. Very few slaves were present, and the Negro population was not large enough to warrant the calculation of separate figures in 1870 and 1880.

CROPS

Corn

Both German pioneers and southerners planted corn as their first crop in the western counties and continued to raise it in large quantities throughout the nineteenth century (Table 35). For the Anglo-Americans, this was not unexpected, particularly in view of their upper south-

TABLE 34

Origins of the Southern White Farmers in Llano, Mason, and Gillespie Counties, 1860

State	Percentage of total	State	Percentage of total
Tennessee	31%	North Carolina	8%
Kentucky	9%	South Carolina	6%
Arkansas	7%	Virginia	5%
Missouri	4%	Maryland	1%
Upper South	51%	Atlantic South	20%
Alabama	12%		
Georgia	7%	Texas	6%
Mississippi	3%		
Louisiana	1%		
Gulf South	23%		

Source: Manuscript census schedules of agriculture and population.

ern origins, but the Germans shared with their kinsmen farther east in Texas a total lack of previous experience with corn, and their adoption of it deserves additional comment.

Corn was reported in the fields around New Braunfels, Castroville, Fredericksburg, and many less important settlements in the earliest years of farming.[10] The Castroville Germans, who raised little else than corn for the first five years, initially made the mistake of planting too late to benefit fully from the spring rains and saw their corn crop destroyed by the summer drought, but at New Braunfels, the German farmers learned the proper method quite early, and planted in March.[11]

[10] C. Stählen, *Neueste Nachrichten, Erklärungen u. Briefe der Auswanderer von Texas*, second unnumbered page; A. Kordül, *Der sichere Führer nach und in Texas* . . ., p. 298; *La Grange Intelligencer*, August 8, 1846, p. 2, col. 4; Hermann Seele, "Zwei Erinnerungsbilder aus der Zeit der deutschen Ansiedlung von West-Texas," *Schütze's Jahrbuch für Texas . . . für 1883*, p. 45; Roemer, *Texas*, pp. 35, 281–282; Alwin H. Sörgel, *Neueste Nachrichten aus Texas . . .*, p. 27; *Galveston News*, February, 1847, and August 6, 1847, as cited in Julia Nott Waugh, *Castro-ville and Henry Castro, Empresario*, pp. 38–39; Bracht, *Texas im Jahre 1848*, p. 149; Louis Reinhardt, "The Communistic Colony of Bettina," *Texas State Historical Association Quarterly*, 3 (1899), 39; Ferdinand H. Lohmann, *Comfort . . . Festschrift zur fünfzig-Jahr Jubelfeier der Ansiedelung*, p. 30; Frederick Law Olmsted, *A Journey through Texas: or A Saddle-Trip on The Southwestern Frontier*, p. 195.
[11] W. Steinert, *Nordamerika vorzüglich Texas im Jahre 1849 . . .*, p. 152;

The recommended procedure for raising corn on new land involved burning the prairie grass and performing the initial plowing of the sod in autumn, followed in spring by a second plowing, harrowing, and planting.[12] The immediate acceptance of corn is explained in part by the recommendation found in many immigrant guidebooks that it was the crop

TABLE 35

Western Counties: Production of Corn, Wheat, Rye, and Oats, by Origins of the Population

ITEM	YEAR	German-born, no slaves	Native of German-born father	All Germans	Southern Anglo-Americans, no slaves
Corn, bushels	1850	462(99%)	--------	--------	474(93%)[a]
per farm and	1860	30(98%)	--------	--------	?
percentage of	1870	272(98%)	--------	--------	311(95%)
farms reporting	1880	34(86%)	35(75%)	34(84%)	113(92%)
Wheat,	1850	2%	--------	--------	7%[a]
percentage of	1860	86%	--------	--------	?
farms reporting	1870	62%	--------	--------	10%
	1880	72%	49%	68%	25%
Rye,	1850	0%	--------	--------	0%[a]
percentage of	1860	0%	--------	--------	?
farms reporting	1870	43%	--------	--------	2%
	1880	8%	1%	6%	1%
Oats,	1850	0%	--------	--------	4%[a]
percentage of	1860	0%	--------	--------	?
farms reporting	1870	5%	--------	--------	0%
	1880	30%	16%	27%	10%

Compiled from the manuscript schedules of the United States Census. The sample counties were: 1850, Gillespie, Comal, Hays, Guadalupe; 1860 and 1880, Gillespie, Mason, Llano; 1870, Gillespie, Mason, Llano, Kerr, Blanco. The sample taken within the counties was 100 percent for 1850 and 1860; 50 percent for 1870 and 1880.
  [a] Calculations based on only twenty-seven farms.

Bracht, *Texas im Jahre 1848*, p. 22; Stählen, *Neueste Nachrichten,* second unnumbered page; *Neu-Braunfelser Zeitung,* March 3, 1854, p. 2, col. 4, and March 4, 1859, p. 3, col. 4.
  [12] Kuno Damian von Schütz, *Texas: Rathgeber für Auswanderer nach diesem Lande . . .,* pp. 68–69.

best suited to newly broken soil.[13] Prince von Solms-Braunfels, the leader of the Verein colonization, advised the raising of corn in the early years of pioneering because of its ease of cultivation, quick maturation, and high yield.[14] It not only became a staple of the German frontier economy, but also found a place of lasting importance in their diet and as livestock feed. Cornbread was one of the major foods among the Germans, particularly in the early years,[15] but they departed from the customary means of preparation used by Anglo-Americans by leavening the bread and mixing in a measure of wheat flour.[16]

Germans continued to devote much of their attention to corn long after the pioneer period had passed, which is perhaps best understandable in terms of its value as a cash crop. As early as 1848 a settler in New Braunfels, after noting that corn was the major crop there, added that the surplus was being sold,[17] and in the same year, numerous ox-wagons loaded with corn were observed on the road heading from this German colony to San Antonio.[18] In 1851 over sixty thousand bushels were sent to market by the farmers of Comal County,[19] and one of the chief buyers was the United States Army.[20] One farmer went so far as to say the corn culture would cease entirely if it were not for the military market.[21] Still, the almost absolute dominance of corn in the crop association of the Germans declined after about 1850, making place for other crops. Olmsted reported that a fall in corn prices had prompted experiments in cotton around New Braunfels in the mid-1850's,[22] while another writer attributed the rise of wheat cultivation in the

[13] A. Siemering, *Texas als Ziel deutscher Auswanderung . . .*, p. 21; and [Verein zum Schutze deutscher Einwanderer in Texas], *Comite-Bericht des Vereines zum Schutze deutscher Einwanderer in Texas*, pp. 43–44.

[14] Carl von Solms-Braunfels, *Texas, Geschildert in Beziehung . . .*, pp. 29, 96.

[15] Kordül, *Der sichere Führer*, pp. 290, 303; Roemer, *Texas*, pp. 118, 124; [Verein], *Comite-Bericht des Vereines*, p. 24.

[16] Dr. and Mrs. Ernst Kapp, "Brief aus der Comalstadt 1850," *Jahrbuch der Neu-Braunfelser Zeitung fuer 1936*, p. 31.

[17] Heinrich Ostermayer, *Tagebuch einer Reise nach Texas im Jahr 1848–1849 . . .*, p. 82.

[18] Emmanuel Henri Dieudonné, *Missionary Adventures in Texas and Mexico: A Personal Narrative of Six Years' Sojourn in Those Regions*, p. 36.

[19] *The Texas Monument*, September 17, 1851, p. 2, col. 1.

[20] D. E. E. Braman, *Braman's Information about Texas*, p. 38; Olmsted, *A Journey through Texas*, p. 279.

[21] *Neu-Braunfelser Zeitung*, May 25, 1855, p. 2, col 2.

[22] Olmsted, *A Journey through Texas*, p. 182.

Fredericksburg area to three successive years of drought which had cut back corn harvests.[23]

There can be no question that the German adoption of corn was both rapid and universal and that the crop also attained a place of commercial importance among them, but it is noteworthy that the southern Anglo-Americans produced more of it per farm and devoted a greater part of their tilled acreage to it. Indeed, corn was the *only* crop reported by many southerners.

Wheat and Other Small Grains

The importance of wheat, and to a lesser extent, rye and oats in areas such as Hesse, Nassau, and Alsace, would lead one to expect these grains to be among the crops of the German immigrants in the western settlements. Prince von Solms-Braunfels had, in fact, advised the immigrants of the Verein colonies that European small grains might be raised in the second year of farming, when ample time for plowing and cultivating would be available.[24] Experiments with wheat began as early as 1848 and 1849 in New Braunfels and Fredericksburg, a few years later in Castroville, and about 1860 in Comfort.[25] During the decade from 1850 to 1860 a great expansion of wheat culture took place in the western settlements, and it became an almost universal crop among the Germans of Gillespie County (Table 35). The expansion occurred primarily in the latter part of the decade, as is indicated by the suggestion made by the editor of the *Neu-Braunfelser Zeitung* as late as 1853 and even 1854 that wheat should be raised in the area.[26] In the summer of the former year, an observer in Fredericksburg noted that small fields of wheat were beginning to dot the farm landscape there,[27] and in the autumn of 1854 Germans in the valley of the upper Guadalupe River in present-day Kendall County harvested 150 bushels, with even larger amounts in the valleys of the Cibolo Creek and

[23] Robert Penniger (ed.), *Fest-Ausgabe zum 50-jährigen Jubiläum der Gründung der Stadt Friedrichsburg*, p. 78.

[24] Solms-Braunfels, *Texas*, pp. 29, 98.

[25] Ostermayer, *Tagebuch einer Reise*, p. 92; [Verein], *Comite-Bericht des Vereines*, p. 24; Penniger, *Fest-Ausgabe*, p. 75; Waugh, *Castro-ville*, pp. 38, 53; Lohmann, *Comfort*, pp. 30–32.

[26] *Neu-Braunfelser Zeitung*, January 28, 1853, p. 1, col. 6; August 18, 1854, p. 2, col. 6.

[27] *Ibid.*, June 3, 1853, p. 2, col. 5.

San Marcos River.[28] In the middle of the decade, Olmsted reported
that "considerable wheat" had been raised by the Germans settled
around New Braunfels, in part because of their reluctance to pay the
twelve dollars per barrel demanded for flour imported from Ohio.[29] He
also observed it in the German communities of Quihi near Castroville
and Sisterdale on the upper Guadalupe,[30] while another traveler noted
its culture in the Llano River Valley and in Medina County.[31] The early
harvests were encouraging, and it was found that wheat could withstand
the searing drought better than corn.[32] Experimentation continued, and
one German settler in Fredericksburg was said to have planted small
patches of 110 different varieties of wheat in 1859, using samples provided by the federal government.[33] By the end of the decade, wheat
production had begun to be shifted to the winter,[34] to avoid the worst
drought season. Cattle and horses were pastured on the fields during the
cold months, which prevented the grain from heading too early in the
spring.[35] Winter cultivation of grain had been the rule rather than the
exception in nineteenth-century Germany and presented no special
problem for the immigrant farmers.[36]

By the post-bellum period, wheat had become one of the major cash
crops of the western German farmers, and its production was particularly important in Gillespie County and the upper Guadalupe
Valley around Comfort and Sisterdale.[37] One Anglo-American who
lived in Gillespie County wrote in 1873 that raising wheat was the
"chief employment" of the Germans there,[38] and soon after the war, a
newspaper in San Antonio credited the introduction of wheat culture
with bringing about a great improvement in the agricultural economy of

[28] *Ibid.*, September 8, 1854, p. 2, col. 1; August 18, 1854, p. 2, col. 6.
[29] Olmsted, *A Journey through Texas*, p. 170. The exact price was indicated
in the *Neu-Braunfelser Zeitung*, August 18, 1854, p. 2, col. 6.
[30] Olmsted, *A Journey through Texas*, pp. 196, 279.
[31] Peter August Moelling, *Reise-Skizzen in Poesie und Prosa . . .*, pp. 375, 380.
[32] Penniger, *Fest-Ausgabe*, p. 78.
[33] *Neu-Braunfelser Zeitung*, January 21, 1859, p. 3, col. 3; August 12, 1859,
p. 3, col. 2.
[34] *Ibid.*, November 25, 1859, p. 3, col 3; Moelling, *Reise-Skizzen*, p. 380.
[35] H. F. McDanield and N. A. Taylor, *The Coming Empire: or, Two Thousand
Miles in Texas on Horseback*, p. 152.
[36] August Meitzen, *Der Boden und die landwirthschaftlichen Verhältnisse des
preussischen Staates . . .*, Vol. 7, pp. 218–219, 236.
[37] McDanield and Taylor, *The Coming Empire*, pp. 138, 151–153, 176–177.
[38] Joseph S. Hall (ed.), "Horace M. Hall's Letters from Gillespie County,
Texas, 1871–1873," *Southwestern Historical Quarterly*, 62 (1958–1959), 354.

the Germans.[39] Its place of importance was challenged toward the end of the century by cotton,[40] but in the long run it survived while cotton disappeared from the scene.

As might be expected, the rise of wheat cultivation was paralleled by increasing numbers of grist mills in the German settlements. In New Braunfels, Olmsted reported four grist mills as early as 1854, and others were found in Gillespie County in the Live Oak Creek settlement and at Fredericksburg, and in Medina County at Castroville.[41] The mill on Live Oak Creek was built in the early 1850's by Carl Guenther, who eventually expanded his operations to establish Pioneer Mills of Texas, a major milling firm with offices at San Antonio.[42] Lange's Mill, a stone structure on Threadgill Creek in northwestern Gillespie County, is still standing after more than a century, although it is no longer in use. The first grist mill at Comfort was erected during the Civil War, and another in 1879.[43]

In spite of the large proportion of upper southerners, notably Tennesseans, in the southern white farm population of the western counties, wheat was not one of their major crops, for the census figures leave no doubt that it was much more common among the German farmers (Table 35). Still, the fact that even as many as one-fourth of the Anglo-Americans raised wheat in 1880 is perhaps indicative of their upper southern origins. In this respect, it is noteworthy that the true wheat belt of Texas during this period was not found among the Germans, but rather in the northern portion of the Black Waxy Prairie, centered on Dallas, in an area settled mainly by yeomen from the Upper South. When placed in this state-wide perspective, the German efforts at wheat raising in the Hill Country appear much less significant, and later, when the open expanses of the Great Plains in the Texas Panhandle were placed under wheat cultivation, the German undertaking was truly dwarfed. It cannot be said that Germans either introduced wheat into the state or contributed in a major way to its expan-

[39] *Freie Presse für Texas*, December 15, 1866, p. 2, col. 3.
[40] Penniger, *Fest-Ausgabe*, p. 79.
[41] Olmsted, *A Journey through Texas,* p. 178; Ernst Schuchard, *100th Anniversary, Pioneer Flour Mills, San Antonio, Texas, 1851–1951*, pp. 1–3; Penniger, *Fest-Ausgabe*, p. 78; John C. Reid, *Reid's Tramp: or A Journal of the Incidents of Ten Months Travel through Texas . . .*, p. 84; Braman, *Braman's Information*, p. 38.
[42] Schuchard, *100th Anniversary*, pp. 1–3.
[43] Lohmann, *Comfort*, p. 32.

sion there. What they did do was to reassert their cultural grain preference in the small-scale, diversified manner to which they had been accustomed in Europe. When competition from the Great Plains wheat
belt eventually put an end to commercial production of the crop in the
German areas, it was relegated to its present position of livestock feed
or winter forage crop.

Rye was an important crop in Hannover, Hesse, and other of the
source regions of the western German settlers, though it lacked the
dominance it enjoyed in parts of northwestern Germany. It was not unusual, then, that experiments with rye were carried on at the same time
the early attempts at wheat cultivation were being made. Small acreages of rye were planted by Germans near New Braunfels in the late
1840's and at Fredericksburg in the early 1850's.[44] However, it failed
at first to attain the widespread adoption that wheat enjoyed (Table
35), probably because it was less marketable, and as late as the Civil
War period those few who cultivated it merited special mention in the
local newspapers.[45] Rye apparently caught hold among the Germans in
the immediate post-bellum period, for nearly half of the farmers in the
western sample counties reported it in the 1870 census, while at the
same time it was referred to as one of the chief crops of the Germans
around Castroville in Medina County.[46] In view of the insignificance of
rye in southern agriculture, its virtual absence among the Anglo-American farmers in the western counties was not unexpected, and the domination of its cultivation by the Germans represents another example of
the persistence of a grain preference brought from Europe. While scattered references to dark bread in the German settlements can be
found,[47] the major use of rye was, in the long run, as a winter forage or
hay crop. In the latter part of the century, rye began to be replaced by
oats, which proved more satisfactory for these purposes. Experiments
with oats had been made by the Germans in Gillespie County in the
early 1850's,[48] but widespread cultivation did not occur until over
twenty years later (Table 35), when horses and mules began to replace
oxen as the chief draft animals. Oats were widely raised not only in the

[44] Steinert, *Nordamerika vorzüglich Texas,* pp. 84, 108; Ostermayer, *Tagebuch einer Reise,* p. 95; *Neu-Braunfelser Zeitung,* February 10, 1854, p. 2,
col. 6; May 25, 1855, p. 2, col. 2.
[45] *Neu-Braunfelser Zeitung,* March 17, 1863, p. 1, col. 4.
[46] George H. Sweet, *Texas . . . or the Immigrants' Hand-Book of Texas,* p. 50.
[47] H. H. McConnell, *Five Years a Cavalryman: or, Sketches of Regular Army
Life on the Texas Frontier . . .,* p. 186.
[48] *Neu-Braunfelser Zeitung,* February 10, 1854, p. 2, col. 6.

German source areas, but also in Tennessee and other parts of the South, and the significantly greater percentage of Germans reporting this crop was a little surprising.

Although barley was a well-known grain throughout Germany it was never raised in notable quantities in the western counties, in spite of some early attempts.[49] The numerous German breweries in the area apparently relied on imported grain.

The German immigrants had no European experience with grain sorghum, but even so they reported it much more frequently than the southern farmers (Table 36). In ante-bellum times, they began cultivating sorghum, mainly as a source of molasses, and later in the century it was recognized as an excellent fodder crop.[50]

Cotton

The western German settlements lay on what was to become the outermost fringe of dry-farmed cotton production, and the crop never attained the dominant place in the agricultural economy that it enjoyed farther east. Still, it did rise to a place of importance and deserves proper attention.

A few of the Germans in the vicinity of New Braunfels and Castroville apparently tried their hand at cotton raising even before 1850,[51] but in the census of that year only about 2 percent of the Germans reported it, a figure comparable to the 4 percent of southern Anglo-American yeomen (Table 36). The first German farmer to devote serious attention to cotton in the New Braunfels area was one Mittendorf, who produced nine bales in 1852,[52] much to the delight of the local newspaper editor, who had strongly recommended the crop to his countrymen earlier.[53] Olmsted, who visited New Braunfels several years later, could scarcely contain his elation over seeing a number of fields of free-labor cotton, though he felt that the excessive distance to market was a serious hindrance.[54] Production by Germans in the New

[49] *Ibid.*
[50] Lohmann, *Comfort*, pp. 33–34.
[51] Ostermayer, *Tagebuch einer Reise*, p. 92; Bracht, *Texas im Jahre 1848*, p. 149; *Galveston News*, February, 1847, as cited in Waugh, *Castro-ville*, p. 38. On the other hand, Steinert, *Nordamerika vorzüglich Texas*, p. 152, reported in 1849 that no cotton had yet been raised in the Castroville area.
[52] *Neu-Braunfelser Zeitung*, April 1, 1853, p. 2, col. 4.
[53] *Ibid.*, January 28, 1853, p. 1, col. 6.
[54] Olmsted, *A Journey through Texas*, pp. 141, 182.

TABLE 36

*Western Counties: Production of Grain Sorghum, Cotton, Tobacco,
and Hay, by Origins of the Population*

ITEM	YEAR	German-born, no slaves	Natives of German-born father	All Germans	Southern Anglo-Americans, no slaves
Grain sorghum,	1850	--------	--------	--------	--------
percentage of	1860	--------	--------	--------	--------
farms reporting	1870	57%			19%
	1880	19%	6%	17%	6%
Cotton, bales	1850	3.5(2%)			1.0(4%)[a]
per farm and	1860	2.4(2%)			?
percentage of	1870	3.3(2%)			3.1(16%)
farms reporting	1880	1.9(70%)	1.3(70%)	1.8(70%)	2.4(43%)
Tobacco,	1850	12%			0%[a]
percentage of	1860	0%			?
farms reporting	1870	0%			0%
	1880	3%	3%	3%	0%
Hay, tons per	1850	3.7(66%)			5.2(33%)[a]
farm and	1860	0(0%)			?
percentage of	1870	....(91%)			....(63%)
farms reporting	1880	0(0%)	0(0%)	0(0%)	0(0%)

Compiled from the manuscript schedules of the United States Census. The sample counties were: 1850, Gillespie, Comal, Hays, Guadalupe; 1860 and 1880, Gillespie, Mason, Llano; 1870, Gillespie, Mason, Llano, Kerr, Blanco. The sample taken within the counties was 100 percent for 1850 and 1860; 50 percent for 1870 and 1880.

[a] Calculations based on only twenty-seven farms.

Braunfels area became quite widespread by 1859,[55] and the crop joined corn and wheat as a major cash product. The disadvantage of interior location far from seaport markets was surmounted in pre-railroad days by overland trade in wagons with textile mills in northern Mexico.[56] Cotton maintained its place of importance in post-bellum times, causing one observer to remark on the fields "snow-white with cotton" around New Braunfels in the mid-1870's.[57]

[55] *Neu-Braunfelser Zeitung*, January 7, 1859, p. 3, col. 3. See also the manuscript census schedules of agriculture and population, Comal County, 1860.
[56] *Neu-Braunfelser Zeitung*, January 21, 1859, p. 3, col. 4; October 4, 1861, p. 3, col. 2.
[57] McDanield and Taylor, *The Coming Empire*, p. 104.

Cotton came somewhat later to the German settlements in the Hill Country, though there were scattered references to it in ante-bellum times.[58] By 1870 a modest increase in production was evident among the Anglo-Americans there, but in the same year only 2 percent of the Germans in the sample counties reported cotton, the same as a decade earlier (Table 36). A spectacular expansion occurred during the 1870's, particularly among the Germans, two-thirds of whom were raising cotton by 1880. The dominance of upper southerners in the Anglo-American population helps explain the low percentage of native farmers who reported cotton, but it is rather startling that this crop was so much more common among the Germans by the end of the period under study.

In the vicinity of Comfort, Kendall County, the year 1875 marked the beginning of cotton farming on a commercial basis,[59] while among the Germans of Gillespie County, 1876 seems to have been the pivotal year.[60] In Mason County, on the westward extreme of the German belt, the first major attempt at cotton production was in 1879.[61]

As would be expected, the number of gins increased with the expansion of cotton raising, and in Comal County the number rose from the mid-1850's, when the first gin was built, to twenty by 1885.[62] In the latter part of the same period, others were constructed at Fredericksburg and Comfort, and another was found at Castroville, testifying to the importance of cotton among the Germans in Medina County.[63] A cotton textile mill was built at New Braunfels just after the Civil War,[64] and, even though the structure itself was destroyed by a tornado several years later, the foundation had been laid for the present-day Comal Cottons industry.

There is little question that the expansion of cotton among the Germans was at the expense of wheat,[65] though many farmers con-

[58] Olmsted, *A Journey through Texas,* p. 196.

[59] Lohmann, *Comfort,* p. 34.

[60] *Wöchentliche Texas Post,* January 20, 1876, p. 1, cols. 3–4.

[61] Loughridge (ed.), "Report on the Cotton Production of the State of Texas," p. 148.

[62] "Zur Geschichte der Baumwollkultur in Comal County," *Kalender der Neu-Braunfelser Zeitung fuer 1905,* p. 35; Hermann Seele, *A Short Sketch of Comal County, Texas,* ninth unnumbered page.

[63] Donald H. Biggers, *German Pioneers in Texas,* pp. 114, 132; *Wöchentliche Texas Post,* January 20, 1876, p. 1, cols. 3–4; Lohmann, *Comfort,* p. 34; Ruth C. Lawler, *The Story of Castroville,* p. 5.

[64] *Neu-Braunfelser Zeitung,* October 20, 1865, p. 4, col. 1.

[65] Penniger, *Fest-Ausgabe,* p. 79.

tinued to raise both cash crops. However, the second decade of the
present century witnessed the beginning of a dramatic decline in Hill
Country cotton production, and today virtually none is found in the
western counties, either on German or Anglo-American farms.[66]

Tobacco

The upper southern origin of most of the native farmers in the western counties would seem to have promised tobacco a place among
their crops, but such was not the case. Instead, the phenomenon observed in the eastern settlements was repeated, and the production of
tobacco was dominated by the Germans.

Tobacco raising was not, however, as common on German farms
in the western counties as it was among their kinsmen between the
lower Brazos and Colorado rivers. It was believed by some New Braunfelsers about 1850 that the crop would become one of major importance,[67] and in that year 12 percent of the German farmers raised it
(Table 36). The editor of the newspaper encouraged its cultivation,[68]
but apparently there was never much progress beyond the production
for home use.[69] Less than 10 percent of the Germans in Comal County
raised tobacco by 1860, generally in very small amounts,[70] though
mention was made of a "tobacco factory" in New Braunfels in 1854,
which also sold Havana seed.[71] The only example found of commercial
tobacco raising by the Hill Country Germans was provided by the
activities of Mr. F. Doebbler of Fredericksburg, who even published
an article on the subject.[72]

Garden Vegetables

The western German settlements were characterized from the very
first by numerous kitchen gardens, in which a great variety of vegetables was grown. The immigrants who founded New Braunfels in

[66] *The Texas Almanac 1949–1950*, p. 218.
[67] [Verein], *Comite-Bericht des Vereines*, p. 25.
[68] *Neu-Braunfelser Zeitung*, January 28, 1853, p. 1, col. 6.
[69] Olmsted, *A Journey through Texas*, p. 195.
[70] Manuscript census schedules of agriculture and population, Comal County, 1860.
[71] *Neu-Braunfelser Zeitung*, December 9, 1853, p. 3, col. 2; September 29, 1854, p. 3, col. 6.
[72] J. Burke, *Burke's Texas Almanac and Immigrant's Handbook for 1881*, p. 135; F. Wilhelm Döbbler, "Der Tabaksbau," *Schütze's Jahrbuch für Texas . . . für 1882*, pp. 66–69.

1845 arrived too late in the year to commence work in the fields, and devoted their time instead to the preparation of gardens on their town lots.[73] In the following year,[74] and indeed, throughout the remainder of the century, gardens were found adjacent to most of the houses in the town, and many travelers commented on them.[75] Similar gardens were found both in the rural areas and in the towns of the western German settlements, and the references to them are too numerous to list.[76] A remarkable variety of vegetables was raised, including not only those found in Anglo-American gardens, but also many brought from Germany, such as kohlrabi, mustard, parsley, and leek.[77] In the mid-1850's Olmsted, who had by then become something of a teutonophile, declared that the kitchen garden of one German farmer in Medina County possessed a greater variety of vegetables than he had seen in "any planter's garden, with two exceptions," in the entire South.[78]

It did not take the Germans long to realize that two garden plantings were possible each year in the mild south Texas climate, for winter vegetables were being produced as early as 1853 in New Braunfels. Plantings were made in February and in late summer, and some fresh vegetables were available all winter.[79] Gardening was primarily the work of women, leaving the males free for more strenuous chores.[80]

The produce of the German gardens, particularly those in the towns, was in no small part intended for sale. In and around San

[73] Oscar von Claren, "Ein Brief aus dem soeben gegründeten Neu-Braunfels," *Kalender der Neu-Braunfelser Zeitung fuer 1920,* p. 47; Kordül, *Der sichere Führer,* p. 290; Schütz, *Texas,* pp. 216–217.

[74] *La Grange Intelligencer,* August 8, 1846, p. 2, col. 4.

[75] See, for example, Olmsted, *A Journey through Texas,* pp. 143, 182; Bracht, *Texas im Jahre 1848,* p. 139; Sweet, *Texas,* p. 39. The gardens of New Braunfels were still in rather primitive condition and few in number in the late 1840's according to Steinert, *Nordamerika vorzüglich Texas,* p. 97, and Jakob Thran, *Meine Auswanderung nach Texas unter dem Schutze des Mainzer Vereins,* p. 76.

[76] Such references include Olmsted, *A Journey through Texas,* pp. 279, 281; Ostermayer, *Tagebuch einer Reise,* pp. 138, 148; Bracht, *Texas im Jahre 1848,* p. 136; Penniger, *Fest-Ausgabe,* p. 68.

[77] *Neu-Braunfelser Zeitung,* September 8, 1854, p. 2, col. 1; Ostermayer, *Tagebuch einer Reise,* p. 113; *Wöchentliche Texas Post,* December 2, 1875, p. 1, cols. 4–5.

[78] Olmsted, *A Journey through Texas,* p. 279.

[79] *Neu-Braunfelser Zeitung,* December 9, 1853, p. 3, col. 2; September 21, 1855, p. 2, col. 4; March 3, 1854, p. 2, col. 4; September 8, 1854, p. 2, col. 1.

[80] Friedrich Armand Strubberg, *Friederichsburg, die Colonie des deutschen Fürsten-Vereins in Texas,* vol. 1. p. 18.

Antonio, market gardening was dominated by the Germans,[81] which is not too surprising in view of the fact that they represented a large part of the total population. From as far away as Castroville and New Braunfels, both of which lay about thirty miles distant, Germans brought their fresh vegetables and melons to San Antonio for sale, attracted by the higher prices offered there.[82]

In spite of the fact that the Germans of the western settlements brought to Texas a number of minor vegetables which they had known in Europe, most of them were apparently content to do without the white potato for many years (Table 37). This is particularly surprising, since a large number of the Verein colonists came from areas of Hesse and Nassau, where the potato had been the main food and where its failure during the years of blight in the mid-1840's had played a role in swelling the volume of emigration. Either the cultural preference for white potatoes did not assert itself during the first thirty or forty years in the new homeland, or else it was satisfied through the purchase of imported potatoes. There are references which indicate that potatoes were being raised in the early period,[83] but the census records reveal that only a minority of Germans reported them.[84] The short supply of white potatoes was noted by several settlers,[85] and there is some suggestion that difficulty was experienced in obtaining successful harvests.[86] Imported potatoes were selling for $3.50 per bushel at New Braunfels in the 1870's.[87]

There is good evidence that a great expansion in production of white potatoes took place in the late 1870's and 1880's.[88] Whether or not such belated attention to a crop which had been an integral part of the agricultural system in the German homeland can be thought of as the reassertion of a traditional dietary preference is open to ques-

[81] Olmsted, *A Journey through Texas*, p. 157; Sweet, *Texas*, p. 45.
[82] Waugh, *Castro-ville*, p. 53; Steinert, *Nordamerika vorzüglich Texas*, pp. 82, 100; [Verein], *Comite-Bericht des Vereines*, pp. 31–32.
[83] *Neu-Braunfelser Zeitung*, February 10, 1854, p. 2, col. 6; March 4, 1859, p. 3, col. 4; Olmsted, *A Journey through Texas*, pp. 231, 277.
[84] Manuscript census schedules of agriculture and population, Comal County, 1860, and Table 37.
[85] Carl Blumberg, *Die wahre Wirksamkeit des Mainzer Vereins . . .* p. 10; E. Kapp, "Briefe aus der Comalstadt," p. 31.
[86] Lohmann, *Comfort*, p. 33; Friedrich Schlecht, *Mein Ausflug nach Texas*, p. 151.
[87] *Wöchentliche Texas Post*, December 2, 1875, p. 1, cols. 4–5.
[88] Eleventh Census, 1890, "Statistics of Agriculture," pp. 491–492; published agricultural reports of the census for Gillespie County, 1900–1960. See also Lohmann, *Comfort*, p. 33.

TABLE 37

*Western Counties: Production of Potatoes and Ownership of Oxen,
by Origins of the Population*

ITEM	YEAR	German-born, no slaves	Natives of German-born father	All Germans	Southern Anglo-Americans, no slaves
White potatoes,					
bushels per	1850	14(9%)	--------	--------	8(15%)[a]
farm and	1860	2(1%)	--------	--------	?
percentage of	1870	14(6%)	--------	--------	8(2%)
farms reporting	1880	19(8%)	9(9%)	17(8%)	26(1%)
Sweet potatoes,					
bushels per	1850	40(54%)	--------	--------	34(30%)[a]
farm and	1860	17(72%)	--------	--------	?
percentage of	1870	29(62%)	--------	--------	46(28%)
farms reporting	1880	28(13%)	25(12%)	27(13%)	50(5%)
Ratio of white	1850	1:18	--------	--------	1:9[a]
potatoes to	1860	1:866	--------	--------	?
sweet potatoes	1870	1:21	--------	--------	1:66
	1880	1:2	1:4	1:2	1:12
Oxen	1850	5(84%)	--------	--------	4(78%)[a]
per farm and	1860	8(88%)	--------	--------	4(61%)
percentage of	1870	8(82%)	--------	--------	5(79%)
farms reporting	1880	6(19%)	5(19%)	5(19%)	3(16%)

Compiled from the manuscript schedules of the United States Census. The sample counties were: 1850, Gillespie, Comal, Hays, Guadalupe; 1860 and 1880, Gillespie, Mason, Llano; 1870, Gillespie, Mason, Llano, Kerr, Blanco. The sample taken within the counties was 100 percent for 1850 and 1860; 50 percent for 1870 and 1880.

[a] Calculations based on only twenty-seven farms.

tion, but the fact remains that the volume of white potato production rose sharply and exceeded that of sweet potatoes in heavily German-ized Gillespie County by 1890, never subsequently falling below it. In the most recent census, the county reported over four times as many bushels of white potatoes as sweet potatoes. In adjacent Llano County, where southern Anglo-Americans were dominant in the popu-lation, no such rise in white potato production occurred, and in 1890 sweet potatoes were still dominant by a ratio of over eight to one.[89]

[89] Eleventh Census, 1890, "Statistics of Agriculture," pp. 491–492.

Throughout most of the period under study, sweet potatoes were far more common, dominating by a ratio of almost twenty to one among the German farmers in 1850. They were found in all of the western German settlements beginning in the very first years of occupancy,[90] and, if the census figures can be trusted, Germans raised them more commonly than the southern Anglo-Americans (Table 37). There is little question that the increase in white potato production among the Germans toward the end of the century was at the expense of sweet potatoes, but a similar decline was not noted on Anglo-American farms, and the southerners appear to have maintained their preference for sweet potatoes.

The impressive list of references to gardening among the Germans of the western settlements, when coupled with the admittedly flimsy accusations of Anglo-American neglect of gardens that were cited in the previous chapter, suggests at least that the Germans there may well have devoted more attention to this farming activity. The higher proportion of Germans reporting sweet potatoes tends to support this possibility though unfortunately other census returns were too inadequately reported to be of much help. All that can be said with certainty is that Germans generally had gardens which drew the attention of many observers and that a considerable variety of plants was grown in them. Evidence is not conclusive enough to warrant any definite statement to the effect that Germans were superior to Anglo-Americans as gardeners in the western settlements.

There were, however, certain ways in which the Germans made different dietary uses of garden vegetables. Sauerkraut was put up by the barrel on some German farms to satisfy a food preference unknown to the southerners, and the Germans often ate cucumbers fresh instead of pickling them as the Anglo-Americans preferred to do.[91]

Orchards

Attempts were made quite early by the Germans to plant fruit trees,[92]

[90] Bracht, *Texas im Jahre 1848*, p. 149; *Galveston News*, February, 1847, as cited in Waugh, *Castro-ville*, pp. 38–39; Steinert, *Nordamerika vorzüglich Texas*, p. 83; Lohmann, *Comfort*, p. 33; Franz Kettner, letter to his parents from Castell, August 12, 1853, in Franz Kettner, "Letters of a German Pioneer in Texas," *Southwestern Historical Quarterly*, 69 (1966), 465.

[91] Myrtle Murray, "Home Life on Early Ranches of Southwest Texas," *The Cattleman*, 26, no. 10 (1940), p. 135; 26, no. 12 (1940), p. 48; and 26, no. 7 (1939), p. 33.

[92] Ostermayer, *Tagebuch einer Reise*, pp. 92, 110; *Neu-Braunfelser Zeitung*,

usually as part of their gardens, though little headway had been made
as late as 1850.[93] Experiments were carried out with many trees common in Europe, such as the apple, cherry, and pear,[94] but in the long
run, notable success was obtained only with peaches, and to a lesser
extent with native pecans, plums, figs, and apricots. Even as early as
the 1850's, it was evident that the peach tree offered the best possibilities, and from then on it was dominant in the western Texas German orchards.[95] While it was not uncommon to sell peaches along
with other produce of the market gardens,[96] specialization in tree
crops was rare in the nineteenth century, and extensive orchards like
the one of J. Meusebach in Mason County[97] were the exception rather
than the rule. The twentieth century, however, has witnessed the development of a major peach-growing area among the German-American farmers in certain areas of Gillespie County. Whether or not the
pecan is a domesticated tree is a matter for dispute, and the production
by the nineteenth-century German farmers perhaps should be listed
under a heading of "gathering." Neatly rowed orchards of this splendid native tree can be observed in some of the German areas today,
but in the last century the pecans brought to market were probably
from wild trees. A traveler in 1857 reported that the Germans around
Castroville were selling pecans for three dollars a bushel.[98] The in-
adequacy of census returns makes it impossible to determine whether
tree crops were more common among the German settlers than among
Anglo-Americans, but it is clear that in time they abandoned the fruit
trees typical of Europe and adopted types common to the southern
United States.

January 26, 1855, p. 1, col. 6; *Galveston News*, February 1847, as cited in Waugh,
Castro-ville, p. 39; *La Grange Intelligencer*, August 8, 1846, p. 2, col. 4; Bracht,
Texas im Jahre 1848, p. 149.

[93] Steinert, *Nordamerika vorzüglich Texas*, pp. 97, 152; E. Kapp, "Briefe aus
der Comalstadt," p. 33.

[94] *Neu-Braunfelser Zeitung*, July 28, 1854, p. 2, col. 2; March 3, 1854, p. 2,
col. 4.

[95] *Galveston Zeitung*, April 10, 1851, p. 3, cols. 2–3; *Neu-Braunfelser Zeitung*,
December 11, 1868, p. 3, col. 2; *Freie Presse für Texas*, July 24, 1869, p. 4,
col. 2.

[96] *Neu-Braunfelser Zeitung*, July 2, 1869, p. 3, col. 2.

[97] McDanield and Taylor, *The Coming Empire*, p. 194; Emil Frederick Wurzbach, *Life and Memoirs of Emil Frederick Wurzbach to Which Is Appended
Some Papers of John Meusebach*, p. 31; manuscript census schedules of agriculture, Mason Co., 1880.

[98] Reid, *Reid's Tramp*, p. 84.

Vineyards and Wine-Making

Source materials dealing with the early German settlements in the West give frequent references to the possibilities offered by viticulture, which is understandable because a large number of the immigrants came from the vine regions of Nassau, Hesse, and Alsace. The abundance of wild grapes convinced the early settlers that domesticated types would also thrive, and vine clippings brought from Europe were planted by Germans in the very first year at New Braunfels[99] and shortly thereafter around Castroville.[100] Prince von Solms-Braunfels advised in his guidebook in 1846 that the warm Texas climate allowed the cultivation of grapes on flat land,[101] but the German tradition of hillside viticulture, which is even expressed in their word for vineyard, *Weinberg* or "vine hill," was still evident in the following decade, when someone suggested that the hills on the north side of Fredericksburg would be excellent for vineyards.[102] Experiments continued for a number of years in the western German settlements,[103] but in the end it was realized that the imported European vines would not grow properly in Texas,[104] and viticulture was, with few exceptions,[105] abandoned. In the early 1880's, a San Antonio German complained that grape culture was little more than a *Spielerei*, a hobby, among his countrymen in Texas.[106] Cultural relics, in the form of a few old grape vines which grew from European clippings brought with the immigrants of the last century, can be observed occasionally today, all that remains of an agricultural specialty once believed to have a great future.

The failure of viticulture did not stop the Germans of the western settlements from making wine by using the native wild grapes and berries. Only eight days after Castroville was founded in 1844, a German in the colony reportedly set about the job of producing two casks of wine, which he sold upon completion for twelve cents a bottle.[107] The

[99] Solms-Braunfels, *Texas*, p. 14.

[100] Bracht, *Texas im Jahre 1848*, pp. 149, 285.

[101] Solms-Braunfels, *Texas*, p. 99.

[102] *Neu-Braunfelser Zeitung*, March 11, 1853, p. 3, col. 1.

[103] Ostermayer, *Tagebuch einer Reise*, pp. 92, 110; Kordül *Der sichere Führer*, pp. 290, 298–299.

[104] *Neu-Braunfelser Zeitung*, January 28, 1853, p. 1, col. 6; August 10, 1866, p. 2, col. 5; Waugh, *Castro-ville*, p. 53.

[105] *Neu-Braunfelser Zeitung*, September 17, 1869, p. 3, col. 1; McDanield and Taylor, *The Coming Empire*, p. 194.

[106] Siemering, *Texas*, p. 27.

[107] Diary of Henri Castro, as cited in Waugh, *Castro-ville*, p. 21.

settlers at New Braunfels were also quick to utilize the wild grape,[108] though many of them felt that only vinegar could be produced from such unimproved varieties.[109] Once they had mastered the technique of adding large amounts of sugar,[110] the Germans began making wine quite commonly in all parts of the western settlements.[111] The quantity made was generally modest, intended for home consumption, but the *Texas Almanac* reported in 1867 that some of the farmers around Fredericksburg were sending "as much as ten to twenty barrels of wine" to market,[112] and a traveler in the middle of the following decade was told that fifty thousand gallons were produced in one season alone around Boerne in Kendall County.[113] In drought years, such as 1859 and 1879, the crop of wild grapes was too small to allow large quantities of wine to be made, and as a result the production sometimes varied greatly from year to year.

Wine-making among the Germans of the western counties can certainly be attributed to their European agricultural heritage, but admittedly this activity never played a very important role in the rural economy. It is true that a commercial winery existed as late as the post-World War II period in Fredericksburg, selling products made from wild grapes and berries, but the wine was made primarily for home use, to satisfy a cultural beverage preference. In making this wine they had to abandon both the domesticated grapes and the wine-making methods they knew in Germany, for the gatherers of wild grapes in the Hill Country of Texas had little in common with the commercial vineyard keepers of the Rhine, the Mosel, and the Main.

Haymaking

The census returns indicate that haymaking was more common among the Germans than the southern Anglo-Americans, as would be expected in view of their respective agricultural heritages, though the

[108] Stählen, *Neueste Nachrichten*, second unnumbered page.
[109] Kordül, *Der sichere Führer*, pp. 298–299.
[110] The method used by H. Hoerster of Mason County is described in Murray, "Home Life on Early Ranches of Southwest Texas," *The Cattleman*, 26, no. 7 (1939), p. 36.
[111] *Neu-Braunfelser Zeitung*, February 10, 1854, p. 2, col. 6; January 21, 1859, p. 3, col. 4; Lohmann, *Comfort*, p. 33; McDanield and Taylor, *The Coming Empire*, p. 177; Henry B. Dielmann, "Emma Altgelt's Sketches of Life in Texas," *Southwestern Historical Quarterly*, 63 (1959–1960), 377.
[112] *The Texas Almanac for 1867*, p. 110.
[113] McDanield and Taylor, *The Coming Empire*, p. 138.

latter group can by no means be said to have neglected it (Table 36). The prairie grasses which were found in abundance throughout the western German settlements offered an excellent opportunity for hay-making. As early as 1849 a resident of New Braunfels described how the Germans of that settlement cut the native prairie grass to provide hay for their livestock during cold "northers" in wintertime,[114] in disregard of the advice given by the leader of the colony that forage was adequate all year round with no winter feed needed.[115] Olmsted noted that his horses were fed mesquite-grass hay in New Braunfels, the first of any sort that they had been offered in Texas.[116] Haymaking soon attained a commercial importance of sorts, and one immigrant in the early 1850's reported that he and some friends had sold seven wagon loads, which they had cut on the prairie around New Braunfels, for $2.50 a load.[117] The German farmers in the valley of the Cibolo hauled hay to San Antonio, where the price was $7 per wagon load,[118] and others in the Hill Country of Mason County found their market among soldiers stationed in the vicinity.[119] The amount of hay produced was dependent on drought conditions, with little or none in dry years, and more than one mowing in years with adequate rainfall.[120]

LIVESTOCK

Draft Animals

In the pioneering period, the draft animal of the western settlements was unquestionably the ox (Table 37). The Germans, who were hard-pressed financially, could better afford to purchase oxen than horses, for they cost only thirty-five dollars a pair at New Braunfels in the 1840's as opposed to at least that much for a single horse.[121] In addition, the cost for keeping oxen was lower than for other draft animals,

[114] Ostermayer, *Tagebuch einer Reise*, pp. 78–79.

[115] Solms-Braunfels, *Texas*, pp. 23–24. The same advice was given by Henri Castro to his colonists in his bilingual pamphlet, *Colonisation au Texas (Amérique du Nord): Castro-ville (25 Milles Ouest de San Antonio de Bexar) . . .,* p. 9.

[116] Olmsted, *A Journey through Texas*, p. 145.

[117] Dorus Kromer, *Die Amerikafahrt: Aus den Goldgräberjahren eines Schwarzwälder Bauernsohns*, p. 48.

[118] Dan Fischer (comp.), *The Willmanns in America—1853–1953*, twenty-fourth unnumbered page.

[119] Selma Marie Raunick, Margaret Schade, and E. Marshall, *The Kothmanns of Texas, 1845–1931*, p. 14.

[120] *Neu-Braunfelser Zeitung*, September 21, 1855, p. 2, col. 4.

[121] Kordül, *Der sichere Führer*, pp. 289–290, 302.

since they received less feeding, and they had the added advantage of being undesirable to the roving bands of horse-stealing Comanches,[122] though the Indians sometimes killed oxen at the same time they stole horses.[123] Often as many as three to five yoke of oxen were used to break new land,[124] and they were considered to be particularly satisfactory for this purpose. In the ante-bellum period, and even as late as 1870, the ox was in almost universal use among the Germans, in contrast to the Anglo-Americans of the same area, who relied much more on the horse (Table 38). In 1850, the Germans had an ox/horse ratio of 1:0.4 as opposed to 1:1.4 for the southern yeomen, and even greater differences were detected in the two following census years. The reason for the dissimilar draft animal ratios was probably partly economic, reflecting the larger amount of capital among the Americans, but it was perhaps also of significance that the ox had been the traditional farm draft animal in Germany, in contrast to southern Anglo-America, where the horse was dominant. In addition, the southerners seem to have been less concerned with crops and more with livestock ranching, an economic undertaking well-served by the horse but not the ox. This would also help explain the curious post-bellum phenomenon of a greater adoption of mules by the Germans (Table 38).

Between 1870 and 1880, the number of oxen declined dramatically, just as had occurred in the eastern German settlements, due in large part to their unsuitability to farm machinery. As early as 1869, the newspaper at New Braunfels noted that ten oxen were being sent each day to a local slaughterhouse, which was producing meat for sale in the town, as well as tallow for shipment to England,[125] and even before that, during the Civil War, the high meat prices offered by the military prompted many Germans to sell their oxen.[126]

Even though horses did not become the chief draft animal of the German farmers until the 1870's, they were already common among the immigrants three decades earlier.[127] Although the Germans owned fewer horses than the Americans, the percentage of each group re-

---

[122] August Santleben, *A Texas Pioneer: Early Staging and Overland Freighting Days on the Frontiers of Texas and Mexico*, p. 10.

[123] A San Antonio newspaper clipping of December 11, 1854, reprinted in Olmsted, *A Journey through Texas*, p. 507.

[124] Lohmann, *Comfort*, p. 36; E. Kapp, "Briefe aus der Comalstadt," p. 36.

[125] *Neu-Braunfelser Zeitung*, July 30, 1869, p. 3, col. 2.

[126] *Ibid.*, May 16, 1862, p. 2, col. 4.

[127] See, for example, Steinert, *Nordamerika vorzüglich Texas*, pp. 82, 84, 116; Stählen, "Neueste Nachrichten," second unnumbered page.

TABLE 38

Western Counties: Horses, Mules, and Draft-Animal Ratios,
by Origins of the Population

ITEM	YEAR	German-born, no slaves	Natives of German-born father	All Germans	Southern Anglo-Americans, no slaves
Horses per	1850	2(79%)	--------	--------	4(96%)[a]
farm and	1860	3(83%)	--------	--------	8(89%)
percentage of	1870	4(96%)	--------	--------	9(94%)
farms reporting	1880	6(94%)	4(97%)	6(95%)	7(97%)
Mules and asses	1850	4(15%)	--------	--------	0(0%)[a]
per farm and	1860	2(7%)	--------	--------	1(10%)
percentage of	1870	4(24%)	--------	--------	2(11%)
farms reporting	1880	4(56%)	4(35%)	4(52%)	2(18%)
	1850	1:0.4	--------	--------	1:1.4[a]
Ratio of oxen	1860	1:0.3	--------	--------	1:3.0
to horses	1870	1:0.6	--------	--------	1:2.0
	1880	1:5.2	1:4.5	1:5.1	1:12.2
Ratio of mules	1850	1:5	--------	--------	(no mules)[a]
and asses	1860	1:15	--------	--------	1:60
to horses	1870	1:4	--------	--------	1:39
	1880	1:3	1:3	1:3	1:19

Compiled from the manuscript schedules of the United States Census. The sample counties were: 1850, Gillespie, Comal, Hays, Guadalupe; 1860 and 1880, Gillespie, Mason, Llano; 1870, Gillespie, Mason, Llano, Kerr, Blanco. The sample taken within the counties was 100 percent for 1850 and 1860; 50 percent for 1870 and 1880.

[a] Calculations based on only twenty-seven farms.

porting them was about equal by the outbreak of the Civil War (Table 38).

Cattle

Cattle ranching was first established in the area by Mexican settlers around San Antonio long before southerners began occupying the state. By the time the Germans arrived on the scene, Anglo-Americans had merged their herding tradition with that of the Spanish borderlands and had established ranching in many parts of Texas. It is likely that the European immigrants observed this economic activity as they

moved inland from Indianola to take their posts on the western rim
of civilization.

Whatever the antecedents, the Germans quickly recognized the
suitability of the land in the western settlements for large-scale cattle
raising (Table 39). After only a single year at New Braunfels, one

TABLE 39

*Western Counties: Possession of Cattle and Swine, by Origins
of the Population*

ITEM	YEAR	German-born, no slaves	Natives of German-born father	All Germans	Southern Anglo-Americans, no slaves
Milch cows	1850	7(99%)	-------	-------	22(100%)[a]
per farm and	1860	23(97%)	-------	-------	48(91%)
percentage of	1870	20(98%)	-------	-------	17(90%)
farms reporting	1880	18(96%)	13(94%)	17(96%)	17(81%)
Other cattle	1850	11(89%)	-------	-------	45(96%)[a]
per farm and	1860	48(96%)	-------	-------	93(90%)
percentage of	1870	74(94%)	-------	-------	164(84%)
farms reporting	1880	41(90%)	37(86%)	40(89%)	39(74%)
	1850	16	-------	-------	65[a]
Total cattle	1860	71	-------	-------	140
per farm	1870	90	-------	-------	170
	1880	57	46	55	52
Swine per	1850	14(70%)	-------	-------	40(96%)[a]
farm and	1860	29(91%)	-------	-------	82(82%)
percentage of	1870	19(86%)	-------	-------	50(91%)
farms reporting	1880	13(80%)	9(75%)	12(79%)	21(85%)

Compiled from the manuscript schedules of the United States Census. The
sample counties were: 1850, Gillespie, Comal, Hays, Guadalupe; 1860 and
1880, Gillespie, Mason, Llano; 1870, Gillespie, Mason, Llano, Kerr, Blanco.
The sample taken within the counties was 100 percent for 1850 and 1860; 50
percent for 1870 and 1880.
[a] Calculations based on only twenty-seven farms.

settler wrote that he had 25 head of cattle,[128] and the total number in
the colony rose rapidly from 150 in the first year to 2,000 by 1847[129]
and 5,000 in the following year.[130] By 1849 the immediate vicinity

[128] Stählen, "Neueste Nachrichten," second unnumbered page.
[129] Sörgel, *Neueste Nachrichten*, p. 27.
[130] Bracht, *Texas im Jahre 1848*, p. 89.

of New Braunfels had become overcrowded with large numbers of cattle, and many settlers were leaving the area with their herds to seek more plentiful forage elsewhere.[131] Thousands of cattle were observed on the prairies around the town a few years later.[132] Near the German town of D'Hanis in Medina County, S. G. French noted herds of cattle in 1849,[133] and five years later Olmsted commented that the wealth of the settlers there lay principally in cattle.[134] Similar herds were found among the Germans around Fredericksburg as early as 1846,[135] and in the years that followed, the settlers of that vicinity purchased large numbers of cattle with the profits they made from selling crops.[136] Cattle raising was noted among the Germans in the Llano River Valley in the 1850's.[137] By the outbreak of the Civil War one anonymous American writer commended the Germans of the western settlements for being "among those who are doing as well as any in the trade,"[138] and in 1865 a published list of cattle brands contained hundreds that belonged to German ranchers in Medina, Comal, Bexar, Guadalupe, Kendall, and Gillespie counties.[139] A series of articles in *Cattleman* magazine about 1940 portrayed the life and times of many of these early German ranchers.[140] The open range and rugged longhorn cattle, the trademarks of the industry, were also common among German stock raisers in the western settlements. Cattle grazed on the rough, thin-soiled interfluvial parklands of the Hill Country and the prairies of the adjacent Coastal Plain.

In the 1850's southern Anglo-American ranchers began settling to the north and east of the Germans in Llano, Mason, and Blanco counties, and to the west of them in Kerr, Bandera, and Uvalde counties, ending the isolation of the Germans on the frontier. As was suggested previously, these native-born ranchers relied less on crops than did

[131] Steinert, *Nordamerika vorzüglich Texas*, p. 101.
[132] Kromer, *Die Amerikafahrt*, p. 69.
[133] S. G. French, "A Report in relation to the route . . . from San Antonio to El Paso del Norte . . .," *Reports of the Secretary of War . . .*, pp. 41–42.
[134] Olmsted, *A Journey through Texas*, pp. 280–281.
[135] Roemer, *Texas*, p. 273.
[136] Penniger, *Fest-Ausgabe*, p. 75.
[137] Moelling, *Reise-Skizzen*, p. 380.
[138] *Western Texas the Australia of America: Or the Place to Live*, p. 184.
[139] W. H. Jackson and S. A. Long, *The Texas Stock Directory or Book of Marks and Brands . . .*, Vol. 1.
[140] Murray, "Home Life on Early Ranches of Southwest Texas," *The Cattleman*, 24, no. 8 (1938), through 27, no. 7 (1940). The German ranchers portrayed were O. Thallman, H. Rothe, C. Real, D. Karbach, F. Holekamp, H. Hoerster, J. Linn, E. Jordan, M. Dittmar, H. Keese, and H. Kothmann.

the Germans, and most of them owned no land at all, choosing instead to let their livestock graze on the unclaimed expanses of the public domain or on property belonging to nonresident owners. The census population schedules list many "stock raisers" who, because they owned no land and apparently had no crops, were not included in the agricultural schedules. Among those who did till some land, corn was not uncommonly the only crop reported.

Cattle ranching continued to grow in importance after the Civil War, as new markets opened to the north in Kansas. Visitors to New Braunfels in the 1870's were struck by the cattle scattered on "a thousand hills" near the town,[141] and in the various German communities of the Hill Country, observers noted the importance of ranching.[142] The industry underwent considerable change in the decade that followed, and Germans were leaders in introducing improved breeds,[143] mainly Herefords, and in fencing the open range. Ranching came to be the dominant form of rural economy in most of the western German areas, and today it is the agricultural activity followed by most of the descendants of the original immigrants. In Germany, the pasture had been an adjunct to the fields, but in the Texas Hill Country, precisely the reverse arrangement evolved.

Sheep

In the major source areas of immigrants, especially Hannover, Hesse, and Nassau, sheep were important in the agricultural system of the mid-nineteenth century and were far more numerous than either swine or cattle (Table 4 in Chapter II). The yeomen of the Upper South who settled adjacent to the Germans in the Hill Country were also acquainted with sheep husbandry, and farmers in portions of eastern and middle Tennessee long had exported wool. In both Germany and the South, however, sheep raising had traditionally been on a small scale, designed to supply enough wool for home use, and neither group had experience in extensive sheep ranching.

As early as 1846 Prince von Solms-Braunfels advised the immigrants of his colony that sheep-raising could be a very profitable agri-

---

[141] McDanield and Taylor, *The Coming Empire*, p. 104.

[142] *Ibid.*, pp. 150, 194; James B. Gillett, *Six Years with the Texas Rangers, 1875 to 1881*, p. 72.

[143] Max Krueger, *Pioneer Life in Texas: An Autobiography*, p. 188; Murray, "Home Life on Early Ranches of Southwest Texas," *The Cattleman*, 26, no. 11 (1940), pp. 28–29; *ibid.*, 27, no. 7 (1940), p. 47.

cultural activity in the Texas Hill Country.[144] He had no way of knowing how prophetic his suggestion was to be, for sheep did rise to a position of very great importance among his countrymen in the western settlements. The introduction of improved breeds can perhaps be credited to the Germans, for in the late 1840's one of the settlers at Sisterdale, in present-day Kendall County, had in his possession some sheep brought from Germany, which he crossed with Mexican stock.[145] Flocks, including some improved breeds, were also noted among the Germans in Medina County and in the Llano River valley in the 1850's,[146] and in the first federal census at mid-century, roughly one-tenth of all Germans in the western counties owned some sheep (Table 40). The flocks were generally quite small, however, and considerable difficulty was experienced with predators, primarily wolves.[147]

The credit for developing large-scale sheep ranching in the Texas Hill Country should, however, be given to an Anglo-American, George W. Kendall, who settled near New Braunfels in the early 1850's and devoted the remainder of his life to this undertaking.[148] He was highly regarded among the Germans, and they were quick to follow his example, creating a major center of sheep raising in the Hill Country of Comal and Kendall counties before the Civil War. Most of the stock was of Mexican origin, and the New Braunfels newspaper noted on one day in 1860 that two Germans drove a flock of about two thousand sheep through the town en route from Saltillo, where they had been purchased, to the Hill Country around Sisterdale.[149] The

[144] Solms-Braunfels, *Texas*, p. 17.

[145] This settler was O. von Behr, and his small flock of sheep attracted the attention of many travelers. See, for example, John Russell Bartlett, *Personal Narrative of Explorations and Incidents in Texas, New Mexico, California, Sonora, and Chihuahua*, Vol. 1, p. 55; Ferdinand von Herff, *Die geregelte Auswanderung des deutschen Proletariats mit besonderer Beziehung auf Texas*, trans. A. L. Finck, M.A. thesis, University of Texas, 1949, pp. 68–69; Bracht, *Texas im Jahre 1848*, pp. 90–91; Olmsted, *A Journey through Texas*, p. 193; Steinert, *Nordamerika vorzüglich Texas*, p. 110.

[146] Olmsted, *A Journey through Texas*, p. 259; *Neu-Braunfelser Zeitung*, September 23, 1853, p. 2, col. 6.

[147] *Neu-Braunfelser Zeitung*, September 23, 1853, p. 2, col. 6; Murray, "Home Life on Early Ranches of Southwest Texas," *The Cattleman*, 26, no. 7 (1939), p. 34; A. Siemering, "Schafzucht in Westtexas," *Schütze's Jahrbuch für Texas . . . für 1882*, pp. 69–73.

[148] Kendall described his sheep ranch in considerable detail in a series of articles published in the *Texas Almanac*, editions of 1858 through 1867. For further information, see George Wilkins Kendall, *Letters from a Texas Sheep Ranch*.

[149] *Neu-Braunfelser Zeitung*, July 20, 1860, p. 3, col. 3.

TABLE 40

*Western Counties: Possession of Sheep, Production of Dairy Goods, and
Value of Livestock, by Origins of the Population*

ITEM	YEAR	German-born, no slaves	Natives of German-born father	All Germans	Southern Anglo-Americans, no slaves
Sheep per	1850	9(9%)	--------	-------	5(19%)[a]
farm and	1860	100(10%)	--------	-------	16(5%)
percentage of	1870	95(27%)	--------	-------	165(24%)
farms reporting	1880	209(36%)	30(17%)	191(32%)	204(9%)
Butter, pounds	1850	135(95%)	--------	-------	305(96%)[a]
per farm and	1860	----(74%)	--------	-------	----(?)
percentage of	1870	----(95%)	--------	-------	----(83%)
farms reporting	1880	171(87%)	141(75%)	165(85%)	184(86%)
Cheese	1850	30%	--------	-------	15%[a]
percentage of	1860	0%	--------	-------	?
farms	1870	2%	--------	-------	0%
reporting	1880	1%	1%	1%	0%
	1850	$280	--------	-------	$ 715[a]
Average value	1860	$857	--------	-------	$1418
of livestock	1870	$605	--------	-------	$ 976
	1880	$756	$486	$704	$ 474

Compiled from the manuscript schedules of the United States Census. The
sample counties were: 1850, Gillespie, Comal, Hays, Guadalupe; 1860 and
1880, Gillespie, Mason, Llano; 1870, Gillespie, Mason, Llano, Kerr, Blanco.
The sample taken within the counties was 100 percent for 1850 and 1860; 50
percent for 1870 and 1880.
[a] Calculations based on only twenty-seven farms.

decade before the outbreak of the Civil War witnessed a great increase in the size of the German flocks (Table 40), and the immigrant farmers were attracting publicity as a result of their sheep-raising activities.[150] The large numbers of sheep on each farm necessitated
the hiring of shepherds to watch the flocks, and Mexicans, as well as
newly arrived German immigrants, filled this role. From the original
center in Comal and Kendall counties, commercial sheep husbandry
began to spread before 1860 to the German settlements in other parts
of the Hill Country, and one German immigrant was among the first

[150] *Western Texas the Australia of America*, p. 49.

ranchers in Kerr County to raise sheep, when he brought flocks totalling eight hundred head into the county in 1857.[151]

The great expansion of sheep husbandry continued in post-bellum
times, as the proportion of Germans who owned sheep rose steadily,
and flocks grew even larger. A traveler in the mid-1870's was told
that the area around the German town of Boerne contained thirty to
forty thousand sheep,[152] and some Germans owned over a thousand
head.[153] The industry continued to expand in the present century, when
fine Merinos and other improved breeds replaced the mixed-blood
stock of the earlier period, and today sheep raising remains one of the
major activities of the Hill Country Germans. They were not alone
in the adoption of large scale sheep husbandry, for it also proved attractive to the Anglo-American population of the area.

Among the German settlers, sheep raising has always been combined with cattle ranching, and this naturally raises the question of
whether the rise of the unique combination ranching economy which
is characteristic of this part of Texas[154] can be attributed to the Germans. It is noteworthy that Kendall, the driving force behind the rise
of sheep husbandry, specialized in raising them, to the exclusion of
cattle. It is also of importance that Kendall settled in an area where
Germans were overwhelmingly dominant in the rural population and
made almost exclusive use of them in his hired labor force,[155] circum-
stances which enabled the Germans to be the first to benefit from his
successful experiment. Anglo-Americans did not begin to settle in the
Hill Country until several years later. On the basis of these facts, it is
concluded that Germans were indeed the first to practice combination
ranching. Southern stock raisers in the adjacent counties of Kerr, Bandera, and Blanco were, because of their later arrival and more periph-
eral location in relation to the original center of sheep husbandry,
slightly later in utilizing the advantages of the combined production
of sheep and cattle. It would be incorrect to attribute the rise of combination ranching and its diffusion throughout the Hill Country to the
Germans alone, for the Anglo-Americans were only a few years behind
them in adopting this system. The stereotyped animosity between cat-

---

[151] Murray, "Home Life on Early Ranches of Southwest Texas," *The Cattleman*, 25, no. 7 (1938), pp. 51–52.

[152] McDanield and Taylor, *The Coming Empire*, p. 139.

[153] Krueger, *Pioneer Life in Texas*, p. 186; Siemering, *Texas*, p. 30.

[154] William T. Chambers, "Edwards Plateau; A Combination Ranching Region," *Economic Geography*, 8 (1932), 67–80.

[155] Olmsted, *A Journey through Texas*, p. 183.

tlemen and sheepmen which is often associated with the American West was never found in this area, either among Germans or Anglo-Americans.

Goats

Goats were kept in small numbers by a few of the Germans of the Hill Country as early as the 1840's,[156] but they failed to attain a noteworthy position in the livestock association. The Angora goat, which became very important to the German ranchers later, was brought into the area in 1858 by a Mr. W. Haupt, an American of Pennsylvania German and English descent,[157] but over twenty years later, goat husbandry was still said to be just beginning among the Germans of Comal County,[158] and in Gillespie County only 731 goats were counted in 1880.[159] The great expansion of goat-raising did not occur until the twentieth century, beyond the period covered in this study, at which time the Angora goat acquired a place alongside cattle and sheep in a combination ranching triumvirate.

Swine

Hogs were remarkably numerous in the Upper South, particularly in middle Tennessee, but in the source regions of German settlers, they were far fewer in number and pork was less important in the diet. In keeping with these respective agricultural heritages, the average number of hogs per farm in the western counties was much higher for the southern yeomen (Table 39). Even so, nearly all German farmers kept swine, and the droves were far larger than those they had owned in Europe. In fact, hogs attained major importance among the immigrants.

In the German settlements, swine were being raised in the wooded bottomlands of rivers and creeks around New Braunfels before 1850,[160] and they were even more numerous in the adjacent Hill Country. Hog production for market soon became a major activity for many of the German farmers, and Olmsted noted in one settlement in present-day

[156] Steinert, *Nordamerika vorzüglich Texas*, p. 116; Penniger, *Fest-Ausgabe*, p. 111.
[157] William L. Black, *A New Industry: Or Raising the Angora Goat, and Mohair, for Profit*, pp. 71–72.
[158] A. W. Spaight, *The Resources, Soil, and Climate of Texas . . .*, p. 68.
[159] Penniger, *Fest-Ausgabe*, p. 142.
[160] Ostermayer, *Tagebuch einer Reise*, p. 83.

Kendall County as early as the mid-1850's that "one of the greatest
sources of profit is from droves of hogs, which increase with remarkable rapidity, and pick their living from the roots and nuts of the
river bottoms."[161] In 1854 it was reported that hog raising was rapidly
becoming the most important agricultural pursuit among the Germans
of Gillespie County, and the animals were thriving on the abundant
acorns and pecans in the area.[162] A similar development occurred in
the Llano River Valley settlements in Mason and Llano counties, where
large droves were fattened on post-oak mast. The onset of cool weather
in November and December was the signal for the annual butchering,
and some of the German settlers of the Art community in Mason
County slaughtered seventy-five or one hundred fattened hogs at a
single time.[163] One of the most vivid memories of one newlywed German girl at Art was her initiation into her husband's family at hog-
butchering time in the winter of 1883–1884, when she worked for
weeks helping with the slaughtering and processing of meat, which
had to be salted and peppered before smoking.[164] Cured ham and
bacon, as well as lard, were hauled to market in Austin and San Antonio, or sold at the local forts.[165] The Germans of Medina County
had large droves as early as the 1850's,[166] and those at Castroville
were producing swine for the San Antonio market in the 1870's.[167]

    Neither the widespread ownership of swine nor their production on
a large scale for market was unique to the German settlements, for
the Anglo-Americans were also engaged in hog raising. Swine husbandry is still a major commercial activity in parts of the western German belt today, particularly in Mason County, and through the years
it has fluctuated in importance, reaching peaks during periods of low
beef prices. Pork production for home use continues, and smokehouses
can still be observed on the farms of some German-Americans.

    The large volume of beef and pork production among the Germans

[161] Olmsted, *A Journey through Texas*, p. 195.
[162] *Neu-Braunfelser Zeitung*, January 13, 1854, p. 2, col. 3; February 10,
1854, p. 2, col. 6.
[163] Murray, "Home Life on Early Ranches of Southwest Texas," *The Cattleman*, 26, no. 7 (1939), p. 34; 27, no. 7 (1940), p. 43; Raunick *et al.*, *The Kothmanns*, p. 14.
[164] Personal reminiscences of Emilie Willmann Jordan, 1863–1960, the writer's grandmother.
[165] Murray, "Home Life on Early Ranches of Southwest Texas," *The Cattleman*, 26, no. 7 (1939), p. 34; Raunick *et al.*, *The Kothmanns*, p. 14.
[166] Olmsted, *A Journey through Texas*, p. 279.
[167] Sweet, *Texas*, p. 50.

of the western counties encouraged the survival of sausage-making, an art brought from Europe by the immigrants and virtually unknown to the southern Anglo-Americans. Olmsted made special mention of the beef sausage for sale in New Braunfels in the 1850's,[168] and throughout the German parts of the Hill Country it was found on most dinner tables. Still today sausage can be purchased in many towns of the western German belt, such as Mason, Fredericksburg, Castroville, and New Braunfels. The latter two vie vigorously for the reputation of sausage capital of Texas, and visitors to Castroville are met by a sign proudly proclaiming "our wurst is the best." Present-day German sausage often contains venison in addition to pork and beef.

Milk Cows and Dairy Products

Nearly all settlers of both German and southern origin apparently regarded milk cows as indispensable. Most of the Verein colonists purchased some even before obtaining draft animals,[169] and milk cows were found on virtually every farm in the New Braunfels colony from the very first weeks of settlement.[170] Cow pens were among the initial improvements made on newly occupied farms.[171] The immigrants in Comal County bought milk cows in the older eastern German communities between the lower Brazos and Colorado rivers, and later, in the fall of 1845, from farmers in Bastrop County.[172] A scant month after the founding of the colony, one settler wrote that he had already acquired a cow and calf for a little over eight dollars, and that by milking her out he could get ten to twelve liters of milk each day, noting with pride that his neighbor only got half as much.[173] One year later, the price had risen to ten dollars.[174] The cows grazed on the open range during the day, returning to their pens at night to feed their calves. They were milked both morning and evening. Milk was available all year round, though in summer cows gave about six quarts per day as opposed to only two quarts at the opposite season. Hay and corn were commonly used to supplement forage in the winter months.[175]

[168] Olmsted, *A Journey through Texas*, p. 143.
[169] Ostermayer, *Tagebuch einer Reise*, p. 84.
[170] Schütz, *Texas*, p. 225.
[171] Claren, "Ein Brief," pp. 46–47; Schütz, *Texas*, p. 216.
[172] Seele, "Short Sketch," fourth unnumbered page.
[173] Kordül, *Der sichere Führer*, p. 302.
[174] Stählen, "Neueste Nachrichten," second unnumbered page.
[175] *Neu-Braunfelser Zeitung*, March 11, 1853, p. 3, cols. 5-6.

Nearly all of the German farmers made butter, except in years of extreme drought when the poor condition of natural forage diminished the milk supply to the point where no surplus existed (Table 40). Even in good years, butter making was confined largely to the season of maximum milk production in late spring, usually May.[176] References to the splendid butter found on German farms in the western settlements are quite numerous,[177] and as early as the 1840's many of the farmers carried their produce to sell in the market at San Antonio. The price offered there ranged from fifty cents a pound in the 1850's to only twenty cents shortly after the Civil War.[178] Olmsted's claim that the German farmers were more likely to produce butter than the Anglo-Americans is refuted by the census manuscripts, which revealed as early as 1850 that almost all farmers, regardless of origin, were producing butter and that, in fact, slaveless Americans were making roughly twice as much per farm[179] (Table 40).

A better claim can be made for German domination of cheese making in the early years of settlement, for nearly one-third of them reported it in 1850, as opposed to only about 15 percent of the southern yeomen (Table 40). In Gillespie County, a German-Swiss named J. Anderegg set up a cheese factory in the cellar of his home and produced cheese up to fifty pounds in weight.[180] The German settlers in the Art community in Mason County made cheese by putting rennet, made from the dried stomach of young deer, into milk to curdle it, and then placing the curd between cheese cloth before pressing it.[181] The census figures indicate that cheese making declined drastically among the Germans after the 1850's, but there is good reason to believe that such was not the case. The low proportion of farmers reporting cheese in 1860 and 1880 can be explained by the droughts which marked those years, and in 1870 it is possible that the enumerators simply overlooked cheese, as they did many agricultural products of minor importance. In any case, living descendants of the German immigrants remember cheese making for home use as being fairly

[176] Murray, "Home Life on Early Ranches of Southwest Texas," *The Cattleman*, 26, no. 11 (1940), p. 28.
[177] Ostermayer, *Tagebuch einer Reise*, p. 148; Steinert, *Nordamerika vorzüglich Texas*, p. 82; Olmsted, *A Journey through Texas*, pp. 144, 184, 187, 280.
[178] *Die Union*, November 15, 1866, p. 3, col. 3; Olmsted, *A Journey through Texas*, pp. 186–187.
[179] Olmsted, *A Journey through Texas*, pp. 144, 186, 187.
[180] [Gillespie County Historical Society], *Pioneers in God's Hills*, pp. 1–2.
[181] Murray, "Home Life on Early Ranches of Southwest Texas," *The Cattleman*, 27, no. 7 (1940), p. 43.

common in their families as late as the first quarter of the present century.

Poultry

Early references seem to indicate that poultry, primarily chickens, were found on most farms, both among the Germans and the Anglo-Americans,[182] and the census of 1880, the first to enumerate poultry, lends additional support to this conclusion (Table 41). Apparently,

TABLE 41

Poultry and Eggs in Gillespie, Mason, and Llano Counties, 1880, by Origins of the Population

	Percentage of farms reporting poultry	Number of poultry per farm	Number of eggs per farm per year
German-born	89%	26	83 dozen
Natives,			
German-born father	74%	19	54 dozen
All Germans	86%	25	79 dozen
Southern Anglo-Americans	91%	20	55 dozen

Source: Manuscript census schedules of agriculture and population.

however, the German farmers were producing more eggs, and there are reports as early as the 1840's and 1850's of Germans marketing their surplus eggs, which sold for ten to twenty cents per dozen.[183] Several observers noted, both before and after the Civil War, that the Germans around Castroville were raising poultry to sell.[184]

While chickens were doubtlessly most common, small numbers of turkeys, ducks, and geese were also found on some German farms.[185] There is, however, no basis for Walter Prescott Webb's claim that

[182] Stählen, "Neueste Nachrichten," second unnumbered page; Kordül, *Der sichere Führer,* p. 290; Olmsted, *A Journey through Texas,* p. 280; Ostermayer, *Tagebuch einer Reise,* p. 75; Claren, "Ein Brief," p. 47.

[183] E. Kapp, "Briefe aus der Comalstadt," p. 30; *Die Union,* November 15, 1866, p. 3, col. 3; *Neu-Braunfelser Zeitung,* April 30, 1869, p. 3, col. 1.

[184] Sweet, *Texas,* p. 50; Braman, *Braman's Information,* p. 38.

[185] Sweet, *Texas,* p. 40; Murray, "Home Life on Early Ranches of Southwest Texas," *The Cattleman,* 26, no. 12 (1940), p. 48; Thomas Hughes (ed.), *G. T.T.: Gone to Texas, Letters from Our Boys,* p. 84.

Germans introduced geese into Texas in 1848,[186] especially in light of
the comment made in 1846 by a settler at New Braunfels, who advised
prospective immigrants in Germany that they need not bring along
their fowl, since geese were to be had practically anywhere in the
state.[187]

DIVERSITY

One of the most striking aspects of the agricultural system of the Germans in the western counties was the remarkable variety of crops and
livestock which were produced. They marketed commercially significant quantities of not only corn, wheat, garden vegetables, hay, and
cotton, but also cattle, hogs, sheep, eggs, and dairy products, and it
was not unusual to find nearly all of these combined on a single farm.
After having journeyed through eastern Texas, where the agricultural economy, including that of the Germans settled there, was dominated by cotton and corn, Olmsted could not help but notice "the
greater variety of the crops" which were found on the German farms
around New Braunfels.[188] It was, to be sure, an unfair comparison,
because the Germans of the western counties had settled in an empty,
untested country, where no staple crop economy was pre-existent, a
country in which experiment was required. While their cultural tradition of diversified agriculture may have influenced the Germans to
a certain degree in their choice of crops and livestock, it seems likely
that the necessity to find, by trial and error, plants and animals well
suited to the rim of the desert was much more important.

It is noteworthy, however, that the western German farmers appear to have established a more diversified agriculture than the Anglo-
Americans (Table 42) in the same area. The differences between the
two groups were centered largely in field and garden crops, since, as
was mentioned previously, both adopted the combined raising of
cattle, hogs, and sheep. The key to the greater crop diversity of the
Germans lay mainly in small grains, as is evidenced by the higher
percentage reporting wheat, rye, oats, and sorghum, but by 1880
cotton had also been added to the list of crops found more frequently
on German farms. In the long run, it mattered little that the Germans
raised a greater diversity of crops, for although the experimenting con-

[186] Walter Prescott Webb, "Christmas and New Year in Texas," *Southwestern
Historical Quarterly*, 44 (1940–1941), 360.
[187] Bracht, *Texas im Jahre 1848*, p. 250.
[188] Olmsted, *A Journey through Texas*, p. 140.

TABLE 42

*Crop Diversity in Gillespie, Llano, and Mason Counties, 1880,
by Origins of the Population*

	Percentage of total improved acreage in		
	corn	cotton	wheat
German-born	29%	23%	20%
Natives, German-born father	30%	27%	16%
All Germans	29%	23%	20%
Southern Anglo-Americans	43%	17%	8%

Source: Manuscript census schedules of agriculture and population.

tinued well into the present century, the commercial production of corn, small grains, and cotton were abandoned one by one, leaving only the combination livestock ranching economy which is dominant today over most of the Hill Country. Diversity, the child of experiment, is no more.

SETTLEMENT FORM

Pattern of Settlement

Nearly all of the Verein and Castro colonists came from parts of Germany where houses and other farmstead structures were clustered together in unplanned, irregular villages called *Haufendörfer*. The three most important German settlements in the western counties, New Braunfels, Castroville, and Fredericksburg, all represented attempts by their founders to establish, with some modifications, the nucleated farm villages of the Old World on Texas soil. In New Braunfels and Fredericksburg, the early settlers were granted town lots of about one-half acre in size and outlying farms of ten acres,[189] and it was assumed that the Germans would locate their houses, gardens, barns, and other farmstead structures in the town and go out to their fields to work each day (Figure 13). The ten-acre farms were given to the immigrants at New Braunfels soon after their arrival in 1845, but at Fredericksburg the settlers chose to cultivate one large communal field

---

[189] Roemer, *Texas*, pp. 24, 277. In New Braunfels, the town lots were 96 by 192 feet, a half-acre by Bavarian measure but over 3,000 square feet short by American standards.

FIGURE 13

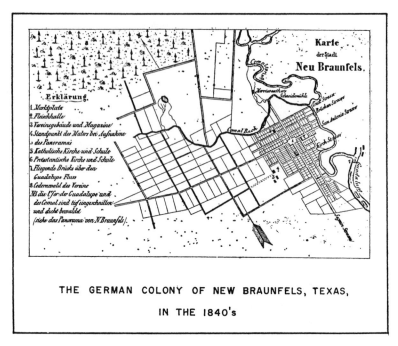

THE GERMAN COLONY OF NEW BRAUNFELS, TEXAS,

IN THE 1840's

Note the cadastral pattern, which shows the half-acre town lots and ten-acre farms granted to the early German immigrants. Reproduced from *Instruction für deutsche Auswanderer nach Texas* . . ., Berlin: D. Reimer, 1851, a publication of the Verein zum Schutze deutscher Einwanderer in Texas.

during the first year, delaying the distribution of farms until 1848.[190] Because these settlements were planned and laid out by surveyors, they differed in a number of respects from the German prototype, perhaps most strikingly in the great width of the streets,[191] but also in the regular geometric checkerboard pattern. At Castroville, the first settlers were given one-third acre town lots and twenty or forty acres

[190] Penniger, *Fest-Ausgabe*, pp. 48, 67, 72.
[191] This feature impressed many contemporary observers, including Oster-mayer, *Tagebuch einer Reise*, p. 77; and Olmsted, *A Journey through Texas*, p. 142.

for farming, depending on their marital status.[192] Initially, Castroville developed in a half-moon pattern around the inside of a bend in the Medina River, because the town lots along the stream were more desirable, but within a few years a regular grid pattern had filled in the intervening space.[193] All three of these German settlements were intended to be not just farm villages, but also market towns of considerable magnitude, and each had an area toward the center left empty for a market square. At Castroville and Fredericksburg these were quite extensive, and one early observer described the proposed market place at Fredericksburg, the Adolphsplatz, as large enough to accommodate a city of ten or twelve thousand inhabitants.[194] In outward appearance, these settlements revealed little of their planned grid pattern in the early years, since houses were scattered randomly on lots drawn by chance, with empty spaces between, giving slight indication of the direction of streets. There was little suggestion of clustering, and tree stumps remained for some time in the roads and market squares.[195]

Other settlements founded by Castro and the Verein were apparently intended to be farm villages tributary to the market towns. At Castell, founded in 1847, the houses were lined up along the north bank of the Llano River, and behind them the ten-acre fields stretched out in narrow rectangles, forming a *Flusshufendorf*[196] similar to the long lots of New France. A house was to be found on each of the adjacent strip farms, with no empty spaces, so the village presented, in spite of the linearity, a less strewn-out appearance than the larger settlements.[197] A similar long-lot pattern can still be observed in the Medina River Valley above and below Castroville. In both instances, the origin of the settlement form probably can be traced to the riverine survey system inherited from the Mexicans, and there seems to be little evidence for suggesting a German antecedent. Franzoseneck, a

[192] Lorenzo Castro, *Immigration from Alsace and Lorraine*, p. 6. The town lots were thirty by sixty *varas* (Sweet, *Texas*, p. 50).

[193] "Special-Karte von Texas nach der neuesten Eintheilung," inset map of Castroville.

[194] Roemer, *Texas*, pp. 276–277.

[195] Steinert, *Nordamerika vorzüglich Texas,* p. 114; Olmsted, *A Journey through Texas*, p. 276; Roemer, *Texas*, pp. 276–277.

[196] *Flusshufendorf*, a term used by students of settlement geography to describe the long-lot pattern with riverine frontage, is perhaps the best word to use here, but it should be pointed out that the Llano River was not navigable and was not a transport route.

[197] Schlecht, *Mein Ausflug nach Texas,* p. 136.

short-lived farm village near New Braunfels, had two rows of houses adjoining a large communal field.[198]

The farm village plan did not take root in Texas and was, almost from the very first, a failure. One year after the founding of New Braunfels, most of the settlers still lived in the town,[199] but some were beginning to move out onto their farms,[200] and several years later many empty houses of farmers who had left could be seen in the town.[201] By the early 1850's the transition was largely completed,[202] and most of the farms which stretched in a row for miles southwest of town along the foot of the Balcones Escarpment were inhabited by their owners.[203] A similar dispersal occurred at Fredericksburg immediately after the distribution of farm lots in 1848,[204] and in Medina County in the mid-1850's,[205] Olmsted observed several hundred Germans living on scattered farms around Castroville. The failure of the farm village system can be attributed to a number of factors. At New Braunfels and Fredericksburg, the exhaustion of natural forage in the vicinity of the town, caused both by excessive numbers of cattle[206] and unwise prairie burning,[207] led many settlers to disperse in search of better grazing areas. In addition, it soon became apparent, in the face of extremely low land prices, that the immigrants were not going to be satisfied with their small ten-acre farms, and the increasing size of farms, coupled with the continued influx of new colonists, pushed the perimeter of settlement ever farther from the town. This expansion occurred, not unexpectedly, in the fertile stream valleys which are scattered through the Hill Country, thereby accelerating the dispersal of settlement by leaving unoccupied interfluves between. The danger of Indian attack, which might have provided enough centripetal force to preserve the farm villages, was nullified in 1847 by the treaty

[198] Ostermayer, *Tagebuch einer Reise,* pp. 106–107.
[199] William A. McClintock, "Journal of a Trip through Texas and Northern Mexico in 1846–1847," *Southwestern Historical Quarterly,* 34 (1930–1931), 34.
[200] Stählen, "Neueste Nachrichten," second unnumbered page.
[201] Ostermayer, *Tagebuch einer Reise,* pp. 99–100.
[202] [Verein], *Comite-Bericht des Vereines,* pp. 32–33.
[203] Seele, "Zwei Erinnerungsbilder," p. 51; Olmsted, *A Journey through Texas,* p. 147; Ostermayer, *Tagebuch einer Reise,* p. 138.
[204] Penniger, *Fest-Ausgabe,* p. 72.
[205] Olmsted, *A Journey through Texas,* p. 278.
[206] Ostermayer, *Tagebuch einer Reise,* p. 99; Steinert, *Nordamerika vorzüglich Texas,* p. 101; Penniger, *Fest-Ausgabe,* p. 75; Moelling, *Reise-Skizzen,* pp. 370, 378.
[207] Sörgel, *Neueste Nachrichten,* p. 28; Dieudonné, *Missionary Adventures,* p. 93; Olmsted, *A Journey through Texas,* p. 147.

between the Verein leaders and the local Comanche chiefs.[208] One scholar of Texas history has maintained that the peaceful relationship between the Indians and the Germans in the early years could be attributed to their settlement in farm villages instead of scattering over the countryside and driving away the wild game as the Anglo-Americans did.[209] The early dispersal of German settlement removes any factual basis for such a claim.

Abandonment of the farm village plan left some curious relics in the cultural landscape, some of which still can be observed at present. One of the most noticeable of these is the large size of the town lots, which had originally been intended to contain entire farmsteads. In the 1870's one visitor in New Braunfels was impressed with the spacious lots, noting that they gave "everyone ample elbow room."[210] The extensive gardens found by many of the homes in the town in the last century were made possible by the large lots and resulted in considerable fruit and vegetable production by otherwise nonagricultural elements in the population, and a similar situation could be observed at Castroville.[211] In Fredericksburg still another use was made of the town lots—as sites for the so-called "Sunday Houses." Farmers who left to settle on their holdings in the surrounding rural areas kept possession of their town lots and later built small frame houses there to use when they came to Fredericksburg for weekend shopping and church-going.

As the German immigrant farmers dispersed over the countryside to occupy the fertile valleys, they established numerous unplanned communities, which betrayed little trace of their farm village heritage. These settlements differed little from those of the Anglo-Americans in the Hill Country and of the Germans farther east in Texas, and were nothing more than loose agglomerations of farmhouses interspersed by unoccupied interfluves. The Pedernales and Live Oak Creek communities, founded in the late 1840's near Fredericksburg, were among the first such settlements, and the number multiplied rapidly in the following decade. Sisterdale, in present-day Kendall County, was described in 1854 by Olmsted as a group of farm dwellings scattered up and down the valley of the Guadalupe River, within long

---

[208] Rudolph L. Biesele, "The German Settlers and the Indians in Texas, 1844–1860," *Southwestern Historical Quarterly*, 31 (1927–1928), 116–129.
[209] Gilbert Giddings Benjamin, *The Germans in Texas*, p. 127.
[210] Sweet, *Texas*, p. 39.
[211] *Ibid.*, p. 50.

FIGURE 14

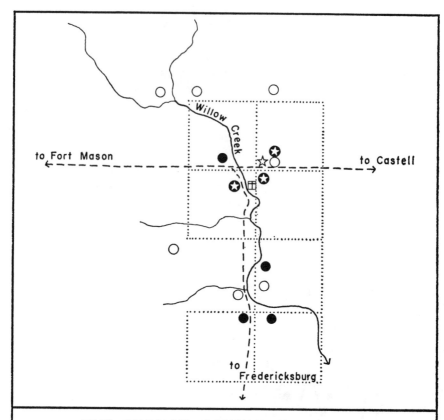

THE GERMAN COMMUNITY OF ART, MASON COUNTY, TEXAS, 1856 – 1885, A TYPICAL UNPLANNED SETTLEMENT

0   1   2

MILES

✪ Houses of original three settlers, 1856
● Houses of other immigrants before 1865
○ Houses of first-generation offspring, 1875–1885
⊞ Church and school, 1858
☆ Store, 1883
.... Original property lines
_ _ _ Wagon roads

TGJ

walking range of one another,[212] and the communities of Quihi in Medina County[213] and Art in Mason County presented a similar appearance (Figure 14). A church, a school, a store or two, and sometimes a grist mill generally were built after a number of years. In some instances, notably in the New Braunfels area, such loose clusterings of farmsteads developed as extended family communities, formed when the children of an original settler built their homes nearby.[214] Other German towns, such as Comfort and Boerne in Kendall County were planned from the very first to be inhabited by nonagricultural elements of the population.

The windmill, which was first introduced in the 1880's, brought water to the dry interfluves of the Hill Country, and in the decades that followed, many of the descendants of the original settlers left the fertile valleys to establish ranches there. This represented the final step in the transition from villages to scattered farmsteads, and it completed the expansion of the German-settled area in the western counties (Figure 7). The development of a pattern of scattered farmsteads meant that, in this respect, the German areas became indistinguishable from those occupied by Anglo-Americans, for true to their traditions, the southern settlers had dispersed over the countryside from the very beginning of their agricultural occupancy of the Hill Country.

Fields, Fences, and the Open Range

In the early years of settlement in the western counties, Germans readily adopted the system of open-range grazing which was characteristic of most parts of Texas.[215] They built only essential fences, those enclosing fields, gardens, and pens, but even so fencing was one of the major expenses of settlement.[216] In some communities, including Fredericksburg, the German pioneers resorted to communal fencing in the first critical year, in order to leave more time free for other work.[217] Each year the settlers improved and expanded their fences, and by 1849 enclosure had progressed so far in some areas around New

[212] Olmsted, *A Journey through Texas*, p. 191.

[213] *Ibid.*, p. 279.

[214] M. Whilldin (ed.), *A Description of Western Texas . . .*, p. 57.

[215] Ostermayer, *Tagebuch einer Reise*, p. 78; Santleben, *A Texas Pioneer*, p. 10; Olmsted, *A Journey through Texas*, p. 191.

[216] Ostermayer, *Tagebuch einer Reise*, p. 86.

[217] Roemer, *Texas*, p. 281; Hermes, "Erlebnisse eines deutschen Einwanderers," p. 27; Ostermayer, *Tagebuch einer Reise*, pp. 106–107.

Braunfels that little open range was left.[218] In the same year, a local
law was passed requiring that swine be kept in pens at all times,[219]
and the newspaper editor suggested that a similar restriction be placed
on milk cows, to prevent tripping over them on dark nights as they
lay sleeping in the streets.[220] To replace the grazing facilities lost
through fencing and to eliminate the straying of livestock, the New
Braunfelsers resorted to a plan which, while not uncommon in Germany, may well have been unique in American agriculture.[221] They
founded a *Hirtengesellschaft,* or pasture club, and as a group purchased grazing land at some distance from the town. Each member
brought his cattle to the communal pasture and left them, for ten cents
a head per month, in the care of hired herders.[222] Most of the settlers
who were interested in large-scale cattle raising moved away from the
New Braunfels area in the next decade to resettle in the Hill Country,
where abundant open range was still to be found, and as a result the
Hirtengesellschaft was dissolved in 1857, after functioning for eight
years.[223]

FENCES
At first, fences were built of wood, generally cedar or oak, in typically American styles. The zig-zag or worm fence was most common
in the early years,[224] though one settler described other types made
either by tying the rails to the posts with strips of leather or by resting
them on supports nailed between two side-by-side posts.[225] Pens were
often enclosed with picket fences, made by driving numerous poles
into the ground so close together as to present an almost solid wall.[226]
As late as 1859, cedar was still the preferred fencing material, but the
Germans were beginning to build fences of flat stones,[227] a style that
was to become extremely common in the following decades, so common as to add distinctiveness to the rural landscape which even today

[218] Ostermayer, *Tagebuch einer Reise,* p. 138.
[219] Steinert, *Nordamerika vorzüglich Texas,* p. 97.
[220] *Neu-Braunfelser Zeitung,* June 22, 1855, p. 2, col. 4.
[221] The uniqueness of the *Hirtengesellschaft* was based on the communal purchase of land, for pasture clubs similar to it in other respects were found in the
Midwest.
[222] *Neu-Braunfelser Zeitung,* March 11, 1853, p. 3, cols. 5–6.
[223] *Ibid.,* March 20, 1857, p. 3, col. 5.
[224] [Verein], *Comite-Bericht des Vereines,* pp. 30, 44; see also a contemporary painting by H. Lungkwitz entitled "Friedrichsburg," which is available at
the Texas State Archives, Austin.
[225] Ostermayer, *Tagebuch einer Reise,* p. 93. See also several contemporary
sketches in Seth Eastman, *A Seth Eastman Sketchbook,* pp. 53, 54.
[226] Eastman, *Sketchbook,* pp. 53, 55, 56.
[227] *Neu-Braunfelser Zeitung,* January 7, 1859, p. 3, col. 3.

can be used to identify the areas of German settlement. Outcroppings of limestone and sandstone, which abound in the area, provided ample amounts of stone. Entire families, including small children, labored for months or even years to construct stone fences on their farms, since the prohibitively high prices, ranging from 300 to 450 dollars per mile in the 1880's[228] prevented most settlers from hiring someone to do the job. By 1860 it was estimated that several hundred miles of stone fences had been built by the Germans in Comal County alone, with many more miles under construction.[229] In the Hill Country, where the open range and cattle roundups persisted into the 1870's, the stone fences were used to enclose not only fields, gardens, and corrals, but also pastures. Across the flat stream valleys, up the steep hillsides, and over the divides the Germans built them, accomplishing what no other ranchers in the entire West were willing or able to do—fencing the open range before barbed wire. The Kothmann family of southeastern Mason County claimed to be the first to enclose their entire ranch in this manner, a task which took four years, from 1873 to 1877, to complete, using stone quarried on their land.[230] At Live Oak Settlement in Gillespie County, another German enclosed twelve hundred acres with a stone fence.[231] The amount of work involved and the volume of stone moved by the German fence builders staggers the imagination, and the contemporary observer cannot help but be awed by the relics of their handiwork. The heyday of stone fence construction was brought to an abrupt end in the 1880's when barbed wire was introduced, but many miles of such fences are still in use.

In contrast to the Germans, who took great pains to enclose their land in prebarbed-wire days, the Anglo-Americans in adjacent areas apparently felt their interests were best served by the maintenance of the open range. This is understandable, since the native ranchers made extensive use of the public domain and land belonging to absentee owners. While Germans purchased huge acreages of interfluvial pasture land in the 1870's and began to enclose it, the Americans made little investment in land and continued to use the open-range system.

Farmstead Structures

The first houses of the German pioneers in the western settlements

228 Spaight, *The Resources*, pp. 68, 116.
229 *Neu-Braunfelser Zeitung,* January 7, 1859, p. 3, col. 3.
230 Raunick *et al.,* *The Kothmanns*, p. 47.
231 [Gillespie County Historical Association], *Pioneers in God's Hills*, p. 75.

were almost invariably crude structures built either of horizontally
laid logs in the American style or of poles driven vertically into the
ground. The similarity between the two groups ended there, for while
the native southerners remained in log cabins for many years before
finally replacing them with modest frame houses, the Germans regarded their initial dwellings as temporary necessities of pioneer life,
to be discarded as quickly as possible. After five or, at the most, ten
years, they built small, sturdy stone houses which, although their architectural styles were southern, displayed many construction methods
brought from Germany, including half-timbering (*Fachwerk*), casement windows, exterior plastering and whitewashing, and thatched
roofs.[232] The appearance of half-timbered construction was particularly
interesting, since it was so common in Hesse, southern Hannover, and
other source regions of the immigrants. Such houses were observed
as early as 1846 in New Braunfels, at which time many of the temporary cabins and huts of the newly arrived immigrants still existed.[233]
In April of 1847, only two houses of stone construction were to be
seen in Fredericksburg, while there were about 150 log cabins,[234] but
nine years later a German settler noted that *only* stone houses were
being built in the town.[235] Olmsted wrote that in the New Braunfels
area in the mid-1850's, log cabins were found in recently settled fringe
areas of the colony, while houses of half-timbered construction were
dominant closer to the town on farms which had been occupied
longer.[236] The houses were most commonly of the story-and-a-half
style, with open porches on the front, outside stairways, and low-
pitched roofs—obviously copied from frame houses of identical architecture which were numerous in Galveston, Indianola, Victoria, and
other Texas towns through which the Germans passed en route to
their new homeland. The floor plans varied considerably, from one-
room houses to double-pen arrangements.

In the period following the Civil War, many larger stone houses
were built by the Germans which, however, employed fewer imported

[232] For a more complete discussion of house construction, see Terry G. Jordan, "German Houses in Texas," *Landscape*, 14 (Autumn 1964), 24–26. Draw-
ings of some of the temporary early houses, as well as houses displaying imported construction methods, can be seen in Eastman, *Sketchbook*, pp. 53–57.
[233] Roemer, *Texas*, p. 118.
[234] Bracht, *Texas im Jahre 1848*, p. 266.
[235] Franz Kettner, letter to his parents in Germany, Fredericksburg, April 2,
1856, in Kettner, "Letters of a German Pioneer," *Southwestern Historical Quarterly*, 69 (1966), 471.
[236] Olmsted, *A Journey through Texas*, pp. 140–141.

construction methods. Half-timbering was abandoned, reportedly because the Germans realized that the native limestone and sandstone used as building material did not need the support of wooden beams. In a few instances, barns of stone were built, but more commonly the nonresidential farmstead structures were small, wooden buildings like those of the Anglo-Americans. After about 1880 or 1890, the Germans abandoned stone construction and began building frame houses devoid of any trace of imported methods, thus completing this aspect of their assimilation. Because of solid construction, many of the original stone and *Fachwerk* houses are still standing and in use, and their unique blend of native architecture and European construction methods will continue to be prominent in the cultural landscape of the German Hill Country for years to come.

Most of the immigrants in the western settlements came from parts of Germany where farmsteads were composed of a number of separate buildings grouped around a central courtyard, the so-called *mitteldeutsches Gehöft*. There was no suggestion whatever in the nineteenth-century literature that any effort was made by the immigrants to establish this form in the Texas colonies. Close scrutiny of recent aerial photographs likewise revealed no trace of it. It seems likely that the *mitteldeutsches Gehöft* is a form better suited to crowded farm villages than to scattered farmsteads, and this may partially explain its absence in the western German settlements.

SCALE OF OPERATION

As might be expected the Germans in the western settlements commenced farming on a very small scale. Instead of the 320 acres promised by the Verein, they received a scant 10, and the Castro colonists fared only slightly better. Early travelers were struck by the small size of the fields and farms in the western German settlements,[237] and one even described the dense concentration of ten-acre holdings near New Braunfels as being settled *"nach vaterländischer Weise,"* "in the manner of the Fatherland."[238] The immigrants expanded their farms rapidly, particularly in the areas away from the towns, attaining an average size of 166 acres by 1850 (Table 43). At the same date, however, Anglo-American yeomen in the western counties owned over two times as much as the Germans. Improved acreages, on the other hand,

---

[237] *Ibid.*, pp. 140–141.
[238] Moelling, *Reise-Skizzen*, p. 370.

TABLE 43

Western Counties: Farm Acreages, by Origins of the Population

ITEM	YEAR	German-born, no slaves	Native of German-born father	All Germans	Southern Anglo-Americans, no slaves
	1850	166	-------	-------	377[a]
Average farm	1860	156	-------	-------	?
size, in acres	1870	253	-------	-------	411
	1880	607	351	557	323
	1850	22	-------	-------	17[a]
Improved acres	1860	20	-------	-------	?
per farm	1870	23	-------	-------	23
	1880	33	19	30	33
	1850	144	-------	-------	361[a]
Unimproved	1860	136	-------	-------	?
acres per	1870	230	-------	-------	388
farm	1880	574	332	527	290
Improved acre-	1850	14%	-------	-------	4%[a]
age as a percent-	1860	14%	-------	-------	?
age of total	1870	9%	-------	-------	6%
farm size	1880	5%	5%	5%	10%

Compiled from the manuscript schedules of the United States Census. The sample counties were: 1850, Gillespie, Comal, Hays, Guadalupe; 1860 and 1880, Gillespie, Mason, Llano; 1870, Gillespie, Mason, Llano, Kerr, Blanco. The sample taken within the counties was 100 percent for 1850 and 1860; 50 percent for 1870 and 1880.

[a] Calculations based on only twenty-seven farms.

were about the same for both groups throughout the period under study.

Small scale of operation did not continue to distinguish the western German farmers, for by a steady expansion they overtook and surpassed the Anglo-Americans in value of farm production by 1870 and in farm value, farm size, and value of livestock by the following census (Tables 40, 43, 44). The decade of the 1870's was one of widespread land purchase by the Germans, attributable in part to their desire to provide an inheritance for their numerous children, and associated with their successful fencing of the range. By the 1880's it was not unusual to find Germans owning thousands of acres.[239] In contrast, the Anglo-

[239] Krueger, *Pioneer Life in Texas*, pp. 172, 186; Murray, "Home Life on

TABLE 44

*Western Counties: Value of Farm, Total Farm Production, and
Implements and Machinery, by Origins of the Population*

ITEM	YEAR	German-born, no slaves	Natives of German-born father	All Germans	Southern Anglo-Americans, no slaves
Average cash	1850	$ 676	--------	--------	$765[a]
value of	1860	$ 478	--------	--------	$900
farm	1870	$ 631	--------	--------	$792
	1880	$1500	$ 823	$1370	$736
Cash value	1850	$ 4.64	--------	--------	$2.38[a]
per acre	1860	$ 3.07	--------	--------	?
of farm	1870	$ 2.49	--------	--------	$1.93
	1880	$ 2.47	$2.34	$ 2.46	$2.28
Average value	1850	--------	--------	--------	--------
of total	1860	--------	--------	--------	--------
farm	1870	$ 550	--------	--------	$486
production	1880	$ 248	$ 169	$ 233	$176
Value of	1850	$ 79	--------	--------	$ 72[a]
implements	1860	$ 107	--------	--------	?
and machinery	1870	$ 135	--------	--------	$ 97
per farm	1880	$ 127	$ 79	$ 118	$ 51

Compiled from the manuscript schedules of the United States Census. The sample counties were: 1850, Gillespie, Comal, Hays, Guadalupe; 1860 and 1880, Gillespie, Mason, Llano; 1870, Gillespie, Mason, Llano, Kerr, Blanco. The sample taken within the counties was 100 percent for 1850 and 1860; 50 percent for 1870 and 1880.

[a] Calculations based on only twenty-seven farms.

American holdings actually decreased during this period and were scarcely more than half the size of German farms by 1880, partly a result of the influx of many new Anglo-American settlers into the area. Within the relatively short period of about thirty years, the German immigrants had overcome their initial deficiency of capital and become the largest-scale operators in the Hill Country.

MARKETS AND DEGREE OF COMMERCIALIZATION

Situated as they were on the outermost fringes of settlement far from

Early Ranches of Southwest Texas," *The Cattleman,* 25, no. 7 (1938), p. 52; Gilbert J. Jordan, *A Biographical Sketch of Ernst and Lizette Jordan,* pp. 25–26.

any markets, the early German colonies in the West held little apparent promise for the development of commercialized agriculture. The outlook was altered for the better with dramatic suddenness, and, ironically, it was precisely their isolation and westernmost location which helped the Germans capture two very important markets within a very few years after initial settlement. First came the federal troops to man the numerous forts which were built, beginning in the late 1840's, to defend the frontier against Indian attack. At the same time, two major roads were opened to the West to handle southerners bound for the gold fields of California. One of these, sometimes called the Upper Emigrant Road, ran northwest from San Antonio through the German-settled Hill Country to Fredericksburg and on beyond, passing only a few miles from the settlements in the Llano River Valley. The other road led directly west from San Antonio through the German towns of Castroville and D'Hanis in Medina County. Both civilians and military personnel moving along these roads purchased supplies from the Germans, and the record of one such transaction, in which corn was bought from the settlers at Castell in 1850, was preserved in the travel notes of John Russell Bartlett.[240] Only in the Mormon settlements in Utah was a similar disadvantage of location converted so rapidly and spectacularly to one of advantage, and like their counterparts in the Great Basin Kingdom, the Germans benefited materially from their situation on the outposts of civilization.

Near Fredericksburg the government built Fort Martin Scott in 1848, and the German farmers of the vicinity provided supplies for it almost from the very first. By 1851 the anticipated arrival of an additional company of troops at the post, coupled with the construction of a new stronghold at Fort Mason, promised the best market ever for the agricultural produce of the area,[241] and the settlers brought corn, hay, cured meat, vegetables, and butter to sell for cash or to barter for sugar and coffee.[242] Newspaper references over the decade of the 1850's indicate that the forts provided the major market for the farmers around Fredericksburg and in the Llano River Valley.[243] Additional posts were built to the west in 1852 at Fort McKavett and Fort

[240] Bartlett, *Personal Narrative*, Vol. 1, pp. 64–66.
[241] *Galveston Zeitung*, March 27, 1851, p. 3, col. 4.
[242] Murray, "Home Life on Early Ranches of Southwest Texas," *The Cattleman*, 26, no. 7 (1939), p. 34; 27, no. 7 (1940), pp. 43, 46; Raunick et al., *The Kothmanns*, p. 14.
[243] *Neu-Braunfelser Zeitung*, March 11, 1853, p. 3, col. 1; September 23, 1853, p. 2, col. 6; May 25, 1855, p. 2, col. 2; October 10, 1856, p. 2, cols. 1-2.

Chadbourne. In Medina County the Germans found a local market at Fort Lincoln, established near D'Hanis in 1849, as well as at Fort Duncan and Fort Inge, which were built in the same year some distance to the west. Several years later, in 1852, Fort Clark was located in the same vicinity and soon became the major military post of that part of Texas.

The Germans not only produced the agricultural supplies for these forts, but also hauled them to their destinations in ox-wagons, dominating the teamster industry of the entire area. German wagon drivers ranged as far east as the Gulf Coast ports and carried supplies even to the posts in far West Texas.[244] During the Civil War, the forts were left virtually unoccupied, but after peace had been established, large numbers of federal occupation troops were sent to man them and the military market was revived.[245] A major new post was established at Fort Concho in 1867, and in the same year the German language newspaper in San Antonio carried advertisements requesting agricultural supplies for the military.[246] The army often made contracts with local German businessmen, who in turn went to their countrymen-farmers to buy the needed supplies.[247] The trade with the forts declined in the 1870's and 1880's as most of the posts were closed down and abandoned.

The rise of cotton production among the Germans of the West was hampered initially by the distance to market at Galveston and New Orleans,[248] and the crop might never have attained commercial importance among them had not their remote western location almost miraculously once again been turned to advantage. For, in the late 1850's, a thriving cotton trade was begun with textile mills in northern Mexico, and the Germans were in the best position to profit from it. The possibilities of Mexican trade were recognized in the 1840's,[249] but not until 1859 was it established on a large scale, coincident with a major rise in cotton production by the German farmers of Comal

[244] G. Jordan, *A Biographical Sketch*, p. 13; R. G. Carter, *On the Border with MacKenzie* . . ., pp. 55–56; Braman, *Braman's Information*, p. 38.

[245] *Texas Almanac for 1867*, p. 110; McDanield and Taylor, *The Coming Empire*, p. 177.

[246] *Freie Presse für Texas*, July 13, 1867, p. 3, cols. 1–2.

[247] *Neu-Braunfelser Zeitung*, March 5, 1869, p. 3, col. 1; Franz Kettner, letter to his parents in Germany, Castell, August 12, 1853, in Kettner, "Letters of a German Pioneer," *Southwestern Historical Quarterly*, 69 (1966), 466.

[248] Olmsted, *A Journey through Texas*, p. 182; *Neu-Braunfelser Zeitung*, May 27, 1853, p. 2, col. 2; *ibid.*, January 7, 1859, p. 3, col. 4.

[249] Herff, *Die geregelte Auswanderung*, pp. 92–93.

County.[250] On one day in November of 1861 fourteen huge wagons, each holding twenty bales of cotton, departed from New Braunfels for the three-week trip to the mills of Saltillo. The blockade of Texas port cities by the Union fleet during the Civil War actually benefited the overland trade, since Mexico was not able to import cotton by sea during this period, and at the height of the war in 1863, the cotton transport through New Braunfels was at its greatest volume in history.[251] This profitable trade continued to prosper after the war,[252] and the trains of ox- and mule-wagons hauled countless loads before being replaced by railroads in the 1870's and 1880's.

The Anglo-American settlers in the western counties, because of their later arrival and their concentration on livestock ranching rather than commercial crop production, did not profit nearly as much as the Germans from the markets offered by the military posts, emigrant roads, and Mexican cotton mills. They were, however, the leaders in seeking out various livestock markets and in opening cattle trails. In this endeavor, the Germans simply followed their example. When the rise of large-scale beef cattle production among the western Germans began in the 1850's, they utilized well-known Anglo-American trails to drive their stock overland to sell at New Orleans and Mobile.[253] Cattle were still being taken to Louisiana as late as 1867.[254] Soon after the Civil War, southern Anglo-American ranchers began driving their livestock north across the prairies to the Kansas railhead towns, trampling out a number of well-known trails. The Hill Country Germans quickly realized the advantages of this new market opened by their American neighbors, and the streets of Kansas cow towns soon rang with the broken English of the Teutonic ranchers from Texas.[255] One branch of the Dodge City or Western Trail ran through Kendall, Gillespie, and Mason counties, providing easy access for the Germans (Figures 6 and 7). Some cattle were also driven over the Upper Emigrant Road to the Pecos Valley of New Mexico, where ranching was

[250] *Neu-Braunfelser Zeitung*, January 21, 1859, p. 3, col. 3; March 4, 1859, p. 3, col. 4.
[251] *Ibid.*, November 29, 1861, p. 3, col. 4; April 24, 1863, p. 2, col. 4.
[252] The best source on post-bellum freighting between the German settlements and Mexico is Santleben, *A Texas Pioneer*, especially pages 10, 22, 106, 114. See also *Neu-Braunfelser Zeitung*, November 5, 1869, p. 2, col. 6.
[253] *Western Texas the Australia of America*, p. 184.
[254] Raunick *et al.*, *The Kothmanns*, p. 41.
[255] *Ibid.*, p. 44; Murray, "Home Life on Early Ranches of Southwest Texas," *The Cattleman*, 26, no. 7 (1939), pp. 34–35.

rapidly expanding, and to the northern portions of Old Mexico.[256] Railroads began to open new markets for the western German settlements ten years after the close of the Civil War, and in 1875 cotton and other agricultural produce were already being hauled from New Braunfels to the head of rail construction some twenty miles to the east.[257] Shortly thereafter the iron rails reached San Antonio, and construction was begun by the Southern Pacific on a line to the west roughly paralleling the old emigrant road which had run through Medina County since gold rush days. The German citizens of Castroville refused to offer the railroad company the financial inducements it demanded, and in punishment the line was run in a semicircle around the town, nowhere approaching closer than five miles. In the Hill Country, the German settlements in Gillespie, Mason, and Llano counties were left without any railroad connections, a condition which persists to the present day.

The markets provided by the traffic on the emigrant roads, the forts, the Mexican cotton mills, the cow towns of Kansas, and the construction of railroads were quite important in encouraging commercialized agriculture among the western Germans, but other markets which developed should not be overlooked. As was pointed out earlier, the city of San Antonio furnished a local market for the sale of fresh fruit and vegetables, dairy and poultry goods, hay, corn, and wheat. Oxwagons carried agricultural produce from New Braunfels to San Antonio even before 1850, and returned laden with merchandise for the farmers of the German colony.[258] The port town of Indianola, though it lay a considerable distance away, exported by sea much agricultural produce of the western settlements in prerailroad days.[259]

The studies of Frederick Jackson Turner and some of his followers[260] have been largely responsible for the concept, still accepted by some, of frontier agriculture as being largely noncommercial. They have outlined a number of neat stages through which newly occupied areas supposedly progress in their economic development, beginning with

[256] Raunick *et al., The Kothmanns*, p. 42.
[257] *Wöchentliche Texas Post*, December 2, 1875, p. 1, cols. 4–5.
[258] Dieudonné, *Missionary Adventures*, p. 36.
[259] Edward King, *The Southern States of North America: A Record of Journeys in . . . Texas . . .*, Vol. 1, p. 145.
[260] Frederick Jackson Turner, *The Frontier in American History*; Frank L. Owsley, "The Pattern of Migration and Settlement on the Southern Frontier," *Journal of Southern History*, 11 (1945), 147–176.

the first pioneers, who relied mainly on a subsistence economy based on herding, progressing through a second stage of semisubsistence crop farmers, and culminating in a stage characterized by commercial crop production. There seems little doubt that the southern Anglo-Americans in the western counties did rely on livestock ranching as their major livelihood from the very first, but among the Germans the theoretical sequence was totally lacking. Even in the early years of settlement, they were engaged in commercial agriculture centered on crops. In fact, the expected sequence was completely reversed, in that livestock husbandry gradually increased in importance until in the present century, it largely eclipsed crop production. The Turnerans might well argue that the Germans were an unusual exception, an alien group not typical of the American frontier, and as far as the southern United States was concerned, they would be correct. In the North, however, immigrants directly from Europe were quite active as pioneers, and it would be most interesting to find out whether they conformed to the stereotype.

INTENSITY AND PRODUCTIVITY

Farming Methods, or Input of Labor and Capital

The cultural heritage of intensive agriculture which the Germans brought with them from Europe manifested itself in a number of ways in the new homeland, but at the same time, many of their traditional intensive farming practices proved unsatisfactory and were modified to meet local conditions or discarded altogether. One of the most interesting expressions of the imported intensive methods was found in the spacing of individual plants in the fields. Both cotton and corn were more closely planted by the Germans in the early years, but in this instance they were not well served by their European heritage, for, as one observer noted, "the greatest mistake which the Germans . . . customarily make is to attempt to plant [corn] too thickly, which . . . can result in crop failure."[261] Olmsted reported, in a similar vein, that in the German cotton fields around New Braunfels the stalks stood closer together than was the case in Anglo-American areas "and were of less extraordinary size."[262] Experience quickly taught the immigrants to adopt a wider spacing, and as early as 1849 corn was being

[261] Bracht, *Texas im Jahre 1848*, p. 47.
[262] Olmsted, *A Journey through Texas*, p. 141.

planted at a more normal interval of four feet.[263] In some instances, the Germans satisfied their natural inclination by planting melons between the rows of corn.[264]

The gardens and field crops were cultivated with Old World meticulousness, and travelers noted that "the more clean and complete tillage they had received contrasted favorably with the patches of corn-stubble, overgrown with crab-grass" of the "poor whites" and slaves. Most of the German cotton fields "looked as if they had been judiciously cultivated, and had yielded a fine crop, differing, however, from that we had noticed on the plantations the day before, in this circumstance —the picking had been entirely completed, and that with care and exactness, so that none of the cotton . . . had been left to waste."[265] One of the original German settlers at Comfort in Kendall County described how, in the early days of cotton cultivation there in the 1870's, everything which might damage the appearance of the cotton, including each dry leaf, was carefully removed,[266] and another farmer near Fredericksburg recalled the German women removing dirt from the cotton bolls with their lips as they picked it.[267]

Intensive methods were revealed in other aspects of agriculture in the western counties, including the expenditures on implements, machinery, and fences, in which Germans far outranked the Anglo-Americans (Tables 44 and 45). In soil conservation, too, the Germans appear to have been leaders, for quite early some of them in Gillespie County had built stone retaining walls to retard erosion,[268] and still today small mounds of earth placed across sloping dirt roads to prevent erosion in the ruts are so closely identified with the German population of the Hill Country as to be called "dutchmen's dumps."

The unreliability of the precipitation in the western German settlements led some of the early settlers to consider the possibilities of irrigation to maintain their intensive farming heritage. In the 1850's an elaborate plan to divert water through a network of ditches onto the gardens of New Braunfels was proposed,[269] and a similar system was

---

[263] Ostermayer, *Tagebuch einer Reise*, p. 90.
[264] Waugh, *Castro-ville*, p. 53.
[265] Olmsted, *A Journey through Texas*, pp. 140–141.
[266] Lohmann, *Comfort*, p. 34.
[267] [Gottfried Ottmers Reunion Committee], *The History of the Gottfried Ottmers Family*, p. 68.
[268] *Ibid.*, p. 18.
[269] *Neu-Braunfelser Zeitung*, May 8, 1857, p. 3, col. 5.

TABLE 45

Fence Expenditures in Gillespie, Mason, and Llano Counties, 1880,
by Origins of the Population

	Average amount spent on fences during previous year	Percentage reporting fence expenditures
German-born	$108	42%
Natives of German-born fathers	$ 76	35%
All Germans	$103	41%
Southern Anglo-Americans	$ 78	28%

Source: Manuscript census schedules of agriculture and population.

actually constructed to serve the German gardens of San Antonio.[270] Shortly before the Civil War, three German farmers near Fredericksburg used the water of a local creek to irrigate their fields before a restraining order was issued on behalf of settlers further downstream.[271] Intensity through the application of irrigation water was an unsatisfactory solution, not only because of legal restrictions, but also because the flow of Hill Country streams was irregular and of inadequate volume. Instead, the Germans turned to dry-farming methods, which were outlined by one farmer in the *Neu-Braunfelser Zeitung* in 1859, a date which places the Texas Germans among the first in the western United States to make such experiments. The methods, all of which were designed to conserve and utilize fully the existing soil moisture, included (1) autumnal plowing, (2) deep plowing, (3) early and deep planting, (4) widely spaced planting, (5) weed removal, and (6) loosening of the soil between rows.[272] The rapid shift to dry-farming practices is remarkable in view of the fact that several of these methods represented complete reversals of European traditions. Closely allied to dry farming was the selection, generally by trial and error, of crops best suited to semi-arid lands, and experiment was the essence of the crop association in the western German settlements for many decades. In the drought year of 1859, the previously mentioned German who tested

[270] *Freie Presse für Texas*, May 16, 1867, p. 2, col. 2.
[271] Biggers, *German Pioneers in Texas*, p. 113.
[272] *Neu-Braunfelser Zeitung*, April 22, 1859, p. 3, cols. 3–4; Walter Prescott Webb, *The Great Plains*, pp. 367–368.

110 varieties of wheat in small patches on his farm found that only seven did well.[273]

The adoption of dry-farming practices was only one of the ways in which the German settlers broke with tradition. Another notable departure was, as had been the case in the eastern settlements, an abandonment of manuring, in keeping with advice offered at the outset of farming in the mid-1840's.[274] In 1854 a German at Fredericksburg wrote that no dung had yet been applied to the fields there, after eight years of cultivation, adding that no one knew how long it would continue to be unnecessary.[275] A similar report was made five years later,[276] and in the mid-1870's a traveler in the German area around Boerne was told that, in twenty years of farming, the lands had "never received an ounce of fertilizer from the tillers."[277] If the census returns for 1880 can be trusted, virtually no farmers, either Anglo-Americans or Germans, made expenditures for fertilizer.

A similar neglect was detectable in the care of livestock, perhaps because the poor quantity of the cattle, sheep, and hogs in the first several decades did not warrant intensive care. The losses of livestock to predators were quite high, as is evidenced by the German farmer in the Llano River Valley who lost almost one-third of his sheep to wolves in the early 1850's.[278] As late as 1880, the losses continued to be considerable, and there was no apparent difference between Germans and Anglo-Americans in this respect (Table 46). There were, however, some efforts made by the Germans to protect and care for their livestock. The unique *Hirtengesellschaft* at New Braunfels with its hired herders has already been discussed, as has the employment of shepherds to guard the large flocks of sheep. Olmsted mentioned one German in Medina County who had provided both winter shelter and feed for his three hundred sheep, and contrasted him favorably with an Anglo-American rancher who had lost fifteen hundred head during recent "northers."[279] Feed was generally given to work animals and dairy cows, and some of the Germans in Mason County fattened beef cattle and hogs on corn and cooked pumpkin before slaughtering.[280]

[273] *Neu-Braunfelser Zeitung*, August 12, 1859, p. 3, col. 2.
[274] Schütz, *Texas*, p. 226.
[275] *Neu-Braunfelser Zeitung*, February 10, 1854, p. 2, col. 6.
[276] *Ibid.*, August 12, 1859, p. 3, col. 2.
[277] McDanield and Taylor, *The Coming Empire*, p. 138.
[278] *Neu-Braunfelser Zeitung*, September 23, 1853, p. 2, col. 6.
[279] Olmsted, *A Journey through Texas*, p. 259.
[280] Murray, "Home Life on Early Ranches of Southwest Texas," *The Cattleman*, 27, no. 7 (1940), pp. 46–47.

German ranchers were apparently some of the first to own improved breeds of livestock. Purebred Durham (Shorthorn) bulls were being purchased in the early 1870's, and by the middle of the decade Herefords, which were to become dominant, began to appear.[281] The Germans were able to concentrate on improved stock about a decade earlier than most Anglo-Americans as a result of their lead in fencing.

Agricultural Clubs

The formation of societies devoted to agriculture must certainly be regarded as an expression of a desire to improve farming methods, and the Germans of the western settlements founded many such clubs, including the first ones in the entire state of Texas (Figure 12). At New Braunfels, the Acker- und Gartenbau-Verein was created in 1852, and it was followed within two years by similar societies at Fredericksburg, Live Oak Creek, and Pedernales, all in Gillespie County,[282] The New Braunfels club offered prizes for superior crops as early as 1854, and at the same date Olmsted reported that it had spent twelve hundred dollars in a single year to introduce new trees and plants.[283] Nor were livestock excluded, as is indicated by the formation of the Verein zum Schutze und zur Beförderung der Viehzucht, or Society for the Protection and Promotion of Animal Husbandry, at New Braunfels, which included among its purposes the tracing of lost livestock.[284] In addition, county-wide agricultural societies were established by the Germans of Gillespie and Medina counties. Among the Anglo-Americans, such clubs were much less numerous and did not begin to appear until the late 1870's.

Productivity, or Output

The more intensive farming methods of the Germans seem to have rewarded them with higher productivity than the Anglo-Americans. It was reported, for example, that the Germans around New Braunfels in ante-bellum days produced more cotton to the acre and that it brought

---

[281] *Ibid.*, 27, no. 7 (1940), p. 47; 26, no. 12 (1940), p. 48; 26, no. 11 (1940), pp. 28–29.

[282] *Neu-Braunfelser Zeitung*, November 19, 1852, p. 2, col. 4; January 20, 1854, p. 4, col. 2; January 27, 1854, p. 3, col. 3; February 10, 1854, p. 3, col. 1.

[283] *Ibid.*, November 3, 1854, p. 1, col. 3; Olmsted, *A Journey through Texas*, pp. 178–179.

[284] *Wöchentliche Texas Post*, December 2, 1875, p. 1, cols. 4–5; *Neu-Braunfelser Zeitung*, May 20, 1859, p. 3, cols. 2–3.

one to two cents per pound more than slave cotton at the Galveston market, on account of its greater cleanliness.[285] Cotton sent to New Orleans in 1859 was classified "very good."[286] The census of 1880 was the first to list acreages of crops as well as volume of production, and it would have offered the only chance of comparing statistically the yields obtained by farmers of different origin, but unfortunately this was one of the most severe drought years on record in the western counties. Yields were so low as to make comparisons of no value. The previous census, 1870, represented a good year climatically, and it offers evidence for the belief that German farms were more productive, in that a greater average value of production was reported, in spite of the fact that the landholdings of the immigrants were smaller (Table 44), resulting in a value of production per acre almost twice as great (Table 47). Further suggestion of greater productivity on German

TABLE 46

Cattle Died, Strayed, or Stolen in Gillespie, Llano, and Mason Counties, 1880, by Origins of the Population

	Total live cattle	Number died, strayed, or stolen in previous year	Percentage died, strayed, or stolen
German-born	15,693	1,504	10%
Natives of German-born fathers	3,021	374	12%
All Germans	18,714	1,878	10%
Southern Anglo-Americans	14,649	1,537	10%

Source: Manuscript census schedules of agriculture and population.

farms is made by a comparison of the average amount of wool obtained from each sheep (Table 48).

In this land of unreliable rainfall, labor in the fields was not always rewarded with bountiful harvests, and in some years almost total crop

[285] Olmsted, *A Journey through Texas*, p. 182; Frederick Law Olmsted, *The Cotton Kingdom*, Vol. 2, p. 263; Hinton Rowan Helper, *Compendium of the Impending Crisis of the South*, p. 144; Ophia D. Smith, "A Trip to Texas in 1855," *Southwestern Historical Quarterly*, 59 (1955–1956), 36.

[286] *Neu-Braunfelser Zeitung*, January 7, 1859, p. 3, col. 3.

failure occurred. Drought, the great equalizer, was an all-too-frequent visitor, striking German and non-German alike. The variability of yields of the three major crops, corn, wheat, and cotton, has been summarized in Table 49.

FARM LABOR AND MACHINERY

Slavery

Out of 130 German farmers in Gillespie, Comal, and Guadalupe counties in 1850, not a single one owned slaves. Ten years later, the same was true of all 377 Germans in Gillespie, Mason, and Llano counties, while 11 percent of the 195 southern Anglo-Americans in the same area had Negroes.[287] The total absence of slaves among the Germans in the western counties attracted the attention of many observers, and their free-labor system was publicized throughout much of the United

TABLE 47

Value of Production per Acre in Gillespie, Mason, Llano, Blanco, and Kerr Counties, 1870, by Origins of the Population

	Value of all farm production per acre
German-born	$2.18
Southern Anglo-Americans	$1.18

Source: Manuscript census schedules of agriculture and population.

TABLE 48

Productivity in Wool Production in Gillespie, Mason, and Llano Counties, 1880, by Origins of the Population

	Weight per fleece
German-born	5.2 lbs.
Natives of German-born fathers	4.7 lbs.
All Germans	5.1 lbs.
Southern Anglo-Americans	4.1 lbs.

Source: Manuscript census schedules of agriculture and population.

[287] Manuscript census schedules of agriculture and population, 1850 and 1860.

TABLE 49

Yields of Selected Crops on German Farms in the Western Counties,
1850–1880

Crop	Reputed yields in good years*	Reputed yields in average years	Census reports of yields in the drought year 1879
Corn, bushels per acre	50–70	25–40	3
Wheat, bushels per acre	40–50	15–30	4
Cotton, bales per acre	1–1 1/2	1/2–3/4	1/5

Sources: Manuscript census schedules of agriculture and population, Gillespie, Mason, and Llano counties, 1880; numerous and diverse other source materials, including traveler accounts, letters, and newspaper reports.
* The reputed yields in good years were remarkably high and may well have been overly imbued with the enthusiasm of local pride.

States and western Europe.[288] Such reports, coupled with the previously mentioned antislavery proclamation made by the German intellectuals at San Antonio in 1854, aroused the suspicion and distrust of Anglo-Americans. These feelings were intensified by abolitionist editorials in the German "Forty-Eighter" newspaper, the *San Antonio Zeitung*, which were written in English for perusal by the Americans.[289] The sentiments of the native southern Texans toward the Germans were well expressed by an editorial in the Know-Nothing *Texas State Times* in 1855, which charged that

the Germans have departed from every rule of propriety and from every shadow of that love of their adopted country by which they should have been actuated, and gone astray after the teachings and bubbles held up to them by traitors and this they cannot deny. Their famous "platform convention" of San Antonio is the first stride towards treason that came before the public eye.[290]

The bulk of the German population at once began an effort to disasso-

[288] *London News* as quoted in the *Texas State Gazette*, May 15, 1858, p. 2, col. 5; *New York Daily Tribune,* January 4, 1856, p. 3, col. 4; Olmsted, *A Journey through Texas,* pp. 140-142 and *Cotton Kingdom,* Vol. 2, pp. 266-267; Helper, *Compendium,* p. 144.
[289] Sister Paul McGrath, *Political Nativism in Texas 1825–1860,* p. 92.
[290] *Texas State Times* (Austin), June 16, 1855, as quoted in McGrath, *Political Nativism,* pp. 93–94.

ciate itself from the pronouncements of the 1854 convention and the
San Antonio Zeitung. A meeting of Germans was held in a town near
New Braunfels, and the resulting resolution not only condemned the
Zeitung editorials, but added that "we recommend to our German
countrymen, to discountenance and suppress all attempts to disturb the
institution of slavery—upon which is founded the prosperity and hap-
piness of our Southern Country . . . ."[291] This very likely represented an
exaggeration of the real feelings of most Germans, and might best be
viewed as a desperate attempt to offset the damage done at San Antonio. It was, rather, probably the case that the majority of the western
Germans preferred not to own slaves, in keeping with their heritage of
family labor. From this it does not follow that they, as a group, were
antislavery and harbored abolitionist sentiments, as some scholars have
claimed.[292] Unlike their countrymen settled farther east in Texas, who
were by virtue of their location in an area of slave-cotton economy con-
fronted with the necessity of being for or against slavery, the Germans
of the western counties were on the frontier, where the "peculiar institution" was less of an issue. Olmsted made what was, perhaps, the most
accurate appraisal of the western Germans when, in 1854, he wrote that
"few of them concern themselves with the theoretical right or wrong of
the institution, and while it does not interfere with their own liberty or
progress, are careless of its existence."[293] The abolitionist image at-
tached to the Germans by some contemporary observers and modern
scholars was the result of the erroneous application of the beliefs of a
small minority of vociferous "Forty-Eighter" intellectuals to the immigrant population as a whole.[294] The German peasant of the nineteenth
century was not a politically oriented being, and nothing could distort
the picture more than to depict the average Texas German farmer in the
western settlements as an active abolitionist.

The only real decision the Germans had to make was whether or
not to support secession and the Confederate cause. Much evidence
has been presented by various scholars to document the presence of

[291] *Texas State Gazette,* July 25, 1855, as quoted in McGrath, *Political Nativism,* pp. 94–95.
[292] Biggers, *German Pioneers in Texas,* pp. 50, 51, 57; Benjamin, *The Germans in Texas,* p. 90; Charles W. Ramsdell, "The Natural Limits of Slavery
Expansion," *Mississippi Valley Historical Review,* 16 (1929), 159.
[293] Olmsted, *A Journey through Texas,* p. 432.
[294] One writer has been so far misled as to state that *most* Texas German immigrants were political refugees of the 1848 revolutions: Robert W. Shook,
"The Battle of the Nueces, August 10, 1862," *Southwestern Historical Quarterly,* 66 (1962–1963), 31.

unionist sentiment among the Germans of some of the western settlements,[295] and there can be little doubt that such feelings were strong
in the frontier counties of Gillespie and present-day Kendall. The German inhabitants of Gillespie County voted almost unanimously against
secession in the 1861 referendum, and the results in heavily German-
ized Medina County also indicated strong opposition to withdrawal
from the Union (Table 50). Two incorrect conclusions have been
drawn from these facts. First, it has been inferred that the western Germans voted in a bloc against secession,[296] a claim refuted by the emphat-
ic prosecession majority recorded in Comal, the most thoroughly German of all the western counties. The *Neu-Braunfelser Zeitung,* one of
the most influential German-language newspapers in Texas, supported
secession and was doubtlessly a contributing factor to the yes-vote in
Comal County. Adjacent Guadalupe County, which had a sizable German element, showed a similar anti-union vote. The overwhelming re-
jection of secession in Gillespie County, while expressive of unionist
sentiment, should nevertheless be viewed in proper context, for to these
Germans on the westernmost frontier, secession meant war, war meant
the withdrawal of troops from the local military posts, and that in turn
meant the loss of a major market for agricultural produce as well as
the removal of protection against the Comanche Indians, who had
proven to be most unfriendly in the half-decade before 1860. Such difficulties did not face the Germans of Comal and Guadalupe counties.
    The second incorrect conclusion, or better, presumption, has been
that the sizeable unionist vote in western counties such as Burnet,
Uvalde, Travis, Bandera, and Llano has been attributed to the "heavy
German population" there,[297] while in fact the manuscript census population schedules reveal that none of these counties had significant
numbers of Germans in 1860. It was the case, rather, that a number of
non-German western counties voted against secession, perhaps an indication of the lack of involvement felt by many frontiersmen toward the
eastern conflict (Table 50). Anglo-American unionist sentiment appears to have been strongest among the slaveless yeomen from the

[295] Frank H. Smyrl, "Unionism in Texas, 1856-1861," *Southwestern Historical
Quarterly,* 68 (1964–1965), 172–195; Claude Elliott, "Union Sentiment in Texas
1861–1865," *ibid.,* 50 (1946–1947), 449–477; Floyd F. Ewing, Jr., "Origins
of Unionist Sentiment on the West Texas Frontier," *West Texas Historical Association Year Book,* 32 (1956), 21–29.
[296] Shook, "The Battle of the Nueces," pp. 31–32; Ewing, "Origins of Union
Sentiment," p. 22; Smyrl, "Unionism in Texas," p. 195.
[297] Ewing, "Origins of Union Sentiment," p. 28.

TABLE 50

The Vote on Secession in Selected Texas Counties, 1861

	Vote for secession	Vote against secession	Percentage of votes against secession
Predominantly German Counties			
Comal	239	86	26%
Gillespie	16	398	96%
Medina	140	207	60%
	395	691	64%
Mixed Counties with Large German Populations			
Bexar	827	709	46%
Blanco	86	170	66%
Guadalupe	314	22	7%
Kerr	76	57	43%
Mason	2	75	97%
	1,305	1,033	44%
Predominantly Non-German Counties			
Bandera	33	32	49%
Burnet	159	248	61%
Hays	166	115	41%
Llano	134	72	35%
Travis	450	704	61%
Uvalde	16	76	83%
	958	1,247	57%

Source: Ernest W. Winkler (ed.), *Journal of the Secession Convention of Texas 1861* (Austin: State Library, 1912), pp. 88–90.

Upper South who dominated the population of much of western and northern Texas.

The split evident within the western German population on the secession issue was carried over into the war period. Comal County Germans contributed three companies of troops for the Confederate Army, but in Gillespie and adjacent counties, there was active resistance to conscription.[298] The reluctance to serve in the military was motivated at least in part by the unwillingness of the Germans on the frontier to leave their homes and families unprotected, and numerous local volunteer guard units were founded in and around Fredericksburg to circumvent the draft. Confederate officials viewed this action with alarm, and troops were dispatched to Gillespie County in 1862 to maintain order. Regrettably, one group of German irregulars became involved in a shooting scrape with the Confederate soldiers, and this clash, generously dubbed the Battle of the Nueces, resulted in the death or capture of nearly every German participant.[299] In the period preceding and following this bloodletting, which took place in August of 1862, numerous atrocities were committed against the German population of the Fredericksburg area by what amounted to an occupation force. The bitterness which these repressions engendered was still detectable over fifty years later.[300] The Germans of Comal County, by reason of their open support of the Confederacy, were spared such persecution. Their loyalty to the southern cause was probably not an expression of support for slavery, because this institution was of little concern or importance to them, but rather an indication of allegiance to their adopted country, which, for reasons beyond their control, had become involved in a war.

Family Labor

Above all, the labor on German farms was a family affair, with women and children joining the men in the fields. One traveler about 1870 was astonished to report that near New Braunfels he had "actually seen a German woman holding the plow drawn by six pair of cattle, while her little son, not more than nine or ten years old, drove the same," adding that "it is a common thing among these people to behold women toiling in the field."[301] Looking from the window of his moving stagecoach, an Englishman witnessed a similar scene several years later, noting that "the women have been afield, ploughing with the reins round their necks and the plough handles grasped in their strong hands," and as it was late in the day, "the German families, mother, father, and the

---

[298] The best source on conditions in Gillespie County is Elliott, "'Union Sentiment in Texas."
[299] For a description of the battle, see Shook, "The Battle of the Nueces."
[300] Biggers, *German Pioneers in Texas*, pp. 57–59; *Fredericksburg Standard*, Centennial Edition, May 1, 1946, sec. 7, pp. 1, 7, 8.
[301] Sweet, *Texas*, p. 40.

whole gamut of children, from four to fourteen, are coming in from work."[302] German women did much of the cotton-picking, and could also be found building stone fences.[303] To judge from the surprised comments of visitors to the German settlements, white females and children were not often seen doing field work among the Anglo-Americans.

Hired Labor

In spite of the fact that most farm labor was supplied by the immediate family, hired help played an important role as early as 1850, when laborers at New Braunfels were paid from fifty cents to one dollar a day, or even as little as eight to fifteen dollars a month.[304] As the capital resources of the immigrants increased, hired labor became more common, and by 1870 a much higher percentage of Germans reported employment of farm workers than the Anglo-Americans, although the average wage was much lower, not equalling that of the Americans until a decade later (Table 51). Not only were Germans active as employers, but also as employees. In a duplication of the procedure observed in the eastern settlements, newly arrived immigrants often worked for several years on the farms of Germans already well established, thereby accumulating both capital and experience. Their tasks were varied, including cutting fence wood, digging gardens, or tending flocks of sheep. Some of the immigrants hired out to George W. Kendall, the Anglo-American sheep-raiser, who had all extra labor on his ranch done by Germans.[305] In 1880 German-born hired workers were observed by census takers in the cotton fields of Gillespie, Medina, Blanco, Bexar, and Comal counties—that is, in nearly all of the western settlements.[306]

Farm Implements and Machinery

In 1846 Prince von Solms-Braunfels advised prospective settlers in Germany who were considering coming to his colony to bring along

[302] King, *The Southern States*, p. 144.
[303] [Ottmers Reunion Committee], *History*, pp. 60, 68; Ostermayer, *Tagebuch einer Reise*, p. 92.
[304] Ostermayer, *Tagebuch einer Reise*, p. 87; Kromer, *Die Amerikafahrt*, p. 41; Olmsted, *A Journey through Texas*, p. 180.
[305] Olmsted, *A Journey through Texas*, p. 183.
[306] Loughridge (ed.), "Report on the Cotton Production of the State of Texas," p. 161.

TABLE 51

*Employment of Farm Laborers in the Western Counties, 1870
and 1880, by Origins of the Population*

Group	Average wages per farm in previous year	Percentage of farms reporting hired help	Average wages per farm in previous year	Percentage of farms reporting hired help
German-born	$ 63	57%	$86	31%
Natives of German-born fathers	--------	--------	$44	36%
All Germans	--------	--------	$77	32%
Southern Anglo-Americans	$147	27%	$77	13%

Source: Manuscript census schedules of agriculture and population, Gillespie, Llano, Mason, Blanco, and Kerr counties, 1870; Gillespie, Llano, and Mason counties, 1880.

wagons, all instruments needed for garden and vineyard cultivation, complete harness outfits, plows, and harrows. Both heavy plows, such as were used in northern Germany, to break the prairie sod, and light plows for subsequent use were recommended.[307] An early settler at New Braunfels echoed the sentiments of the prince, and suggested that his friends in Germany bring plowshares, scythes, sickles, hoes, manure forks—in short, everything they possibly could, to avoid having to rely on American-made implements, which he condemned for their poor quality.[308] Still, the space restrictions on most immigrant ships did not allow large-scale importation of farm tools, and the new settlers had to purchase most of what they needed after arriving. One colonist wrote in the first year that he had bought a wagon for sixty dollars and a plow for ten.[309] Among the immigrants were many who were skilled as craftsmen, and it was not long before they were manufacturing farm implements in the new homeland. By the late 1840's typical German *Leiterwagen*, farm wagons with ladder-like sides, could be seen in the streets of Fredericksburg,[310] and several years later New Braunfels

[307] Solms-Braunfels, *Texas*, pp. 97, 110–111.
[308] Kordül, *Der sichere Führer*, pp. 291–292.
[309] *Ibid.*, p. 287.
[310] Such a wagon was depicted by an artist who visited the town in 1849: Eastman, *Sketchbook*, p. 55.

188 GERMAN SEED IN TEXAS SOIL

alone had seven wagon-makers.[311] Breaking-plows sold for as little as sixteen dollars in the mid-1850's.[312]

Farm machinery had been virtually unknown to the German farmers in Europe, and they arrived in the United States at a time when American ingenuity was just beginning to revolutionize agricultural production with many new labor-saving inventions. Texas, like the remainder of the South, did not benefit as much from the development of farm machinery as other sections of the country, partly because many of the new inventions were designed for crops not common in the southern states. The wheat-raising Germans, however, could and did benefit from this mechanical revolution, and as early as 1854 a few of the Hill Country farmers had begun to purchase threshers to use in grain farming,[313] although machinery was still uncommon some twenty years later.[314] Large-scale adoption of farm machinery did not occur until the mid-1870's, at which time an unusual burst of activity was noted in the implement and machinery trade.[315] At about the same date, a traveler observed mechanical reapers and mowers, cultivators, and harrows on the farm of one Hill Country German, noting that he used many of the most improved implements.[316] A few years later, it was estimated that the Germans of Gillespie County owned some thirty threshing machines.[317] Census figures indicate that Germans were investing far more capital in farm implements and machinery than were the Anglo-Americans, almost 250 percent more by 1880 (Table 44).

TENURE AND LOCATIONAL STABILITY

The first Germans to settle in the western counties, in both the Castro and Verein colonies, received grants of land as part of the agreement under which they immigrated. In Castro's settlements, these holdings were quite modest in size, not exceeding 40 acres, but the Verein promised 160 acres to single men and 320 to the heads of families. When it became apparent that the lands of the Fisher-Miller Grant were too remote for immediate occupancy, the Verein purchased tracts at the

[311] Olmsted, *A Journey through Texas*, p. 142.
[312] Franz Kettner, letter to his parents in Germany, Fredericksburg, April 23, 1855, in Kettner, "Letters of a German Pioneer," *Southwestern Historical Quarterly*, 69 (1966), 468.
[313] Olmsted, *A Journey through Texas*, p. 195.
[314] McDanield and Taylor, *The Coming Empire*, pp. 152–153.
[315] *Wöchentliche Texas Post*, December 2, 1875, p. 1, cols. 4–5.
[316] Whilldin (ed.), *A Description of Western Texas*, p. 80.
[317] W. G. Kingsbury, *Beschreibung von Süd-, West- und Mittel-Texas*, p. 4.

present sites of New Braunfels and Fredericksburg and distributed them in ten-acre plots at no charge. The larger holdings of the immigrants in the Fisher-Miller Grant were legally voided when it was discovered that the Verein had no title to the land there, but the government of the state of Texas by special act restored title to the individual German settlers in the early 1850's. Most of the holdings of 160 and 320 acres were never settled by their German owners, because of their remoteness, and instead the scrip were sold, often for as little as forty dollars.[318] In one guidebook of the mid-1850's, forty-seven such grants were listed for sale by Germans.[319] Since the 10-acre farms were considered inadequate, most immigrants were obliged to acquire additional land on their own initiative, and those Germans who arrived after the collapse of the Verein received no free land.

There were a number of procedures by which immigrants with little or no capital resources could become landowners. As was pointed out earlier, many worked as hired agricultural laborers until they had adequate funds to buy their own farms. Some rented land and purchased it out of the profits they made,[320] and still others, who were skilled at some trade, earned the needed capital by practicing their crafts, which were much in demand, for a number of years.[321] A large number of immigrants temporarily became teamsters to make enough money to buy land, and, as mentioned previously, Germans dominated the freighting industry in their part of Texas.

Whatever the methods used, the Germans rapidly acquired the funds necessary for purchasing their farms, for by 1850 over 90 percent in Comal, Gillespie, and Guadalupe counties owned land. Throughout the period under study, the German farmers of the western settlements maintained an extremely high rate of ownership, far higher than that of their southern Anglo-American counterparts in the same area (Table 52), many of whom were landless livestock raisers utilizing the public domain.[322] The purchase of land was facilitated by the low prices asked in the early years, which ranged as low as $1.50 per acre around New Braunfels in 1848. In the same vicinity five years later, prices had risen to $5 or $10 per acre, but up in the Hill Country, land remained quite cheap. Near Fredericksburg the price was only $1 per

---

[318] G. Jordan, *Biographical Sketch*, p. 16.
[319] J. De Cordova, *The Texas Immigrant and Traveller's Guide Book*, pp. 39–42.
[320] Amand Goegg, *Ueberseeische Reisen*, p. 136.
[321] Ostermayer, *Tagebuch einer Reise*, p. 84.
[322] Manuscript census schedules of population, 1860 and 1870.

acre in 1855.[323] A settler in Mason County paid as little as $.35 at the same date and only $.75 for similar land twenty years later.[324]

Closely associated with the greater interest shown by the Germans in land purchase was their stability or tendency to remain settled in one place and impregnate the cultural landscape with an appearance of permanency.[325] It is true that most of the original settlers at New

TABLE 52

Land Tenure in the Western Counties,
by Origins of the Population

| | Percentage owning land | | | |
	1850[a]	1860[b]	1870[b]	1880[b]
German-born	91%	92%	90%	97%
Natives of German-born fathers	--------	--------	--------	90%
All Germans	--------	--------	--------	96%
Southern Anglo-Americans	77%	41%	40%	75%

Source: Manuscript census schedules of agriculture and population.
[a] Comal, Gillespie, Guadalupe, and Hays counties.
[b] Gillespie, Mason, and Llano counties.

Braunfels later departed to move up to the Hill Country,[326] but it should be borne in mind that they regarded their stay in that town as a temporary stopover en route to the lands promised them farther inland. Once the German immigrant found a piece of property to his liking, he generally remained there. This trait was discussed by one Anglo-American writer in the 1880's, who noted that the Germans in Medina County were so disinclined to sell land that there was hardly a quotable market price available for property in that area.[327] Another observer in the Hill Country a few years earlier chided his fellow Anglo-Americans for being "prepared to pull up stakes and depart any time," noting in con-

[323] Franz Kettner, letters to his parents in Germany, Castell, August 12, 1853, and Fredericksburg, April 23, 1855, in Kettner, "Letters of a German Pioneer," *Southwestern Historical Quarterly,* 69 (1966), 465, 468.
[324] G. Jordan, *Biographical Sketch,* pp. 16, 25.
[325] Bracht, *Texas im Jahre 1848,* p. 107; Ostermayer, *Tagebuch einer Reise,* p. 174.
[326] Olmsted, *A Journey through Texas,* p. 177.
[327] Spaight, *The Resources,* p. 219.

trast that "when the German stops, he is fully determined to make things suit him, and immediately goes to work to that end and accomplishes it."[328] An English-speaking resident of Mason County reported in the mid-1860's that "the Germans generally live upon their own lands, and hence are more disposed to improve them.[329] The tendency to buy land and hold onto it allowed Germans to displace much of the American population of Guadalupe County, to the east of New Braunfels, by the turn of the century, a process already underway in the 1850's.[330] The stability of the rural population enabled the Germans to mark their striving for permanency indelibly on the countryside. The ranches of the Hill Country Germans, with their stone houses and mile upon mile of stone fences had an air of permanency about them that was totally missing in the Anglo-American areas. Upon observing Castroville in the 1850's, one traveler was moved to comment that "it did not present an appearance of rapid improvement, but there was that about it which bespoke permanency and prosperity."[331]

[328] McDanield and Taylor, *The Coming Empire,* p. 193.
[329] James E. Ranck, "Mason County," *The Texas Almanac for 1867* . . . , p. 136.
[330] Olmsted, *A Journey through Texas,* p. 184.
[331] Reid, *Reid's Tramp,* p. 84.

Chapter Six

Conclusion: The Importance of Cultural Heritage in the Agricultural Systems of Immigrant Groups

The comparative study of German and non-German farmers in two portions of nineteenth-century Texas has revealed a number of striking differences and similarities. One of the principal conclusions derived from the preceding two chapters is that the systems of agriculture established by German immigrants were different in some important ways from those of the southern Anglo-Americans and their cultural kinsmen, the Negroes. In both the eastern and western settlements, in the Cotton Kingdom and on the rim of the desert, this distinctiveness was based largely upon certain aspects of the European agricultural heritage which survived in the new homeland. A second, and equally important conclusion is that many imported farming traits did not survive the transplanting and were replaced, often quite rapidly, by practices common to southern agriculture. The result was a blend of adopted and imported traits, a partial assimilation, which caused the Texas Germans to differ not only from southern Anglo-American farmers, but also from their countrymen back in Europe.

In outward appearance, the agricultural systems established by the immigrants bore a much closer resemblance to those of their adopted countrymen in Texas than to their European counterparts. One can only be impressed by the rapidity with which the Germans accepted the gross traits of southern farming—crops, livestock, and settlement pattern. Outwardly, in what might best be called the "visible agriculture," the German farmers showed, with a few exceptions, only minor differences from their Anglo-American counterparts, even as early as

1850. It was in the more subtle aspects of the agricultural systems that major and persistent differences were detected, differences not always manifested in the cultural landscape, but important nonetheless. The distinctiveness of the Germans rested largely on a number of traits which were observed in both eastern and western settlements throughout the period under study. These included the greater intensity, productivity, and locational stability of the German farmers, as well as their higher rate of landownership. All of these major differentiating factors are closely interrelated, in that the more intimate attachment to the land, which was manifested in the greater locational stability and avoidance of tenancy, was associated with the fact that the German put more into the land in the form of labor and capital and got more from it in terms of produce. On this basis, one is tempted to conclude that the Germans were *superior* as farmers in Texas, a temptation rather natural for observers in the conservation-minded twentieth century. However, when viewed in the context of ante- and postbellum times, the concept of superiority seems much less valid. There is no reason to suppose that greater intensity, productivity, and locational stability were more desirable, economically or otherwise, as far as the nineteenth-century southern farmer was concerned. Extensive methods, when coupled with the abundance and cheapness of land and the possibility of moving with ease from place to place, offered a comfortable living at a minimum of expense and labor. Only in retrospect, as a citizen of an over-populated world, in which an ever-higher value is placed on the soil which nourishes man, can one view the Germans as superior farmers.

Persistent divergences were also detected in other aspects of the respective agricultural systems. The German immigrant farmers were apparently more active in market gardening, inasmuch as they were the leaders in supplying vegetables and fruit for Galveston, Houston, and San Antonio, the three major towns in Texas during the period under study, and they devoted more attention to wine-making and the production of white potatoes. In both western and eastern settlements, the Germans showed greater interest than the southerners in the cultivation of small grains, though their efforts to raise rye and wheat in the area between the lower Brazos and Colorado rivers failed due to the recurrence of rust and blight. Other differences were noted which, while quite significant, were unlike those mentioned previously in that they tended to disappear during the course of the forty or fifty years under study. One example was the smaller scale of operation which characterized the German farms in ante-bellum times, and another was the lesser tendency of the immigrants to own slaves.

Curiously enough, there were several differences observed in both eastern and western areas which were precisely the opposite of what might have been expected. For example, the Germans dominated the production of tobacco, in spite of the presence in the same areas of large numbers of farmers from the Upper South, and the same was true of cotton-raising in the ante-bellum eastern settlements and post-bellum western counties. By the same token, the Germans, who had a heritage of semisubsistence farming, operated on a higher level of commercialization than the Americans before the Civil War. In addition, the adoption of the mule as a draft animal after 1865 was apparently more common among the Germans.

In general, greater contrasts were noted between the immigrant Germans and native southern farmers in the western counties. For example, the Hill Country Germans had a more diversified crop economy and, in ante-bellum times, a distinctly higher number of oxen in proportion to horses than the Americans in adjacent areas, while at the same time they utilized imported construction methods and even attempted to establish the farm-village system. In contrast, the Germans of the eastern settlements adopted an undiversified crop association dominated by corn and cotton like that of their Anglo-American neighbors, made no effort to introduce Old World settlement forms or construction methods, and had an ox/horse ratio almost identical to that of the southern yeomen.

While it is true that the present study provides support for the general idea of German distinctiveness in nineteenth-century Texas agriculture, it does not follow that all such claims have been verified. No basis was found for the contention that Germans devoted more attention to kitchen gardening and tree culture than the southerners, and certainly statistical evidence refutes the notion that they were superior in milk and butter production. Identification of the Germans with the cause of abolitionism was found to be a fallacy, heightened by the ownership of slaves by a significant percentage of immigrants in the eastern settlements. The claim that the Germans, as a group, were unionists seems to be quite without foundation. It is true that unionism was strong in some German counties, but it is wrong to assert that all immigrants were so inclined. In fact, the percentages of Germans and Anglo-Americans voting against secession in the western counties were about equal.

Germans cannot be credited with the introduction into Texas of any major crops or livestock. Claims made by various scholars and contemporary observers that Germans brought gardening, orchard-keeping, dairying, and geese into the state have no evidential bases. Every major crop raised by the Germans was produced in greater volume elsewhere in Texas by southern Anglo-Americans.

The similarities observed between farmers of German and southern origin were, in many ways, even more striking than the differences. Corn, cotton, and sweet potatoes, the three major crops of the South, attained widespread and rapid acceptance among the immigrant farmers, as did the native fruit trees and breeds of livestock. Typically southern farmstead architecture and settlement pattern, including the open-range system, were likewise adopted. Dunging of fields, winter housing of livestock, and stall feeding were never introduced by the immigrants. In all these major respects, and in other less important ways, the Germans became southerners almost from the very first.

On the basis of the findings presented in chapters IV and V, the various aspects of the imported agricultural systems of an immigrant group can be divided into four classes with respect to their survival tendencies:

1. Traits which never took root in the new homeland because little or no attempt was made by the immigrant group to perpetuate them. These would include the dunging of fields, the cultivation of barley, and the provision of winter quarters for livestock.

2. Traits which were introduced but, often despite persistent attempts, failed to succeed and were discarded. These were represented by such items as viticulture, European fruit trees, small grain production in the eastern settlements, and the farm-village plan and communal herding in the western colonies.

3. Traits which were introduced, either through the desire of the immigrants or through financial necessity, and survived for about one generation. Included would be a small scale of operation, typified by smaller farms, fewer livestock, lower volume of crop production, and lower value of farm production than the Anglo-Americans; and German construction methods for farmstead structures in the western settlements. In this respect, there is good evidence that the free-labor system of the Germans was beginning to break down after about twenty years in the eastern settlements, as many

settlers who had been in Texas for several decades were purchasing slaves. It would have been interesting to observe what would have happened in another twenty years had slavery not been abolished.

4. Traits which were successfully introduced and, often in a modified form, acquired a lasting place in the agricultural system in the new homeland. As indicated previously, these would include such important items as intensive methods, high productivity, a locationally stable rural population, a high rate of landownership, and the cultivation of small grains in the western settlements. In addition, less significant traits, such as wine-making, the raising of white potatoes, and cheese production would also fit into this category.

A number of factors worked in combination to help decide the fate of any given aspect of the imported agricultural system—to determine which of the four categories claimed it. The first of these was the *physical environment* and its evaluation by the immigrant group. Certainly, Texas as a whole presented some great contrasts to Germany in this respect, perhaps most notably in climate, but the immigrants who settled the western counties had the greatest environmental adjustment to make. The partial assimilation which occurred in the eastern German areas can be attributed in large part to cultural contacts and economic pressures, but in the western counties, which was an empty, untested land at the time of the Germans' arrival, it was their evaluation of the physical environment that prompted many changes. On the rim of the desert, the question was not merely one of economic viability, but also one of ecological suitability. This was a land best served by experiment, by improvisation, in which cultural baggage survived or was discarded through the process of trial and error. In the eastern settlements environmental difficulties of a different nature were encountered, in the form of rust and blight, for example, which were frequent visitors in wheat and rye fields of the Germans. In both areas, the warm climate was an advantage, in that it made unnecessary many of the precautions which were taken in preparation for the winter season in higher latitudes. The following practices were apparently discarded or never introduced at least partially because they were ecologically unsuitable or unnecessary:

1. winter housing of livestock
2. large farmstead structures
3. viticulture
4. dunging of fields

5. farm villages
6. mid-latitude fruit trees
7. small grains (in eastern settlements)
8. crop-livestock association dominated by crops (in western settlements)
9. close planting of crops (in western settlements)
10. small scale of operation (in western settlements).

Such was not the fate, however, of all practices which were plagued by ecological difficulties or which were of minimal value in the new homeland. Persistent attempts to overcome environmental problems associated with the raising of white potatoes were finally rewarded with success after several decades, and this crop attained a place of lasting importance in the German kitchen gardens. Haymaking, which was deemed unnecessary by a consensus of contemporary spokesmen, nevertheless persisted among the Germans.

The second major factor affecting the survival of imported agricultural traits was the *cultural-economic milieu* and the manner in which it was viewed by the immigrant farmers. In this respect also, the Germans in the two parts of Texas were faced with quite different situations. Those in the eastern settlements found themselves in an area which was already at the time of their arrival a social and economic part of the South, with the basic procedures of the southern agricultural system well established, an area where a proven, viable rural economy was pre-existent. In such a case, once the immigrant group has made the decision to participate competitively in the production of goods for market and not to remain aloof in the isolation of folk-islands, the cultural and economic pressures to conform agriculturally are very great. The Germans in the western counties, on the other hand, were the almost sole occupants of a frontier area, isolated in colonies composed exclusively of their European countrymen, and cultural contacts with native southerners were accordingly much less frequent than was the case farther east. But even there, on the rim of the desert, the economic pressure to conform existed, for once the Germans chose to engage in the production of crops and livestock for market, they obligated themselves to supply the items which were in demand.

An evaluation of their cultural-economic milieu prompted the Germans to discard, either at once or after some years, many agricultural practices known in Europe, either because they were detrimental to the economic viability of the system of farming in the new homeland or because practices observed among the native southerners appeared in their eyes to be better. Included would be:

1. low degree of commercialization
2. small scale of operation
3. stall feeding of livestock
4. supervised herding of livestock.

Reason, of course, does not always govern the actions of mankind, and imported farming practices which proved to be ecologically suitable were not always perpetuated or discarded after a strictly logical evaluation of the new cultural-economic milieu. Some survived apparently for little more than sentimental reasons, while others persisted because they were perhaps too deeply ingrained in the culture to be abandoned once they were found to be no longer economically necessary. In this category would fall such diverse items as:

1. intensive farming methods
2. high productivity
3. locational stability of the rural population
4. wine and cheese making
5. European construction methods (in western settlements)
6. white potatoes

It is of significance, however, that none of these *interfered* with or endangered the economic viability of the agricultural systems. The more intensive farming methods meant, in mid-nineteenth century Texas, only that the Germans were perhaps putting more labor and capital into their land than was necessary to assure a comfortable living. Locational stability only saddled them with the obligation to care for the land in order that their descendants could inherit it in good condition.

Most of the imported agricultural traits which survived were modified somewhat to meet local conditions. The production of wheat and rye in the western areas came, in time, to serve primarily forage functions; haymaking was adapted to utilize the unimproved prairie grasses; the intensive application of labor and capital was channeled in directions unknown in Germany, toward the purchase of farm machinery, the double-cropping of garden vegetables, the careful picking of cotton, and the perfection of dry-farming methods; wine-making was changed to be applied to wild grapes; kitchen orcharding was modified to utilize trees uncommon in northwestern Europe; the tra-

ditional stability of the rural population was directed toward the purchase of land and fencing of the open range; and German construction methods were adapted to local architectural styles and building
materials.

An interesting phenomenon was observed concerning those imported traits which survived either permanently or for at least a generation. In almost every case, these traits were absent in the first years
of settlement, only to appear five, ten, and even twenty or thirty years
later, in what might be called "cultural rebound." In the western settlements, for example, significant wheat cultivation was first established
about seven to ten years after initial occupancy of the land, German
construction methods after about five years, rye only after a quarter
of a century, oats and white potatoes not before the 1870's. That is
to say, fewer imported German agricultural traits could be observed
in the first years of settlement than in the period that followed.

Cultural rebound is difficult to prove, unless it involves something
as striking as half-timbered construction. It might well be argued, for
example, that the rise of wheat cultivation among the western Germans was a response to local conditions of market and climate rather
than an expression of Old World grain preferences. For some supposedly imported traits to have become established only after two
decades or more in the new homeland was so remarkable as to create
doubt whether such belated attention actually constituted cultural rebound or merely adaptations and borrowings not associated with the
European heritage. The evidence is usually circumstantial, in that
some trait which had been known in Europe appeared after a number of years among the immigrant farmers but not among native agriculturists.

Still, cultural rebound would not be too unexpected, for the initial
pioneer years were difficult ones, and the settlers temporarily did without many things which were not absolutely essential. In addition, many
of the German immigrants had been carefully instructed in the methods of American pioneering by reading the better guidebooks, which
included, in some cases, detailed directions for the construction of log
cabins, and recommendations for corn as the best crop to plant initially.
The leader of the Verein colony, Prince von Solms-Braunfels, anticipated the process of cultural rebound when he suggested that attention might be devoted to German crops and the construction of more
pretentious houses in the second or third year of settlement, while ad-
vising the immigrants under his supervision that log cabins and corn

should be the rule in the first year. Cultural rebound would not, of course, be limited to Germans and other immigrant groups directly from Europe, but would be applicable to the native Americans as well. The process involves the partial reversal of an initial, "artificial" assimilation. If it is valid, as seems to be the case, it deserves additional study, for it conflicts somewhat with the generally accepted idea of how immigrant groups are assimilated. In this respect, it is noteworthy that some traits which appeared after a period of dormancy were later discarded.

The agricultural distinctiveness of any immigrant group is dependent in no small part on the degree to which the imported practices differ from those of the native groups among which they settle, on the cultural *context* in which the immigrants are placed. The Germans were an alien group to Texas, whose agricultural heritage was greatly different from that of the native southerners in the state, and, as a result, those imported farming traits which survived tended to differentiate them from the Americans. Their "Europeanness," their lack of contact with the New World evolution of southern agriculture over a period of more than two hundred years, allowed them to be distinctive as farmers in Texas. It was thus a "built-in" difference shared by many groups of farmers from northwestern and central Europe.

Immigrants who are placed in agricultural surroundings similar to those of their old homeland are less apt to be so distinctive. German wheat farmers would not be so noticeable on the prairies of Kansas, vinegrowers from the Rhine might lose their identity in the vineyard areas of California, and Norwegian dairymen perhaps would be unremarkable in Wisconsin. Similarly, the important place of swine in the German livestock economy did not differentiate them from the southern Anglo-Americans in Texas, who consumed pork in even larger quantities, and along the same lines, the tendency of both groups to devote attention to gardening and dairy products, notably butter, wiped out differences which might otherwise have shown up in these respects. For this reason, the European immigrant farmers who settled the northern United States in the nineteenth century were less distinctive, because the agricultural systems of their European homelands differed less from those of the northern portions of the country than from those of the southern states. The farther one goes back in American agricultural history, the less the differences between farming practices in northwestern Europe and the northern United States, so that in the colonial period, for example, farmers from Germany and the British Isles who settled in eighteenth-century Pennsylvania were still so closely in touch with their European agricultural heritages that no great differences existed between them. It is quite possible that the Pennsylvania Germans could have imported and preserved many more European farming traits than did the immigrants who settled in Texas and still have been less distinctive in their new surroundings, simply because of the difference in context. By the same token, one would not expect to find much contrast between the German and Czech farmers who settled about the same time in nineteenth-century Texas.

The partial assimilation of the German farmers in Texas was facilitated by a number of processes through which they were acquainted with the southern agricultural system. Often, initial contact was made even before they left Germany, by reading the numerous *emigrant guidebooks*, some of which gave very accurate descriptions of agriculture in mid-nineteenth century Texas. These books were generally brought along by the settlers, and the better ones served as crude farming manuals in the new homeland. A second channel of communication was through *direct contact* with the southern Anglo-American population of Texas. This was particularly important in the eastern settlements, where Germans lived in the same areas as the Americans, and especially before the mid-1840's when the number of Germans was still relatively small. Perhaps the most important mechanism for assimilation was the previously mentioned *"apprenticeship" period,* in which many newly arrived immigrants worked for several years on the farms of other Germans who had come previously and already been partially assimilated agriculturally. This process allowed new settlers to acquire through experience many of the ways of southern farmers, and it was particularly effective since no language barrier existed. The numerous immigrants who came to the eastern settlements after the Civil War were able to make the necessary agricultural adaptations quite rapidly because of the presence of a large body of ante-bellum German settlers in the same area. A fourth means by which assimilation was furthered was through the numerous *agricultural societies* founded by the Germans in Texas. The clubs had regular meetings at which farmers discussed many of the problems they faced as immigrant farmers in a strange, new physical-cultural environment, and the necessity for discussions of this nature may well have been one explanation of the greater prevalence of such societies among the Germans. However, these clubs also helped perpetuate distinctiveness, inasmuch as their membership was almost exclusively German, thereby segregating the farm population on the basis of origins.

The census of 1880 was the first to list the specific nativity of the parents of each inhabitant, and, conveniently enough, it was also about that decade when the native-born offspring of the German immigrants began reaching young adulthood and becoming independent farmers. Unfortunately, they were not yet numerous enough in the eastern settlements to warrant the presentation of separate figures, but in the western areas, where the bulk of immigration had been in ante-bellum times, a considerable number of the first generation German-Americans were engaged in farming. The only major agricultural difference detected between them and their immigrant parents was in the scale of operation. They had less land, fewer livestock, a lower value of farm production, less farm machinery, less improved acreage, and a smaller volume of crop production than did their German-born fathers, which is not at all surprising in view of the fact that most of them were still in their twenties and just beginning as farmers. There is also some indication that they were less inclined to plant small grains. At the same time, and in spite of their more meager capital resources, they owned more farm machinery, had a higher rate of landownership, and a higher average of cash value of farm than the southern Anglo-Americans of all ages, and they equalled them in farm size, value of production, fence expenditures, and value of livestock. In addition, the native-born German-Americans practiced a more diverse agriculture, and a greater percentage of them reported cotton, wheat, and oats than the Anglo-Americans. The ox/horse, mule/horse, and white-potato/sweet-potato ratios were also markedly different.

The first generation of native German-American farmers as presented in the statistics is deceptively small, for it excludes all who came from Germany with their parents as small children. Such persons never knew the agricultural systems of Europe, and their formative years were spent in Texas, but in the census they are recorded only as German-born. In actuality, they were invisible members of the first generation of native farmers, and it is regrettable that they cannot be identified and included as such.

There is some reason to believe that the German-American farmers of Texas still retain a measure of distinctiveness today. The clues for this lie in certain easily observable features of the social life. Societies of various sorts are still found throughout the German areas, devoted to such things as singing, shooting, mutual aid, and even gymnastics. Meeting halls of the Order of the Sons of Hermann, a social brotherhood of German-American men and women, which also has insurance functions, dot the countryside of the German belt, as do local chapters of the Germania Farm Mutual Aid Association. The Cat Spring Agricultural Society in Austin County observed its centennial in 1956 and continues to function as a social club. The last German-language newspaper ceased publication in the 1950's, but in the streets and stores of towns like Fredericksburg, spoken German can still be heard, though it has long since been infiltrated by English words and expressions. In a few churches, German services are still held. The majority of Texas Germans adhere to the Lutheran and Catholic faiths of their immigrant ancestors, though the Methodists made early and significant inroads in some areas. Voting patterns within the state suggest that the German element is also distinctive in this respect. In short, the German-Texans have by no means lost all of their cultural identity in the century or more that they and their forefathers have lived in the state.

The degree to which the Germans remain socially distinctive indicates the possibility that their agricultural practices might also still differ somewhat from those of other Texas farmers. To be sure, assimilation has continued, aided by land-grant colleges and county agents, and the German-American farmers and ranchers today are doubtlessly even less distinctive than their grandfathers in the 1880's. But perhaps some of the "invisible" differences persist yet, particularly as concerns intensity and productivity. It is perhaps significant that some German-American farmers today believe that the Germans, as a group, are better farmers than the Anglo-Americans.

. . . . *Appendix* . . . .

The sampling procedure employed was approved by the Survey Research Laboratory of the University of Wisconsin. For 1870 a simple random sample of 50 percent was obtained by taking every other farm on the agricultural schedules, while for 1880, a 20 percent random sample was achieved by recording every fifth farm. The following tables were used to estimate the sampling error for all *percentage* comparisons between the various farmer groups for both years. The tables assume an "adequate"-sized random sample, and the very large percentages (50 and 20) actually taken for the two years resulted in even less sampling error than is allowed for in the tables. Mr. Harry Sharp of the Survey Research Laboratory supplied the tables.

For example, it was predicted on the basis of 1850 and 1860 calculations, that German-born farmers in Austin and Waller counties were more likely to own their land than were southern Anglo-Americans. Calculations based on the sample of farms taken for 1880 indicated that 86 percent of German-born farmers owned their land and 62 percent of the southern whites, a difference of twenty-four percentage points. In the sample, there were 213 German-born and 129 southern whites. By consulting Table A under "percentages around 20 and 80 percent," and reading down the vertical column to 200 (German sample) and across the horizontal scale to 100 (Anglo-American sample), the number six is found. Since six is less than twenty-four, the probability is less than .10 that the observed difference between the two subgroups was due to sampling error.

TABLE A

Used When the Differences in Percentages of the Two Subgroups Was Predicted in Advance, on the Basis of the 1850 and 1860 Calculations and on Past Research and Theory

Sampling Errors of Differences: One-tail   P = .10*

Sample size	300	200	100	75	50	25
			For percentages from 35 to 65 per cent			
300	5	6	7	8	10	14
200		7	8	9	10	14
100			9	10	11	14
75				10	12	15

(continued from preceding page)

Sample size	300	200	100	75	50	25
50					13	16
	For percentages around 20 and 80 per cent					
300	4	5	6	7	8	
200		5	6	7	8	
100			7	8	9	
75				9	10	
50					10	
	For percentages around 10 and 90 per cent					
300	3	4	4	5		
200		4	5	5		
100			6			

* When the percentage-point difference between two subgroups in the sample is of the magnitude indicated in the appropriate cell, or greater, and when the difference is one which *was predicted*, the probability is less than .10 that the observed difference between the subgroups was due to sampling error.

TABLE B

Used When the Differences in Percentages of the Two Subgroups Could Not Be Predicted in Advance

Sampling Errors of Differences: Two-tail   P = .10*

Sample size	300	200	100	75	50	25
	For percentages from 35 to 65 per cent					
300	7	8	9	11	13	17
200		8	10	11	13	17
100			12	13	14	18
75				13	15	19
	For percentages around 20 and 80 per cent					
300	5	6	8	8	10	
200		7	8	9	11	
100			9	11	12	
75				12	12	
	For percentages around 10 and 90 per cent					
300	4	5	6	7		
200		5	6	7		
100			7			

*When the percentage differences between two subgroups in the sample is of the magnitude indicated in the appropriate cell, or greater, and when the difference is one which *was not predicted,* the probability is less than .10 that the observed difference between the subgroups was due merely to sampling error.

· · · · *Bibliography* · · · ·

· · · · *Bibliography* · · · ·

I. PUBLISHED MATERIAL

A. BOOKS, ARTICLES, AND PAMPHLETS

1. General Sources

Achenbach, Hermann. *Tagebuch meiner Reise nach den Nordamerikanischen Freistaaten oder: Das neue Kanaan.* Düsseldorf: G. H. Beyer and J. Wolf, 1835.

Adams, Ephraim D. (ed.). *British Diplomatic Correspondence Concerning the Republic of Texas—1838–1846.* Austin: Texas State Historical Association, 1918.

Allen, Irene T. *Saga of Anderson.* New York: Greenwich Book Publishers, 1957.

Almonte, Juan N. "Statistical Report on Texas," *Southwestern Historical Quarterly,* Vol. 28 (1924–1925), pp. 177–222. Edited and translated by C. E. Castaneda.

Arnow, Harriette Simpson. *Flowering of the Cumberland.* New York: The Macmillan Company, 1963.

————. "The Pioneer Farmer and His Crops in the Cumberland Region," *Tennessee Historical Quarterly,* Vol. 19 (1960), pp. 291–327.

————. *Seedtime on the Cumberland.* New York: The Macmillan Company, 1960.

"Austin County," in *Schütze's Jahrbuch für Texas . . . für 1883.* Austin: A. Schütze, 1882. P. 120.

Der Auswanderer nach Texas. Ein Handbuch und Rathgeber für Die, welche sich in Texas ansiedeln wollen, unter besonderer Berücksichtigung Derer, welche sich dem Mainzer oder Antwerpener Verein anvertrauen . . . Bremen: C. Schünemann, 1846.

Banta, William, and J. W. Caldwell, Jr. *Twenty-Seven Years on the Texas Frontier.* Council Hill, Oklahoma: n.p., 1933. First published in 1893.

Barker, Eugene C. "The Influence of Slavery in the Colonization of Texas," *Southwestern Historical Quarterly,* Vol. 28 (1924–1925), pp. 1–33.

————. *The Life of Stephen F. Austin.* Nashville and Dallas: Cokesbury Press, 1925.

————. *Mexico and Texas 1821–1835.* Dallas: P. L. Turner, 1928.

Bartlett, John Russell. *Personal Narrative of Explorations and Incidents in Texas, New Mexico, California, Sonora, and Chihuahua.* 2 vols. New York: D. Appleton & Company, Inc., 1854.

Batte, Lelia M. *History of Milam County, Texas.* San Antonio: Naylor, 1956.

Behr, Ottomar von. *Guter Rath für Auswanderer nach den Vereinigten Staaten von Nord America mit besonderer Berücksichtigung von Texas . . . nach eigner Erfahrung geschrieben.* Leipzig: Robert Friese, 1847.

Benjamin, Gilbert Giddings. *The Germans in Texas.* New York: D. Appleton & Company, Inc., 1910.

Berghaus, Heinrich. "Der Freistaat Texas," *Allgemeine Länder- und Völkerkunde.* Vol. 6. Stuttgart: Hoffmann, 1844. Pp. 358–394.

Beyer, Moritz. *Das Auswanderungsbuch oder Führer und Rathgeber bei der Auswanderung nach Nord Amerika und Texas.* Leipzig: Baumgartner, 1846.

Biesele, Rudolph L. "Early Times in New Braunfels and Comal County," *Southwestern Historical Quarterly,* Vol. 50 (1946–1947), pp. 75–92.

————. "The First German Settlement in Texas," *Southwestern Historical Quarterly,* Vol. 34 (1930–1931), pp. 334–339.

————. "The German Settlers and the Indians in Texas, 1844–1860," *Southwestern Historical Quarterly,* Vol. 31 (1927–1928), pp. 116–129.

————. *The History of the German Settlements in Texas 1831–1861.* Austin: Von Boeckmann-Jones, 1930.

————. "Industry: The First German Settlement in Texas," *Deutsch-Amerikanische Geschichtsblätter,* Vol. 32 (1932), pp. 523–528.

————. "The Texas State Convention of Germans in 1854," *Southwestern Historical Quarterly,* Vol. 33 (1929–1930), pp. 247–261.

Biggers, Donald H. *German Pioneers in Texas.* Fredericksburg: Fredericksburg Publishing, 1925.

Billingsly, W. C. "Llano County," in *The Texas Almanac for 1867. . . .* Galveston: Richardson, 1866. P. 132.

Billington, Ray Allen. *Westward Expansion: A History of the American Frontier.* 2nd ed. New York: The Macmillan Company, 1960.

Black, William L. *A New Industry: Or Raising the Angora Goat, and Mohair, for Profit.* Fort Worth: Keystone, 1900.

Blasig, Anne. *The Wends of Texas.* San Antonio: Naylor, 1954.

Blumberg, Carl. *Die wahre Wirksamkeit des Mainzer Vereins für die Auswanderung nach Texas geschildert in einem Briefe vom 3. November 1846 . . .* n.p.: n.p., [c. 1847].

Boethel, Paul C. *History of Lavaca County.* Austin: Von Boeckmann-Jones, 1959.

Bogue, Allan G. *From Prairie to Corn Belt.* Chicago: University of Chicago Press, 1963.

Bollaert, William. *William Bollaert's Texas.* Edited by W. Eugene Hollon and Ruth Lapham Butler. Norman: University of Oklahoma Press, 1956.

Bracht, Viktor. *Texas im Jahre 1848.* Elberfeld and Iserlohn: Julius Baedeker, 1849.

Braman, D. E. E. *Braman's Information about Texas.* Philadelphia: J. B. Lippincott, 1858.

Bromme, Traugott. "Der Freistaat Texas," Chapter IV in *Rathgeber für Auswanderungslustige. Wie und wohin sollen wir auswandern: nach den Vereinigten Staaten . . . oder dem Freistaat Texas. . . .* Stuttgart: Hoffmann, 1846.

————. "Der Staat Texas," Chapter III in *Hand- und Reisebuch für Auswanderer nach den Vereinigten Staaten von Nord-Amerika, Texas,. . . .* 5th ed. Bayreuth: Buchner, 1848.

Bruce, Kathleen. "Virginian Agricultural Decline to 1860: A Fallacy," *Agricultural History*, Vol. 6 (1932), pp. 3–13.

Brunner, Edmund de Schweinitz. *Immigrant Farmers and Their Children.* Garden City, New York: Columbia University Press, 1929.

Bryan, Francis T. "Report on a Reconnaissance of a Route from San Antonio, via Fredericksburg to El Paso," in *Reports of the Secretary of War, with Reconnaissances of Routes from San Antonio to El Paso. . . .* Senate Executive Document No. 64, 31st Congress, 1st Session. Washington, D.C.: Union Office, 1850.

Buck, Paul H. "The Poor Whites of the Ante-Bellum South," *American Historical Review*, Vol. 31 (1925), pp. 41–54.

Bugbee, Lester G. "Slavery in Early Texas," *Political Science Quarterly*, Vol. 13 (1898), pp. 389–412, 648–668.

———. "The Texas Frontier—1820–1825," *Publications of Southern History Association*, Vol. 4 (1900), pp. 102–121.

Büttner, Johann G. *Briefe aus und über Nordamerika. . . .* Vol. I. Dresden and Leipzig: Arnold, 1847.

Canstatt, Oscar. *Die deutsche Auswanderung, Auswandererfürsorge und Auswandererziele.* Berlin-Schöneberg: Ernst Hahn, 1904.

Carroll, H. Bailey. "Texas Collection," *Southwestern Historical Quarterly*, Vol. 60 (1956–1957), pp. 401–415.

Carter, R. G. *On the Border with MacKenzie. . . .* New York: Antiquarian Press, 1961.

Carter, W. T. *The Soils of Texas.* Texas Agricultural Experiment Station, Bulletin No. 431, July, 1931. College Station: A. & M. College of Texas, 1931.

Castro, Heinrich. *Texas im Jahre 1845: Castrostadt, eine französische Colonie, welche . . . am Flusse Medina . . . durch Heinrich Castro begrundet worden ist.* n.p.: n.p., [c. 1845].

Castro, Henri. *Colonisation au Texas (Amérique du Nord): Castro-ville (25 Milles Ouest de San Antonio de Bexar), Fondée le 3 Septembre 1844. Colonisation in Texas (Nord Amérika). Castro-ville (25 Meilen Westlich von San Antonio de Bexar), Gegründet den 3 Septembre 1844.* Antwerp: J.-E. Buschmann, 1845.

———. *Le Texas.* Antwerp: J.-E. Buschmann, 1845.

Castro, Lorenzo. *Immigration from Alsace and Lorraine: A Brief Sketch of the History of Castro's Colony.* San Antonio: Herald Office, 1871.

[Cat Spring Agricultural Society]. *The Cat Spring Story.* San Antonio: Lone Star Printing, 1956.

———. *Century of Agricultural Progress 1856–1956.* Translated from the German by A. L. Schuette, E. P. Krueger, and E. A. Miller. San Antonio: Lone Star Printing, 1956.

Chambers, William T. "Edwards Plateau: A Combination Ranching Region," *Economic Geography*, Vol. 8 (1932), pp. 67–80.

Claghorn, Kate H. *"Agricultural Distribution of Immigrants." U.S. Industrial Commission Report*, Vol. 15 (1901), pp. 492–646.

Clapham, J. H. *The Economic Development of France and Germany, 1815–1914.* 4th ed. Cambridge, England: University Press, 1961.
Claren, Oscar von. "Ein Brief aus dem soeben gegründeten Neu-Braunfels," in *Kalender der Neu-Braunfelser Zeitung fuer 1920.* New Braunfels: Zeitung, 1920. Pp. 46–52.
Clark, Andrew H. *Three Centuries and the Island.* Toronto: University of Toronto Press, 1959.
Clark, Blanche Henry. *The Tennessee Yeomen 1840–1860.* Nashville: Vanderbilt University Press, 1942.
Clauss, C. Hugo. "Boerne und das Cibolo-Thal in Kendall County," in *Schütze's Jahrbuch für Texas . . . für 1882.* Austin: A. Schütze, 1881. Pp. 29–31.
Connor, Seymour V. "Log Cabins in Texas," *Southwestern Historical Quarterly,* Vol. 53 (1949–1950), pp. 105–116.
———. *The Peters Colony of Texas.* Austin: Texas State Historical Association, 1959.
Constant, L. *Texas. Das Verderben deutscher Auswanderer in Texas unter dem Schutze des Mainzer Vereins.* Berlin: Reimer, 1847.
Cooley, A. O. "Gillespie County," in *The Texas Almanac for 1867. . . .* Galveston: Richardson, 1866. Pp. 109–110.
Cox, Cornelius C. "From Texas to California in 1849: Diary of C. C. Cox," *Southwestern Historical Quarterly,* Vol. 29 (1925–1926), pp. 36–50. Edited by Mabelle Eppard Martin.
Cozzens, Arthur B. "Conservation in German Settlements of the Missouri Ozarks," *Geographical Review,* Vol. 33 (1943), pp. 286–298.
Craven, Avery O. *Soil Exhaustion in the Agricultural History of Maryland and Virginia, 1606–1860.* Urbana: University of Illinois Press, 1925.

Davis, Charles S. *Cotton Kingdom in Alabama.* Montgomery: Alabama State Department of Archives and History, 1939.
Davis, T. H. "Llano County," in *The Texas Almanac for 1861. . . .* Galveston: Richardson, 1860. Pp. 172–173.
De Cordova, J. *Texas: Her Resources and Her Public Men. . . .* Philadelphia: E. Crozet, 1858.
———. *The Texas Immigrant and Traveller's Guide Book.* Austin: De Cordova and Frazier, 1856.
Deiler, John Hanno. *Geschichte der Deutschen Gesellschaft von New Orleans.* New Orleans: Im Selbstverlage, 1897.
"Deutschland," in *Meyers Konversations-Lexikon.* 5th ed. Vol. 4. Leipzig and Vienna: Bibliographisches Institut, 1897.
Diamond Jubilee Souvenir Book of Comfort, Texas, Commemorating 75th Anniversary, August 18, 1929. n.p.: n.p., 1929.
Dickinson, Robert E. *Germany: A General and Regional Geography.* New York: E. P. Dutton & Co., Inc., 1953.
———. "Rural Settlement in the German Lands," *Annals of the Association of American Geographers,* Vol. 39 (1949), pp. 239–263.
Dielmann, Henry B. "Emma Altgelt's Sketches of Life in Texas," *Southwestern Historical Quarterly,* Vol. 63 (1959–1960), pp. 363–384.

Dieudonné, Emmanuel Henri. *Missionary Adventures in Texas and Mexico: A Personal Narrative of Six Years' Sojourn in Those Regions.* Translated from the French. London: Longman, Brown, Green, Longmans, and Roberts, 1858.

Döbbler, F. Wilhelm. "Der Tabaksbau," in *Schütze's Jahrbuch für Texas . . . für 1882.* Austin: A. Schütze, 1881. Pp. 66–69.

Dresel, Gustav. *Houston Journal: Adventures in North America and Texas 1837–1841.* Edited and translated by Max Freund. Austin: University of Texas Press, 1954.

Dunlevy, A. "Colorado County," in *The Texas Almanac for 1859. . . .* Galveston: Richardson, 1858. Pp. 170–171.

Dunt, Detlef. *Reise nach Texas, nebst Nachrichten von diesem Lande; für Deutsche, welche nach Amerika zu gehen beabsichtigen.* Bremen: Carl W. Wiehe, 1834.

Durand, Loyal, Jr. "Dairy Barns of Southeastern Wisconsin," *Economic Geography,* Vol. 19 (1943), pp. 37–44.

Eastman, Seth. *A Seth Eastman Sketchbook, 1848–1849.* Introduction by Lois Burkhalter. Austin: University of Texas Press, 1961.

Eaton, Clement. *The Growth of Southern Civilization.* New York: Harper & Brothers, 1961.

Ehemann, Kurt. *Das Bauernhaus in der Wetterau und im SW-Vogelsberg.* Forschungen zur deutschen Landeskunde, Vol. 61. Remagen: Bundesanstalt für Landeskunde, 1953.

Eichholz, W. T. "Die deutschen Ansiedlungen am Colletto," in *Schütze's Jahrbuch für Texas . . . für 1884.* Austin: A. Schütze, 1883. Pp. 83–86.

Ekkehart, Klaus. *Deutsche Bauerngeschichte.* Gotha and Leipzig: Arno Reissenweber, 1934.

Elliott, Claude. "Union Sentiment in Texas 1861–1865," *Southwestern Historical Quarterly,* Vol. 50 (1946–1947), pp. 449–477.

Engerrand, George C. *The So-Called Wends of Germany and Their Colonies in Texas and in Australia.* University of Texas Bulletin No. 3417, Bureau of Research in the Social Sciences, Study No. 7. Austin: University of Texas, 1934.

"Erinnerungen an die Trümmer der Adels-Colonie in Texas u.s.w.," *Der deutsche Pionier,* Vol. 1 (1869), pp. 143–146, 181–185, 212–216.

Erlenmeyer, A., and P. M. Muller. "Gillespie," in *The Texas Almanac for 1858. . . .* Galveston: Richardson, 1857. Pp. 65–66.

Everett, Milton. *Central West Texas.* Texas Department of Agriculture, Bulletin No. 17. Austin: 1911.

Ewing, Floyd F., Jr. "Origins of Unionist Sentiment on the West Texas Frontier," *West Texas Historical Association Year Book,* Vol. 32 (1956), pp. 21–29.

Faust, Albert B. *The German Element in the United States.* 2 vols. Cambridge, Massachusetts: Riverside Press, 1909.

Fischer, Dan (compiler). *The Willmanns in America—1853–1953.* n.p.: n.p., 1953.

Fornell, Earl Wesley. *The Galveston Era: The Texas Crescent on the Eve of Secession.* Austin: University of Texas Press, 1961.

Fournel, Henri. *Coup d'Oeil historique et statistique sur le Téxas.* Paris: Delloye, 1841.

Frank, Samuel H. "Comal," in *The Texas Almanac for 1859.* . . . Galveston: Richardson, 1858. Pp. 169–170.

French, S. G. "A report in relation to the route over which the government train moved from San Antonio to El Paso del Norte, made in pursuance to orders received from Major E. B. Babbitt, A.Q.M.U.S.A., dated May 30, 1849," in *Reports of the Secretary of War, with Reconnaissances of Routes from San Antonio to El Paso.* . . . Senate Executive Document No. 64, 31st Congress, 1st Session. Washington, D.C.: Union Office, 1850.

Fröbel, Julius. *Aus Amerika: Erfahrungen, Reisen und Studien.* 2 vols. Leipzig: J. J. Weber, 1857–1858.

Fugate, Francis L. "Origins of the Range Cattle Era in South Texas," *Agricultural History,* Vol. 35 (1961), pp. 155–158.

Gehrke, William H. "The Ante-Bellum Agriculture of the Germans in North Carolina," *Agricultural History,* Vol. 9 (1935), pp. 143–160.

Geiser, Samuel W. "Dr. Ernst Kapp, Early Geographer in Texas,"*Field and Laboratory,* Vol. 14, No. 1 (1946), pp. 16–31.

————. *Naturalists of the Frontier.* Dallas: Southern Methodist University Press, 1937.

"Germans in Texas," *New York Daily Tribune* (January 4, 1856), p. 3, col. 4.

"The Germans in Texas. The Germans in Fredericksburg, their First Settlement and Present Prosperous Condition," in *Texas Almanac for 1872.* Galveston: Richardson, 1871. Pp. 76–77.

[Gillespie County Historical Society]. *Pioneers in God's Hills.* Austin: Von Boeckmann-Jones, 1960.

Gillett, James B. *Six Years with the Texas Rangers, 1875 to 1881.* Austin: Von Boeckmann-Jones, 1921.

Goegg, Amand. *Ueberseeische Reisen.* Zürich: J. Schabelitz, 1888.

Goeth, Ottilie Fuchs. *Was Grossmutter erzaehlt.* San Antonio: Passing Show Printing Co., 1915.

Goltz, Theodor von. *Agrarwesen und Agrarpolitik.* 2d ed. Jena: 1904.

————. *Geschichte der deutschen Landwirtschaft.* 2 vols. Stuttgart and Berlin: J. G. Cotta, 1902–1903.

Gray, Lewis Cecil. *History of Agriculture in the Southern United States to 1860.* 2 vols. New York: Peter Smith, 1941.

Grund, Francis Joseph. *Handbuch und Wegweiser für Auswanderer nach den Vereinigten Staaten von Nordamerika und Texas.* 2d ed. Stuttgart and Tübingen: J. G. Cotta, 1846.

Hall, Horace M. "Horace M. Hall's Letters from Gillespie County, Texas, 1871–1873," *Southwestern Historical Quarterly,* Vol. 62 (1958–1959), pp. 336–355. Edited by Joseph S. Hall.

Halle, Ernst von. *Baumwollproduktion und Pflanzungswirtschaft in den Nordamerikanischen Südstaaten.* 2 vols. Leipzig: Duncker & Humblot, 1897–1906.

Hannemann, Max. "Das Deutschtum in den Vereinigten Staaten, Seine Verbreitung und Entwicklung seit der Mitte des 19. Jahrhunderts," in *Petermanns Mitteilungen Ergänzungsheft Nr. 224.* Gotha: Justus Perthes, 1936.

Hartkopf, F. "Weinbau in Texas," in *Schütze's Jahrbuch für Texas . . . für 1882.* Austin: A. Schütze, 1881. Pp. 123–125.

Hatcher, Mattie Austin. *The Opening of Texas to Foreign Settlement, 1801–1820.* University of Texas Bulletin No. 2714. Austin: University of Texas, 1927.

Hawgood, John A. *The Tragedy of German-America.* New York and London: G. P. Putnam's Sons, 1940.

Hecke, J. Val. *Reise durch die Vereinigten Staaten von Nordamerika in den Jahren 1818 und 1819. . . .* 2 vols. Berlin: H. Ph. Petri, 1820–1821.

Hedrick, Ulysses P. *A History of Horticulture in America to 1860.* New York: Oxford University Press, 1950.

Helbok, Adolf. *Deutsche Siedlung, Wesen, Ausbreitung und Sinn.* Halle/Saale: Max Niemeyer, 1938.

Helper, Hinton Rowan. *Compendium of the Impending Crisis of the South.* New York: A. B. Burdick, 1860.

Henderson, Mary V. "Minor Empresario Contracts for the Colonization of Texas," *Southwestern Historical Quarterly,* Vol. 32 (1928), pp. 1–28.

Herff, Ferdinand von. *Die geregelte Auswanderung des deutschen Proletariats mit besonderer Beziehung auf Texas.* Frankfurt am Main: Franz Varrentrapp, 1850. Translated by Arthur L. Finck, Jr., M.A. thesis, University of Texas, Austin, 1949.

Hermes, Wilhelm. "Erlebnisse eines deutschen Einwanderers in Texas," in *Kalender der Neu-Braunfelser Zeitung fuer 1922.* New Braunfels: Zeitung, 1922. Pp. 18–30.

Hesse-Wartegg, Ernst von. *Nord-Amerika, seine Städte und Naturwunder, sein Land und seine Leute.* Leipzig: Gustav Weigel, 1880.

Hewes, Leslie. "Cultural Fault Line in the Cherokee Country," *Economic Geography.* Vol. 19, (1943), pp. 136–142.

———. "Tontitown: Ozark Vineyard Center," *Economic Geography,* Vol. 29 (1953), pp. 125–143.

Hinueber, Caroline von. "Life of German Pioneers of Early Texas," *Texas State Historical Association Quarterly,* Vol. 2 (1899), pp. 227–232.

Hogan, William R. *The Texas Republic: A Social and Economic History.* Norman: University of Oklahoma Press, 1946.

Höhne, Friedrich. *Wahn und Ueberzeugung. Reise des Kupferschmiede-Meisters Friedrich Höhne in Weimar über Bremen nach Nordamerika und Texas in den Jahren 1839, 1840 und 1841.* Weimar: Wilhelm Hoffmann, 1844.

Hollander, A. N. J. den. *De landelijke arme Blanken in het Zuiden der Vereenigde Staten.* Groningen: J. B. Wolters, 1933.

————. "The Tradition of 'Poor Whites'," in *Culture in the South*. Edited by W. T. Couch. Chapel Hill: University of North Carolina Press, 1934.

[Houston and Texas Central Railway Company]. *Texas the Best Land for the Emigrant*. n.p.: n.p., [c. 1885].

Hughes, Thomas (ed.). *G. T. T., Gone to Texas: Letters from Our Boys*. London: Macmillan & Co., Ltd., 1884.

Huson, Hobart. *Refugio: A Comprehensive History of Refugio County from Aboriginal Times to 1953*. 2 vols. Woodsboro, Texas: Rooke Foundation, 1953.

Jackson, W. H., and S. A. Long. *The Texas Stock Directory or Book of Marks and Brands*. . . . Vol. I. San Antonio: Herald Office, 1865.

Jäger, Eugen. *Die Agrarfrage der Gegenwart*. 4 vols. Berlin: Puttkammer & Mühlbrecht, 1882–1893.

Jordan, Gilbert J. *A Biographical Sketch of Ernst and Lizette Jordan*. Dallas: 1931.

Jordan, Terry G. "German Houses in Texas," *Landscape*, Vol. 14 (Autumn, 1964), pp. 24–26.

Jordan, Weymouth T. "Agricultural Societies in Ante-Bellum Alabama," *Alabama Review*, Vol. 4 (1951), pp. 241–253.

————. *Ante-Bellum Alabama: Town and Country*. Tallahassee: Florida State University Press, 1957.

Kapp, Dr. and Mrs. Ernst. "Briefe aus der Comalstadt 1850," in *Jahrbuch der Neu-Braunfelser Zeitung fuer 1936*. New Braunfels: Zeitung, 1936. Pp. 15–38.

Kapp, Frederick. "The History of Texas, Early German Colonization, Princes and Nobles in America, The Future of the State, a Lecture by Frederick Kapp," *New York Daily Tribune* (January 20, 1855), p. 6, cols. 1, 2, 3.

Kapp, Friedrich. *Aus und über Amerika, Thatsachen und Erlebnisse*. 2 vols. Berlin: Julius Springer, 1876.

————. "Die Geschichte der deutschen Ansiedelungen des westlichen Texas und dessen Bedeutung für die Vereinigten Staaten," *Atlantische Studien von Deutschen in Amerika*, Vol. 1 (1853), pp. 173 ff.

Kemmerer, Donald L. "The Pre-Civil War South's Leading Crop: Corn," *Agricultural History*, Vol. 33 (1949), pp. 236–238.

Kendall, George Wilkins. *Letters from a Texas Sheep Ranch*. Edited by Harry J. Brown. Urbana: University of Illinois Press, 1959.

————. "Sheep Raising in Texas," in *The Texas Almanac, 1858–1867*. Galveston: Richardson, 1857–1866.

Kenney, Martin M. *An Historical and Descriptive Sketch of Austin County, Texas . . . forming the Centennial Address, Delivered at the Celebration near Bellville, July 4th, 1877* [sic]. Brenham: Banner Print, 1876.

Kettner, Franz. "Letters of a German Pioneer in Texas," *Southwestern Historical Quarterly*, 69 (1965–1966), 463–472. Edited and translated by Terry G. Jordan and Marlis Anderson Jordan.

Killebrew, J. B., and J. M. Safford. *Introduction to the Resources of Tennessee*. Nashville: Tavel, Eastman & Howell, 1874.

King, Edward. *The Great South: A Record of Journeys in Louisiana, Texas* . . .. Hartford, Connecticut: American Publishing Company, 1875.
―――. *The Southern States of North America: A Record of Journeys in . . . Texas* . . .. Vol. I. London: Blackie & Son, 1875.
Kingsbury, W. G. *Beschreibung von Süd-, West- und Mittel-Texas* . . .. Translated by Albert Burckhardt. n.p.: n.p., [c. 1878].
Kleberg, Rosa. "Some of My Early Experiences in Texas," *Texas State Historical Association Quarterly,* Vol. 1 (1898), pp. 297–302; Vol. 2 (1898), pp. 170–173.
Kollmorgen, Walter M. *The German Settlement in Cullman County, Alabama: An Agricultural Island in the Cotton Belt.* Washington, D.C.: U.S. Department of Agriculture, Bureau of Agricultural Economics, 1941.
―――. *The German-Swiss in Franklin County, Tennessee: A Study of the Significance of Cultural Considerations in Farming Enterprises.* Washington, D.C.: U.S. Department of Agriculture, Bureau of Agricultural Economics, Report 7, 1940.
―――. "Immigrant Settlements in Southern Agriculture: A Commentary on the Significance of Cultural Islands in Agricultural History," *Agricultural History,* Vol. 19 (1945), pp. 69–78.
―――. "A Reconnaissance of Some Cultural-Agricultural Islands in the South," *Economic Geography,* Vol. 17 (1941), pp. 409–430; Vol. 19 (1943), pp. 109–117.
Kordül, A. *Der sichere Führer nach und in Texas* . . . Rottweil am Neckar: J. P. Setzer, 1846.
Kromer, Dorus. *Die Amerikafahrt: Aus den Goldgräberjahren eines Schwarzwälder Bauernsohns.* Edited by Heinrich E. Kromer. Leipzig: L. Staackmann, 1935.
Krueger, Max. *Pioneer Life in Texas: An Autobiography.* n.p.: n.p., [c. 1928].
Krzymowski, Richard. *Geschichte der deutschen Landwirtschaft.* Berlin: Duncker & Humblot, 1961.

Lafrentz, L. F. "Deutsche Ansiedlungen in Comal County nach der Gründung von Neu-Braunfels," in *Jahrbuch der Neu-Braunfelser Zeitung fuer 1929.* New Braunfels: Zeitung, 1929. Pp. 15–30.
―――. "Die Deutschen in Texas vor der Massen-Einwanderung im Jahre 1844," *Deutsch-Texanische Monats-Hefte.* A series of articles in Vol. 11 (1906) through Vol. 12 (1908).
Lamb, Robert Byron. *The Mule in Southern Agriculture.* University of California Publications in Geography, Vol. 15. Berkeley & Los Angeles: University of California Press, 1963.
Lathrop, Barnes F. *Migration into East Texas 1835–1860.* Austin: Texas State Historical Association, 1949.
Lawler, Ruth C. *The Story of Castroville.* N.p.: n.p., 1957.
Linden, Fabian. "Economic Democracy in the Slave South: An Appraisal of Some Recent Views," *Journal of Negro History,* Vol. 31 (1946), pp. 140–189.

218 GERMAN SEED IN TEXAS SOIL

List, Friedrich. *Die Ackerverfassung, die Zwergwirthschaft und die Auswanderung.* Stuttgart and Tübingen: J. G. Cotta, 1842.

Löher, Franz. *Geschichte und Zustände der Deutschen in Amerika.* Cincinnati: Eggers and Wulkop; Leipzig: K. F. Köhler, 1847.

Lohmann, Ferdinand H. *Comfort: Ein kurzer Überblick über das Leben und Treiben der Bewohner von der Gründungszeit bis zur Gegenwart. Festschrift zur fünfzig-Jahr Jubelfeier der Ansiedelung.* Comfort, Texas: Wilhelm Fellbaum, 1904.

Lotto, F. *Fayette County: Her History and Her People.* Schulenburg: 1902.

Loughridge, R. H. (ed.). "Report on the Cotton Production of the State of Texas, with a Discussion of the General Agricultural Features of the State," in *Report on Cotton Production in the United States. . . .* Vol. 5 of the Tenth Census of the United States, 1880. Washington, D.C.: Government Printing Office, 1884.

Ludecus, Eduard. *Reise durch die Mexikanischen Provinzen Tumalipas, Cohahuila und Texas im Jahre 1834, In Briefen an seine Freunde.* Leipzig: Joh. Friedr. Hartknoch, 1837.

Luhn, F. W. "Bericht des Farmers F. W. Luhn aus Holstein über seine Erfahrungen in Texas . . .," in *Jahrbuch der Neu-Braunfelser Zeitung fuer 1925.* New Braunfels: Zeitung, 1925. Pp. 27–42.

Lynch, Russell Wilford. *Czech Farmers in Oklahoma.* Bulletin, Oklahoma A. & M. College, Vol. 39, No. 13. Stillwater: Oklahoma A. & M. College, 1942.

Lynch, W. O. "The Westward Flow of Southern Colonists before 1861," *Journal of Southern History,* Vol. 9 (1943), pp. 303–327.

Martiny, Rudolf. "Die Grundrissgestaltung der deutschen Siedlungen," in *Petermanns Mitteilungen Ergänzungscheft,* No. 197. Gotha: Justus Perthes, 1928.

McClintock, William A. "Journal of a Trip through Texas and Northern Mexico in 1846–1847," *Southwestern Historical Quarterly,* Vol. 34 (1930–1931), pp. 20–37, 141–158, 231–256.

McConnell, H. H. *Five Years a Cavalryman: or, Sketches of Regular Army Life on the Texas Frontier, Twenty Odd Years Ago.* Jacksboro, Texas: J. N. Rogers, 1889.

McDanield, H. F., and N. A. Taylor. *The Coming Empire: or, Two Thousand Miles in Texas on Horseback.* New York, Chicago, & New Orleans: A. S. Barnes, 1877.

McGrath, Sister Paul. *Political Nativism in Texas 1825–1860.* Washington, D.C.: Catholic University of America, 1930.

Meitzen, August. *Der Boden und die landwirtschaftlichen Verhältnisse des preussischen Staates . . ..* 8 vols. Berlin: Paul Parey, 1868–1908.

———. *Das deutsche Haus.* Berlin: Dietrich Reimer, 1882.

[Methodist Church]. *A Century of German Methodism in the Llano River Valley of Texas, 1852–1952.* Fredericksburg, Texas: Fredericksburg Pub. Co., 1952.

———. *Kurze Beschreibung des 75. Jubiläums und Geschichte der Llano-Gemeinde.* Fredericksburg, Texas: Fredericksburg Pub. Co., 1931.

Meusebach, John. See Wurzbach, Emil Frederick.

Meusebach, John O. *Answer to Interrogatories* . . .. Austin: Eugene Von Boeckmann, 1894.

Meyer, Hans. *Das Deutsche Volkstum.* Leipzig and Vienna: Bibliographisches Institut, 1903.

Meyer, J. G. "Die Colonie Neu Baden in Robertson County," in *Schütze's Jahrbuch für Texas . . . für 1883.* Austin: A. Schütze, 1882. Pp. 146–160.

Mgebroff, Johannes. *Geschichte der Ersten Deutschen Evangelisch-Lutherischen Synode in Texas.* Chicago: Wartburg Pub. House, 1902.

Moelling, Peter August. *Reise-Skizzen in Poesie und Prosa, Gesammelt auf einer siebenmonatlichen Tour durch die Vereinigten Staaten von Nord-Amerika.* Galveston: Office des "Apologeten," [c. 1858].

Moore, A. W. "A Reconnaissance in Texas in 1846," *Southwestern Historical Quarterly,* Vol. 30 (1926–1927), pp. 252–271.

Moore, John H. *Agriculture in Ante-Bellum Mississippi.* New York: Bookman Associates, 1958.

Müller-Wille, Wilhelm. "Feldsysteme in Westfalen um 1860," *Deutsche Geographische Blätter,* Vol. 42 (1939), pp. 119–131.

———. "Haus- und Gehöftformen in Mitteleuropa," *Geographische Zeitschrift,* Vol. 42 (1936), pp. 121–138.

Murray, Myrtle. "Home Life on Early Ranches of Southwest Texas," *The Cattleman.* A series of articles, beginning in Vol. 24, No. 8 (January, 1938), and ending in Vol. 27, No. 7 (December, 1940).

Niederauer, C. "Weinbau," in *Schütze's Jahrbuch für Texas . . . für 1884.* Austin: A. Schütze, 1883. Pp. 71–72.

Niehaus, Heinrich. "Agricultural Conditions and Regions in Germany," *Geographical Review,* Vol. 23 (1933), pp. 23–47.

North, Douglass C. *The Economic Growth of the United States 1790–1860.* Englewood Cliffs, New Jersey: Prentice-Hall, Inc., 1961.

North, Thomas. *Five Years in Texas: or, What you did not hear during the war from January 1861 to January 1866* . . .. Cincinnati: Elm Street Printing Co., 1871.

Och, Joseph T. *Der deutschamerikanische Farmer* . . .. Columbus: Ohio Waisenfreund, 1913.

Olmsted, Frederick Law. *The Cotton Kingdom.* 2 vols. New York: Mason Brothers, 1861.

———. *A Journey in the Back Country.* New York: Mason Brothers, 1860.

———. *A Journey through Texas: or, A Saddle-Trip on the Southwestern Frontier.* New York: Dix, Edwards and Co., 1857.

Ostermayer, Heinrich. *Tagebuch einer Reise nach Texas im Jahr 1848–1849* . . .. Biberach: Im Verlage des Verfassers, 1850.

[Ottmers Reunion Committee, Gottfried]. *The History of the Gottfried Ottmers Family.* Fredericksburg, Texas: Fredericksburg Pub. Co., 1955.

Owsley, Frank L. "The Pattern of Migration and Settlement on the Southern Frontier," *Journal of Southern History,* Vol. 11 (1945), pp. 147–176.

————. *Plain Folk of the Old South*. Baton Rouge: Louisiana State University Press, 1949.

Owsley, Frank L. and Harriet C. "The Economic Basis of Society in the Late Ante-Bellum South," *Journal of Southern History*, Vol. 6 (1940), pp. 24–45.

————. "The Economic Structure of Rural Tennessee, 1850–1860," *Journal of Southern History*, Vol. 8 (1942), pp. 161–182.

Padilla, Juan Antonio. "Texas in 1820," *Southwestern Historical Quarterly*, Vol. 23 (1919–1920), pp. 47–68. Translated by Mattie Austin Hatcher.

Parisot, Pierre Fourier. *The Reminiscences of a Texas Missionary*. San Antonio: Johnson Bros., 1899.

Penniger, Robert (ed.). *Fest-Ausgabe zum 50-jährigen Jubiläum der Gründung der Stadt Friedrichsburg*. Fredericksburg, Texas: A. Hillmann, 1896.

Philippovich, E. (ed.). *Auswanderung und Auswanderungspolitik in Deutschland*. Schriften des Vereins für Socialpolitik, Vol. 52. Leipzig: Duncker & Humblot, 1892.

Prunty, Merle. "The Renaissance of the Southern Plantation," *Geographical Review*, Vol. 45 (1955), pp. 459–491.

Rabe, Joh. E. *Eine Erholungsfahrt nach Texas und Mexico. Tagebuchblätter von Joh. E. Rabe*. Hamburg and Leipzig: Leopold Voss, 1893.

Racknitz, Johann von. *Kurze und getreue Belehrung für deutsche und schweizerische Auswanderer, welch an der Begründung der Colonie Johann v. Racknitz, im mexicanischen Freistaate Tamaulipas gelegen, Theil nehmen wollen . . . .* Stuttgart: Imle und Krauss, 1836.

Radig, Werner. *Die Siedlungstypen in Deutschland*. Berlin: Henschel, 1955.

Ramsdell, Charles W. "The Natural Limits of Slavery Expansion," *Mississippi Valley Historical Review*, Vol. 16 (1929), pp. 151–171.

Ranck, James E. "Mason County," in *The Texas Almanac for 1867 . . ..* Galveston: Richardson, 1866. Pp. 135–136.

Ransleben, Guido E. *A Hundred Years of Comfort in Texas*. San Antonio: Naylor, 1954.

Rather, Ethel Z. "De Witt's Colony," *Texas State Historical Association Quarterly*, Vol. 8 (1904), pp. 95–192.

Raunick, Selma Marie, Margaret Schade, and E. Marshall. *The Kothmanns of Texas 1845–1931*. Austin: Von Boeckmann-Jones, 1931.

Raup, H. F. "The Italian-Swiss Dairymen of San Luis Obispo County, California," *Yearbook of the Association of Pacific Coast Geographers*, Vol. 1 (1935), pp. 3–8.

Regenbrecht, Adalbert. "The German Settlers of Millheim (Texas) before the Civil War," *Southwestern Historical Quarterly*, Vol. 20 (1916–1917), pp. 28–34.

Reid, John C. *Reid's Tramp: or A Journal of the Incidents of Ten Months Travel through Texas . . ..* Selma, Alabama: John Hardy, 1858. Reprinted at Austin: Steck Co., 1935.

Reinhardt, Louis. "The Communistic Colony of Bettina," *Texas State Historical Association Quarterly*, Vol. 3 (1899), pp. 33–40.

Richardson, Rupert N. *Texas: The Lone Star State.* 2d. ed. New York: Prentice-Hall, Inc., 1958.

Rock, James L., and W. I. Smith. *Southern and Western Texas Guide for 1878.* St. Louis: A. H. Granger, 1878.

Roemer, Ferdinand von. *Texas: Mit besonderer Rücksicht auf deutsche Auswanderung und die physischen Verhältnisse des Landes nach eigener Beobachtung geschildert.* Bonn: Adolph Marcus, 1849.

Rose, Victor M. *Some Historical Facts in Regard to the Settlement of Victoria, Texas, Its Progress and Present Status.* Laredo: Daily Times, 1883. Reprinted at San Antonio: Lone Star Printing, 1961. Edited by J. W. Petty and K. S. O'Connor.

Rosenthal, A. J. "Fayette County," in *Schütze's Jahrbuch für Texas . . . für 1883.* Austin: A. Schütze, 1882. Pp. 41–44.

Ross, Georg M. von. *Des Auswanderers Handbuch. Getreue Schilderung der Vereinigten Staaten von Nordamerika und Zuverlässiger Rathgeber für dahin Auswandernde jeden Standes.* Elberfed: Julius Bädeker, 1851.

————. *Der Nordamerikanische Freistaat Texas, nach eigener Anschauung und nach den neuesten und besten Quellen für deutsche Auswanderer.* Rudolstadt: G. Froebel, 1851.

Rush, Benjamin. *An Account of the Manners of the German Inhabitants of Pennsylvania . . . ..* Rev. ed. Edited by I. Daniel Rupp. Philadelphia: Samuel P. Town, 1875.

St. Romain, Lillian Schiller. *Western Falls County, Texas.* Austin: Texas State Historical Association, 1951.

Santleben, August. *A Texas Pioneer: Early Staging and Overland Freighting Days on the Frontiers of Texas and Mexico.* Edited by I. D. Affleck. New York and Washington: Neale Publishing, 1910.

Sauer, Carl O. "The Settlement of the Humid East," in *Climate and Man.* U.S. Department of Agriculture Yearbook, 1941. Washington, D.C.: Government Printing Office, 1941. Pp. 157–166.

Scherpf, G. A. *Entstehungsgeschichte und gegenwärtiger Zustand des neuen, unabhängigen, amerikanischen Staates Texas . . . ..* Augsburg: Matth. Rieger, 1841.

Schlecht, Friedrich. *Mein Ausflug nach Texas.* Bunzlau: Appun, 1851.

Schreiber, Albert M. *Mesquite Does Bloom.* San Antonio: Standard Printing, 1942.

Schuchard, Ernst. *100th Anniversary, Pioneer Flour Mills, San Antonio, Texas, 1851–1951.* San Antonio: Naylor, 1951.

Schultz, Joh. Heinr. Siegfried. *Die deutsche Ansiedelung in Texas . . . ..* Bonn: Friedrich Encke, 1845.

Schütz, Kuno Damian von. *Texas: Rathgeber für Auswanderer nach diesem Lande . . . ..* Wiesbaden: Chr. W. Kreidel, 1847.

Schütze, Julius. "Meine Erlebnisse in Texas," *Texas Vorwaerts* (Austin), February 1, 1884, p. 2, cols. 2–4.

Schwarz, Gabriele. *Allgemeine Siedlungsgeographie.* 2d ed. Berlin: Walter de Gruyter, 1961.

Seele, Hermann. "Ein Beitrag zur Geschichte von Neu Braunfels," in

Schütze's Jahrbuch für Texas . . . für 1882. Austin: A. Schütze, 1881. Pp. 31–65.

———. *Die Cypresse und Gesammelte Schriften.* New Braunfels: Zeitung, 1936.

———. "Die deutsche Colonie New Braunfels im Mai 1845," in *Schütze's Jahrbuch für Texas . . . für 1884.* Austin: A. Schütze, 1883. Pp. 93–104.

———. *A Short Sketch of Comal County, Texas,* New Braunfels: Zeitung, 1885.

———. "Zwei Erinnerungsbilder aus der Zeit der deutschen Ansiedlung von West-Texas," in *Schütze's Jahrbuch für Texas . . . für 1883.* Austin: A. Schütze, 1882. Pp. 44–61.

Shook, Robert W. "The Battle of the Nueces, August 10, 1862," *Southwestern Historical Quarterly,* Vol. 66 (1962–1963), pp. 31–42.

Siemering, A. "Die lateinische Ansiedlung in Texas," *Der deutsche Pionier,* Vol. 10 (1878), pp. 57–62.

———. "Lebensbilder aus dem Süden," *Deutsche Monats-Hefte,* Vol. 7 (1856), pp. 277–293.

———. "Schafzucht in Westtexas," in *Schütze's Jahrbuch für Texas . . . für 1882.* Austin: A. Schütze, 1881. Pp. 69–73.

———. *Texas als Ziel deutscher Auswanderung . . ..* Hamburg: J. F. Richter, 1882.

Smith, Ophia D. "A Trip to Texas in 1855," *Southwestern Historical Quarterly,* Vol. 59 (1955–1956), pp. 24–39.

Smyrl, Frank H. "Unionism in Texas, 1856–1861," *Southwestern Historical Quarterly,* Vol. 68 (1964–1965), pp. 172–195.

Solms-Braunfels, Carl von. "Berichte des Prinzen Karl zu Solms-Braunfels an den Mainzer Adelsverein," in *Kalender der Neu-Braunfelser Zeitung fuer 1916.* New Braunfels: Zeitung, 1916. Pp. 15–64.

———. *Texas, Geschildert in Beziehung auf seine geographischen, socialen und übrigen Verhältnisse mit besonderer Rücksicht auf die deutsche Colonisation . . ..* Frankfurt am Main: Johann David Sauerländer, 1846.

Sommer, Karl von. *Bericht über meine Reise nach Texas im Jahre 1846.* Bremen: 1847.

Sörgel, Alwin H. *Für Auswanderungslustige! Briefe eines unter dem Schutze des Mainzer Vereins nach Texas Ausgewanderten.* Leipzig: Expedizion des Herold, 1847.

———. *Neueste Nachrichten aus Texas: Zugleich ein Hülferuf an den Mainzer Verein zum Schutze deutscher Einwanderer in Texas.* Eisleben: Georg Reichardt, 1847.

[The South Western Immigration Company]. *Texas: Her Resources and Capabilities . . ..* New York: E. D. Slater, 1881.

Spaight, A. W. *The Resources, Soil, and Climate of Texas: Report of Commissioner of Insurance, Statistics, and History.* Galveston: A. H. Belo, 1882.

Stählen, C. *Neueste Nachrichten, Erklärungen u. Briefe der Auswanderer von Texas.* Heilbronn: n.p., 1846.

Steinert, W. *Nordamerika vorzüglich Texas im Jahre 1849 . . ..* Berlin: K. W. Krüger, 1850.

Stöhr, Louise. "Die erste deutsche Frau in Texas," *Der deutsche Pionier,* Vol. 16 (1884), pp. 372–375.

Strickland, Rex W. "Miller County, Arkansas Territory: The Frontier That Men Forget," *Chronicles of Oklahoma,* Vol. 18 (1940), pp. 12–34, 154– 170; Vol. 19 (1941), pp. 37–54.

Strubberg, Friedrich Armand. *Friedrichsburg, die Colonie des deutschen Fürsten-Vereins in Texas.* 2 vols. Leipzig: Friedrich Fleischer, 1867.

Sweet, George H. *Texas . . . or the Immigrants' Hand-Book of Texas.* New York: E. O'Keefe, 1871.

Taylor, Paul S. *An American-Mexican Frontier: Nueces County, Texas.* Chapel Hill: University of North Carolina Press, 1934.

———. "Plantation Agriculture in the United States: Seventeenth to Twentieth Centuries," *Land Economics,* Vol. 30 (1954), pp. 141–152.

Thran, Jakob. *Meine Auswanderung nach Texas unter dem Schutze des Mainzer Vereins. Ein Warnungs-Beispiel für Auswanderungslustige.* Berlin: Eduard Krause, 1848.

Thurmond, A. S. "Goliad County," in *The Texas Almanac for 1867.* Galveston: Richardson, 1866. Pp. 110–111.

Tiling, Moritz. *History of the German Element in Texas from 1820–1850.* Houston: Rein and Sons, 1913.

Townshend, Samuel Nugent. *Our Indian Summer in the Far West: An Autumn Tour of Fifteen Thousand Miles in Kansas, Texas, New Mexico, Colorado, and the Indian Territory.* London: Charles Whittingham, 1880.

Trenckmann, W. A. *Austin County: Beilage zum Bellville Wochenblatt . . ..* Bellville, Texas: Wochenblatt, 1899.

Treu, Georg. *Das Buch der Auswanderung, enthaltend . . . der Bekanntmachungen . . . des Texas-Vereins . . ..* Bamberg: Fränkischer Merkur, 1848.

Trewartha, Glenn T. "The Green County, Wisconsin, Foreign Cheese Industry," *Economic Geography,* Vol. 2 (1926), pp. 292–308.

———. *An Introduction to Climate.* New York: McGraw-Hill Book Company, Inc., 1954.

Turner, Frederick Jackson. *The Frontier in American History.* 3rd ed. New York: Henry Holt and Company, Inc., 1958.

Tyler, George W. *The History of Bell County.* San Antonio: Naylor, 1936.

[United States Census Office]. Seventh Census, 1850; Eighth Census, 1860; Ninth Census, 1870; Tenth Census, 1880; Eleventh Census, 1890; Twelfth Census, 1900. Washington, D.C.: 1850–1900.

[United States Department of Agriculture]. "Agricultural and Horticultural Societies and Clubs," in *Report of the Commissioner of Agriculture for the Year 1867.* Washington, D.C.: Government Printing Office, 1868.

———. *A Directory of Departments, Boards, Societies, Colleges, and Other Organizations in the Interest of Agriculture, Horticulture, Stock-Raising, Bee-Keeping, Fish-Culture, and Kindred Industries.* Report No. 39. Washington, D.C.: Government Printing Office, 1885.

———. *List of Agricultural Colleges, and of Farmers' Clubs, and Agricul-*

tural, Horticultural, and Pomological Societies . . . . Washington, D.C.: Government Printing Office, 1872.

―――. *List of Agricultural Societies and Farmers' Clubs, Established to Promote the Agricultural, Horticultural, and Pomological Interests of the Farmer . . . .* Report No. 12. Washington, D.C.: Government Printing Office, 1876.

[United States Immigration Commission]. *Immigrants in Industry: Recent Immigrants in Agriculture.* Reports of the Immigration Commission, Vol. 22, Part II. Washington, D.C.: Government Printing Office, 1911.

[Verein zum Schutze deutscher Einwanderer in Texas]. *Comite-Bericht des Vereines zum Schutze deutscher Einwanderer in Texas.* Wiesbaden: J. A. Stein, 1850.

―――. *Gesammelte Aktenstücke des Vereins zum Schutze deutscher Einwanderer in Texas.* Mainz: Victor von Zabern, 1845.

―――. *Instruction für deutsche Auswanderer nach Texas, nebst der neuesten Karte dieses Staates . . . .* Berlin: D. Reimer, 1851.

―――. *Texas. Ein Handbuch für deutsche Auswanderer. Mit besonderer Rücksicht auf diejenigen, welche ihre Ueberfahrt und Ansiedlung durch Hilfe des Vereins . . . bewirken wollen.* Bremen: A. D. Geisler, 1846.

Walther, F. E. *Texas in sein wahres Licht gestellt, als geeignetster Colonisationsplatz für deutsche Auswanderer . . . .* Dresden and Leipzig: Arnold, 1848.

Wappäus, J. E. *Deutsche Auswanderung und Colonisation.* Leipzig: J. G. Hinrichs, 1846.

Waugh, Julia Nott. *Castro-ville and Henry Castro, Empresario.* San Antonio: Standard Printing, 1934.

Weaver, Herbert. *Mississippi Farmers 1850–1860.* Nashville: Vanderbilt University Press, 1945.

Webb, Walter Prescott. "Christmas and New Year in Texas," *Southwestern Historical Quarterly,* Vol. 44 (1940–1941), pp. 357–379.

―――. *The Great Plains.* New York: Grosset & Dunlap, n.d. Paperback edition of the original 1931 edition.

Webb, Walter Prescott, and H. Bailey Carroll (eds.). *The Handbook of Texas.* 2 vols. Austin: Texas State Historical Association, 1952.

Weber, Adolf Paul. *Deutsche Pioniere. Zur Geschichte des Deutschthums in Texas.* San Antonio: Selbstverlag, 1894.

Weilbacher, A. "Zubereitung von Wein aus der Mustang-Traube," in *Schütze's Jahrbuch für Texas . . . für 1884.* Austin: A. Schütze, 1883. Pp. 187–193.

Westermanns Atlas zur Weltgeschichte. Part II: "Mittelalter." Braunschweig: Georg Westermann, 1956.

Western Texas the Australia of America: Or the Place to Live. Cincinnati: E. Mendenhall, 1860.

Weston, George M. *The Poor Whites of the South.* Washington, D.C.: 1856.

Weyand, Leonie Rummel, and Houston Wade. *An Early History of Fayette County.* La Grange, Texas: Journal, 1936.

Wharton, Clarence Ray. *History of Fort Bend County.* San Antonio: Naylor, 1939.

Whilldin, M. (ed.). *A Description of Western Texas, Published by the Galveston, Harrisburg & San Antonio Railway Company, The Sunset Route.* Galveston: The News, 1876.

Whiting, W. H. C. "Whiting Diary: March from Fredericksburg to El Paso del Norte," *Publications of the Southern History Association,* Vol. 9 (1905), pp. 361–373.

Winkler, Ernest W. (ed). *Journal of the Secession Convention of Texas 1861.* Austin: State Library, 1912.

Wooster, Ralph A. "Foreigners in the Principal Towns of Ante-Bellum Texas," *Southwestern Historical Quarterly,* Vol. 66 (1962–1963), pp. 208–220.

Wrede, Friedrich W. von. *Lebensbilder aus den Vereinigten Staaten von Nordamerika und Texas. . ..* Cassel: Selbstverlag, 1844.

Wurzbach, Emil Frederick. *Life and Memoirs of Emil Frederick Wurzbach to Which Is Appended Some Papers of John Meusebach.* Translated by Franz J. Dohman, San Antonio: Artes Graficas, 1937.

"Zur Geschichte der Baumwollkultur in Comal County," in *Kalender der Neu-Braunfelser Zeitung fuer 1905.* New Braunfels: Zeitung, 1905. P. 35.

2. Bibliographic Sources

Carroll, H. Bailey. *Texas County Histories: A Bibliography.* Austin: Texas State Historical Association, 1943.

Carroll, H. Bailey, and Milton R. Gutsch. *Texas History Theses.* Austin: Texas State Historical Association, 1955.

Clark, Thomas D. (ed.). *Travels in the New South.* 2 vols. Norman: University of Oklahoma Press, 1962.

———. *Travels in the Old South.* 3 vols. Norman: University of Oklahoma Press, 1959.

Elliott, Claude (ed.). *Theses on Texas History.* Austin: Texas State Historical Association, 1955.

Griffin, A. P. C. *A List of Works Relating to the Germans in the United States.* Washington, D.C.: 1904.

Pochmann, Henry A., and Arthur R. Schultz. *Bibliography of German Culture in America to 1940.* Madison: University of Wisconsin Press, 1953.

Streeter, Thomas W. *Bibliography of Texas 1795–1845.* Cambridge: Harvard University Press, 1960.

[Works Progress Administration, Division of Women's and Professional Projects]. *Check List of Records Required or Permitted by Law in Texas.* San Antonio: The Historical Records Survey, January, 1937.

B. NEWSPAPERS, YEARBOOKS, AND ALMANACS

Allgemeine Auswanderungs-Zeitung (Bremen and New York), January-May, 1848.
The Austin County Times (Bellville, Texas), 1883–1886.
Bastrop Deutsche Zeitung (Bastrop, Texas), 1873–1874.
Burke, J. *Burke's Texas Almanac and Immigrant's Handbook.* Houston: W. M. Hamilton, 1875–1885.
The Civilian and Galveston Gazette (Galveston, Texas), 1843.
Deutsch-Amerikanischer Volks-Kalender der Freie Presse für Texas. San Antonio: Freie Presse, 1904, 1905.
Deutsch-Texanische Monats-Hefte (San Antonio and Fredericksburg), 1895–1910.
Fredericksburg Standard (Fredericksburg, Texas), Centennial Edition, May 1, 1946.
Freie Presse für Texas (San Antonio), 1866–1876.
Galveston-Zeitung (Galveston, Texas), 1851–1855.
Jahrbuch der Neu-Braunfelser Zeitung (New Braunfels: Zeitung), 1925–1939.
Kalender-Jahrbuch der Neu-Braunfelser Zeitung (New Braunfels: Zeitung), 1924.
Kalender der Neu-Braunfelser Zeitung (New Braunfels: Zeitung), 1905–1923.
La Grange Intelligencer (La Grange, Texas), 1844–1846.
Neu-Braunfelser Zeitung (New Braunfels, Texas), 1852–1885.
New York Daily Tribune (New York City), 1855–1856.
The Radio Post (Fredericksburg, Texas), Centennial Edition, May 4, 1946.
San Antonio Zeitung (San Antonio, Texas), 1854.
Schütze, Albert (ed.). *Schütze's Jahrbuch für Texas und Emigranten-Führer.* Austin: Albert Schütze, 1882–1884.
——. *Schütze's Monatsbuch für Texas.* Austin: Albert Schütze, September, 1904.
The Southern Intelligencer (Austin, Texas), 1857–1859.
The Texas Almanac. Galveston: Richardson, 1857–1873.
Texas Almanac. Dallas: A. H. Belo Corp., editions of 1949–1950, 1961–1962.
The Texas Monument (La Grange, Texas), 1851.
Texas State Gazette (Austin, Texas), 1855–1858.
Texas Vorwaerts (Austin, Texas), 1884.
Die Union (Galveston, Texas), 1866–1868.
Wöchentliche Texas Post (Galveston, Texas), 1870–1877.

C. MAPS

Haberlandt, A. Map of house types in Central Europe, found in *Illustrierte Völkerkunde,* Vol. 2, Part 2, following p. 176. Edited by Georg Buschan. Stuttgart: Strecker and Schröeder, 1926.

"Special-Karte von Texas nach der neuesten Eintheilung." Elberfeld: Julius Bädeker, 1849.

Willke, H. "Karte von den Vermessungen im Grant und in der Gegend zwischen demselben und Neu Braunfels, zusammengestellt & gezeichnet von H. Willke," in *Instruction für deutsche Auswanderer nach Texas . . .* Berlin: D. Reimer, 1851.

II. UNPUBLISHED MATERIAL

Andrews, Rena Mazyck. "German Pioneers in Texas: Civil War Period." M.A. thesis, University of Chicago, December, 1929.

Fields, S. S. B. (assessor) "Assessors Return from Fayette County for the Year 1840." Texas State Archives, Austin.
Freeman, George (assessor). "Assessment of Taxes in Colorado County for 1840." Texas State Archives, Austin.

Hall, Ada Marie. "The Texas Germans in State and National Politics, 1850–1865." M.A. thesis, University of Texas, June, 1938.

Jordan, Terry G. "A Geographical Appraisal of the Significance of German Settlement in Nineteenth-Century Texas Agriculture." Ph.D. dissertation, University of Wisconsin, June, 1965.
—. "The German Element of Gillespie County, Texas." M.A. thesis, University of Texas, August, 1961.

Kuykendall, J. Hampton (assessor). "Return List of Taxes, Austin County, A. D. 1840." Texas State Archives, Austin.

Schuette, Arthur Luedecke. "The German Settlers of Cat Spring and Their Scientific Study of Agriculture." M.A. thesis, Southwest Texas State Teachers College (San Marcos), 1945.

[Texas, State of]. Climatic records in the Office of the State Climatologist, United States Weather Bureau, Airport Station. Austin, Texas.

United States Census, Manuscript schedules of population and agriculture. 1850: Austin, Comal, Fayette, Gillespie, Guadalupe, and Hays counties, Texas; 1860: Austin, Comal, DeWitt, Gillespie, Llano, and Mason counties, Texas; 1870: Austin, Blanco, Gillespie, Kerr, Llano, and Mason counties, Texas; 1880: Austin, Gillespie, Llano, Mason, and Waller counties, Texas. In the Texas State Archives, Austin.

. . . . *Index* . . . .

230